POSTCARD HISTORY SERIES

The Straits of Mackinac

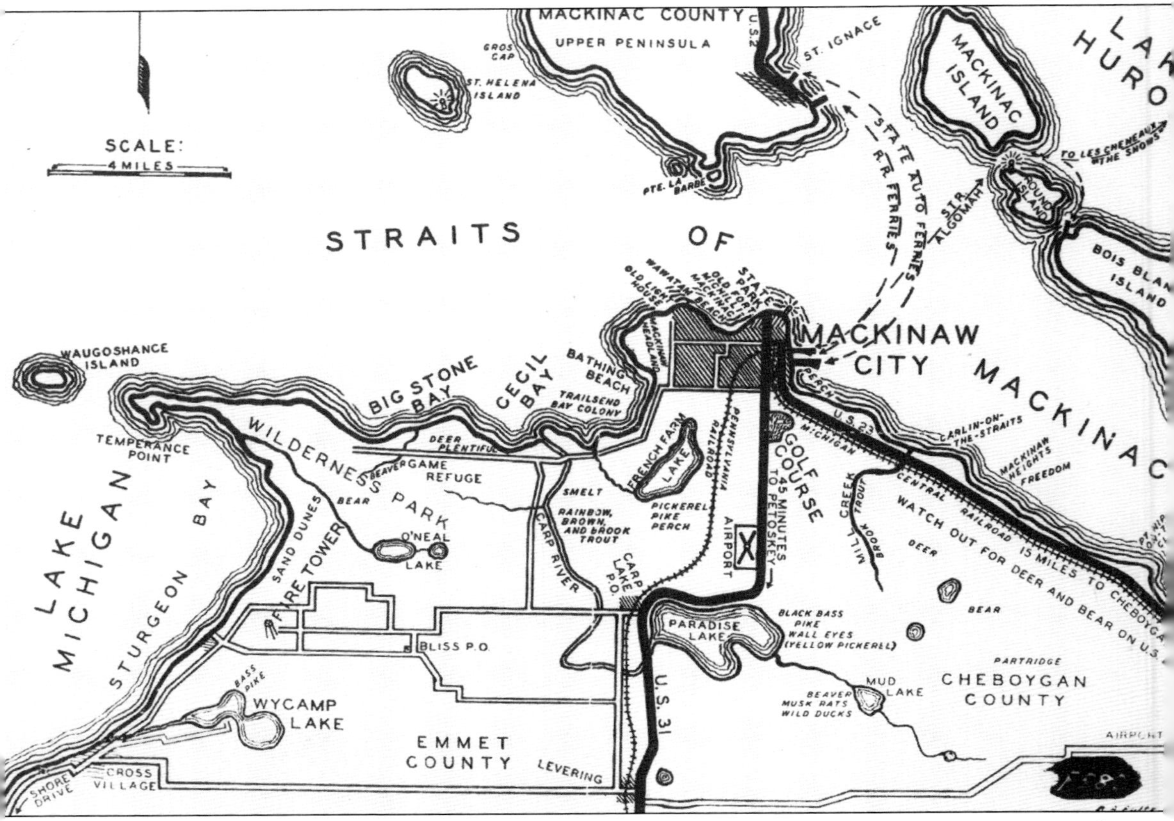

This postcard "map" shows a close-up of the Straits of Mackinac—the scenic waterway that connects Lake Michigan and Lake Huron and separates Michigan's two peninsulas. St. Ignace and Mackinac Island are located on the north side of The Straits, while Mackinaw City sits at the "Tip of the Mitt" on the south side. Just off this map and to the southeast of Bois Blanc Island is the city of Cheboygan. (Author's collection.)

ON THE FRONT COVER: A group of Native Americans poses in this 1931 postcard on the grounds of the Indian Village gift shop and trading post at St. Ignace. Early native people on the north side of The Straits included Ojibwa, Ottawa, and Huron. (Author's collection.)

ON THE BACK COVER: This postcard map shows the relationship of the upper Great Lakes to the two peninsulas of Michigan. (Author's collection.)

POSTCARD HISTORY SERIES

The Straits of Mackinac

Madeline Okerman Adie

ARCADIA
PUBLISHING

ISBN 978-0-7385-9189-6

Published by Arcadia Publishing
Charleston, South Carolina

Printed in the United States of America

Library of Congress Control Number: 2012938888

For all general information contact Arcadia Publishing at:
Telephone 843-853-2070
Fax 843-853-0044
E-mail sales@arcadiapublishing.com
For customer service and orders:
Toll-Free 1-888-313-2665

Visit us on the Internet at www.arcadiapublishing.com

To Eric and Helen,
Colin, and Mark,
a legacy . . .

The grandfathers and the grandmothers
are in the children;
teach them well.

—Ojibwa proverb

Contents

Acknowledgments

I would like to extend my congratulations to the employees and dedicated people and organizations associated with the Mackinac Straits Health System (MSHS) for their new, state-of-the-art, expanded facility, the Mackinac Straits Hospital and Health Center, overlooking historic East Moran Bay in St. Ignace, Michigan. This new facility is a magnificent community achievement, improving medical and health services for The Straits area. The Sault Ste. Marie Tribe of Chippewa Indians donated the land for the new facility, and their Sault Tribal Health and Human Services organization is located on the second floor. Partial royalties from the sale of this book will go continuously and directly to the MSHS to help fund small needs within the hospital.

My thanks to Rod Nelson, the CEO of the MSHS, the MSHS Board, and the MSHS Foundation Board for approving this project and affording me the opportunity to contribute in this way. Members of these boards at the beginning of this endeavor were Steve Autore, Bob Brown, Prentiss M. Brown Jr., Dennis Cawthorne, Greg Cheeseman, Margaret Doud, David Goldthorpe, Mike Hart, Kirk Lipnitz, Wes Maurer, Paula McNamara-Underwood, Mark Mercer, Ronald Mitchell, Lynn Moore, Dan R. Musser III, James North, Walter North, Fred Paquin, Sandi Parish, Dave Schmidt, Cheryl Schlehuber, Patricia Serwach, Pat Shannon, Dr. Edward Smith, Richard Smith, Robert W. Smith, David Swope, and Fr. Jim Williams. I also wish to thank Shannon Doran, Tami Hartwig, RN, Colleen Horn, and Kim North, who graciously helped me along the way.

Also, with great appreciation, I wish to acknowledge and thank Mackinaw City native John Marsh for sharing my enthusiasm about Mackinac postcards. John's wife, Georgia, patiently "allowed" us to spend hours and hours pouring over John's extensive collection and even more time just talking about Mackinaw/Mackinac history. Many images in this book are from his collection, for which I thank him wholeheartedly. Unless otherwise noted, all images are from the author's collection.

INTRODUCTION

They called it Michilimackinac. Early French Canadians spelled what they heard Native Americans say, and because there was no early Native American written language, listeners of native words rendered their own spelling and translated sounds phonetically. Depending upon the specific native dialect or the interpretation of the listener, the Indian term Mi-shi-ne-mackinong became Mishinnimakinong. It was also recorded as Missilimakinak, Missilimackinac, Missilimonkina, Michilimachina, and Michilimackinac. Subsequently abbreviated, it was recorded to be Macina, Maquina, Mackinac, and Mackinaw. According to one historian, studies have revealed over 60 variations in the spelling.

Originally, Michilimackinac was a province of New France, or eastern Canada, with territory stretching from the Atlantic Ocean to the far western stretches of Lake Superior. As new territories were established and new borders formed, Michilimackinac shrunk to the approximate historical triangle of present-day St. Ignace, Mackinac Island, and Mackinaw City. The narrow water passageway separating the land areas became known to nautical folks as the Strait of Mackinac. As time went on, somehow an "s" was added to the name, becoming the Straits of Mackinac, or simply "The Straits."

This historical water passageway connects two Great Lakes, Lake Michigan (Lac des Illinois) and Lake Huron (Mer Douce/Lac des Hurons), and separates Michigan's Upper and Lower Peninsulas. Geographically, cartographers have charted the Straits of Mackinac on the west from Waugoshance Island in Lake Michigan eastward through the narrow submerged valley between Mackinaw City and St. Ignace and continuing east/southeast down the south channel of Lake Huron to the city of Cheboygan. Crossing this scenic waterway north and south is Interstate 75 and Michigan's "Mighty Mac"—the Mackinac Bridge—linking history as well as land. The water area of The Straits is approximately five miles wide between Mackinaw City and St. Ignace and has varying depths of 100 feet or more. Topographic pictures of the submerged valley through the Mackinac Straits are fascinating to see, with the eastern end of the valley looping northward around Mackinac Island. The Straits will usually freeze during Michigan winters, making it very slow going or next to impossible for year-round navigation. But warm weather brings all kinds of maritime vessels: sailing ships, ferry boats, motor craft, and Great Lakes freighters.

Different historical accounts reveal different interpretations of how Michilimackinac received its name. Currently, the most popular version of "great turtle" comes from the presumed original naming of Mackinac Island, based on the rise and shape of the island when viewed by Native Americans from land, which resembled the shape of a giant tortoise. Another rendition tells us that Mishinnimakinong literally translated means "the land of the great fault"; fault meaning a geographical crevice or crack. Both on Mackinac Island and in the St. Ignace area, earth crevices likely of glacial origin were mysteries to the native people. A third version is professed by Henry Rowe Schoolcraft (1793–1864), an Indian agent at early Sault Ste. Marie and Mackinac Island who studied Native American cultures. He learned a great deal from his wife, Jane Johnston, a descendent of an Ojibwe chief. Schoolcraft tells us that Michilimackinac means "place of the great spirits," relating to departed ancestors of native peoples. One of the older nicknames for Mackinac Island is "fairy isle." Perhaps most interesting is the account by Andrew J. Blackbird, also known as the Ottawa chief Mack-aw-de-be-nessy of the Petoskey/Harbor Springs region, from the 1880s. Blackbird asserted that Michilimackinac was never correctly translated by nonnative historians. He tells us that a small, independent tribe of aboriginal people occupied what is now Mackinac Island and had great enemies within the eastern Iroquois Nation. Annihilated by their powerful enemies, the Mi-shi-ne-macki-naw-go people were honored by their Ottawa neighbors in the naming of the island they once inhabited: Mishinimakinong, or "place of the Mishinimaki."

Whatever the origin of the name, it adds to the abundant history and scenic splendor of the Straits of Mackinac. A melting pot of people explored and inhabited the area. At peace with nature, early native people were soon visited by French explorers, fur trappers and traders, and Jesuit missionary priests called "black robes." Next came the French military, establishing forts adjacent to the busy fur-trading posts. British troops came next, ousting the French. And, finally, Americans defeated the British in bloody skirmishes to raise their own new flag over a conquered stockade. These were the first families of Michilimackinac, and they knew that this waterway was their lifeblood—giving plentiful access to all of Mother Nature's gifts.

To the native people, land was a place to live, to respect, to be a part of, and to hold sacred. To them, there were few territories and few boundaries. Many neighboring tribes in different parts of Michilimackinac lived in harmony with each other. For others, it was different. Driven from eastern lands by the fierce Iroquois, the Michilimackinac native people appreciated this new home as a gift from the Great Spirit until the encroaching cultures of Europeans and Americans introduced new concepts of land and property ownership.

The Michilimackinac native people trace their ancestry to the Lenni Lenape tribes, known as the "grandfathers," from lands adjacent to the Atlantic Ocean. These Algonquian language people migrated westward to the upper Great Lakes region and separated into a confederation of tribes called the Three Fires, consisting of Anishinabe (Ojibwa/Chippewa), Odawa (Ottawa), and Potawatomi, or Weshnabek as they called themselves. Ousting the earlier Miami and Sauk Indians, these three new tribes inhabited three different areas. The Chippewa moved to what is now Michigan's Upper Peninsula, the Odawa settled along the eastern shores of Lake Michigan, and the Potawatomi migrated to southern Michigan and northern Indiana. Another significant tribe in the area, from the Iroquois language family, was the Huron, later called Wyandot when they migrated from Mackinac to the Detroit area with Antoine de la Mothe Cadillac around 1701. An ostracized tribe and fierce enemies of the Iroquois nations of New York, the Huron received their name from the French for the special way they wore their hair.

Native people had different names for white people of various European nationalities. The Ojibwa, Ottawa, and Potawatomi called an Englishman *saganash* or *sogonosh*. The Algonquian tribes of Michilimackinac believed in spirits, which, good or bad, were called *manitou*. A great or good spirit was *kitchi-manitou*, and a bad spirit was *matchi-manitou*. Kitchie-manitou made the laws of nature for all beings, creatures, and things to live in harmony. These "great laws" governed the earth, sun, moon, and stars as well as water, wind, fire, and rock. They governed the movement of life—birth, growth, and decline. All were sacred to native people.

Historians tell us that most likely the first European white man to arrive in The Straits area, other than perhaps Étienne Brûlé, was Jean Nicolet de Belleborne. Born in Normandy, France, around 1598, Nicolet sailed to Canada in 1618 to work for a fur-trapping company. As a coureur de bois, or "runner/ranger of the woods," he lived among the native tribes for several years learning their languages and customs. On an exploration in 1634, in search of a trade route to the Orient, Nicolet traveled through the Straits of Mackinac, ending up on the shores of present-day Wisconsin. This particular journey of Nicolet's became a major fur-trading route for the French, and the industry soon came to dominate French and Native American cultures.

The Jesuit black robes followed, determined to minister to the tribes while developing missions in the fur-trading communities. Their missions included modestly built chapels and churches, where Mass was said and native people were baptized. To protect the bustling fur commerce, military forts were constructed nearby to monitor and protect French commercial interests. The Jesuit priests had their work cut out for them, as they constantly competed for the souls of the native people, who were bombarded by unscrupulous traders offering trinkets, colorful beads, blankets, and whiskey.

Voyageur, French for "traveler," was a term originally applied to all Michilimackinac explorers, fur traders, and trappers but was subsequently defined as only those men who operated the canoes, or bateaux, of fur traders. Voyageurs also led dogsled travel and were experts in maneuvering through treacherous waterways. Red stocking caps and bright sashes were common attire for these hardy souls, who were often gone for 12 months or more on fur-trapping expeditions.

The attractive trading-post price of beaver, mink, ermine, fox, marten, and otter furs made this a lucrative and frequently dangerous occupation. Hats from beaver fur were an exploding fashion in France, which kept this commerce alive until the Michilimackinac beaver population was almost extinct. Incredibly powerful and with great stamina, these "canoe-men" were able to navigate the unpredictable waters of Michilimackinac and hoist heavy cargo on their backs for portages over land lasting several miles. Voyageurs could paddle for hours on end, singing French songs to the wind and only stopping for occasional "pipe breaks." Meals of pemmican, pounded lard and dried berries, were their staple food.

When Native Americans joined the fur trade, they were eager to exchange their pelts for European goods such as cooking pots, clothing, and metal knives and other weapons. A proprietor at a fur-trading post was a "bourgeois," directing the activities of his subordinates. The lower-class fur trappers were nicknamed *mangeur de lard*, or "pork eater." Another member of the fur-trading community was the coureur de bois, mentioned earlier, who ventured into the wilderness without proper licensing. These hardy souls rarely became ill, but when they did, the bourgeois became a physician, administering castor oil, a rationed diet, and special salts inducing the victim to recover. Many place names in Michigan are reminiscent of these voyageurs, including Grosse Point, Grosse Isle, Au Train, Bete Grise, Bois Blanc Island, Presque Isle, and Point aux Barques.

Historical islands in The Straits include majestic Mackinac Island (Michilimackinac), which lies just a short distance from the shores of St. Ignace. Bois Blanc Island, French for "white wood," lies just a short distance south and east of Mackinac Island. Pronounced "Bob-low" by locals, this densely wooded beauty is home to about 50 year-round residents and is not to be confused with the Bob-Lo Island near Detroit. Between Mackinac Island and Bois Blanc Island is the small, uninhabited Round Island, or Nissawinagong ("Middle Island"), whose Round Island Light welcomes thousands of tourists every year. Round Island and parts of Bois Blanc and Mackinac Islands were used as sacred burying grounds by early native people. Farther west in Lake Michigan, St. Helena Island, or Mish-aou-o-ning ("the beautiful island") is also uninhabited except for a few who volunteer to help maintain the St. Helena Island Lighthouse. West of St. Helena Island, at the western entrance to The Straits, is Waugoshance Island. Waugoshance Point and Waugoshance Island extend approximately seven miles west from the mainland into northern Lake Michigan. This small chain of rock and gravel islands is surrounded by a large shoal, which due to changing water levels, appears a bit magical, with tiny parcels of land disappearing and reappearing. Waugoshance Island, meaning "fox," and adjacent islands belong to Michigan's Wilderness State Park, a protected wildlife and wilderness area.

The first vessel ever seen on the waters of The Straits other than Native American canoes and fur-traders' bateaux was the French sailing ship *Griffon*, in 1679. The first steamer, *Walk-in-the-Water*, named after a Native American chief, did not arrive until 1819, followed by passenger steamers, railcar and passenger-car ferries, and tall ships. Today, a 1,000-foot Great Lakes freighter it is a sight to behold as it makes its way through the Straits of Mackinac. On foggy or stormy days, there is sometimes a line of vessels waiting for passage under the Mackinac Bridge.

Located on the southern shore of The Straits, at the tip of Michigan's Lower Peninsula, is Mackinaw City, the site of McGulpin Point Light, Old Mackinac Point Light, and Colonial Michilimackinac, a reconstructed military fort established in 1715 by the French also known as Old Mackinaw. The city of Cheboygan is also in the Lower Peninsula, sitting scenically on the south channel of Lake Huron at the mouth of the Cheboygan River. Known for its logging history, Cheboygan was also home to early Native American villages and ambitious fur traders. On the northern shore of The Straits, in Michigan's Upper Peninsula, is St. Ignace, the second-oldest city in Michigan. Once home to early Native American settlements, it is also the site of Fr. Jacques Marquette's Catholic mission, founded around 1671.

With this brief introduction to the history of The Straits, it is the author's hope that readers will dig deeper and continue to keep this history alive. Volumes have been published on all aspects of the area's history, with each writer expressing his or her own interpretation of early events. The varied legends and varied opinions make Michilimackinac history particularly fascinating.

Fortunately, much of contemporary history was recorded with picture postcards. Beginning about 1901, ordinary American citizens had black and white photographs taken and then printed onto stout paper with space on the back for a mailing address and message called real photo postcards. Postcards have progressed and improved over the years, from private mailing cards and real photo postcards to the "Linen Era" and the photochrome card seen today. Picture postcards give us a glance of the past and show that the Straits of Mackinac area is a gold mine of pictorial history.

One

First People
Anishinabe

In the beginning, or *mad-ji-tang*, they called themselves Anishinabek, plural for "first peoples." Belonging to the Algonquian language group of the St. Lawrence Seaway region, these Native Americans eventually migrated to the upper Great Lakes. In later years, nonnative people called these tribes the Chippewa, Ottawa, and Potawatomi.

Long before Europeans arrived, the Anishinabe established a new homeland in a territory they called Mish-en-i-mok-in-ong, primarily to escape the neighboring Iroquois. After their arrival, these Algonquian people divided themselves into three groups called the "People of the Three Fires": the Ojibwa ("Keepers of the Faith"), the Odawa ("Keepers of Trade"), and the Potawatomi ("Keepers of the Fire").

There are several spellings of the Ojibwa tribal name, including Odjibwa, Ojibwe, and Ojibway, depending on the appropriate reference to culture, people, or language. English-speaking people corrupted the name to Chippewa, which has become a popular place-name in Michigan. The Ojibwa were reported to be the most numerous of the tribes in The Straits, and one theory states that they received their name from the manner in which they constructed, or "puckered-up," their moccasins.

Closely linked to the Ojibwa are the Odawa, or Ottawa, who were best known for their skill as barterers or traders of desired commodities such as animal furs. Their largest settlement was south of The Straits in an area called L'Arbre Croche ("Crooked Tree") along the northeastern shores of Lake Michigan from present-day Cross Village to Harbor Springs. Earlier spellings included Ot-tah-way, Ottoway, and Odawak.

Originally named Bodewadomi, the third member of the Three Fires, the Potawatomi, lived near The Straits before migrating to the southern end of Lake Michigan and northern Indiana. Their name means "people of the fire," but they called themselves Weshnabek, "the people."

Other Algonquian tribes of Michilimackinac history included the Miami, Sauk, Fox, Menomini, and Winnebago and one significant tribe from the Iroquoian language group, the Huron.

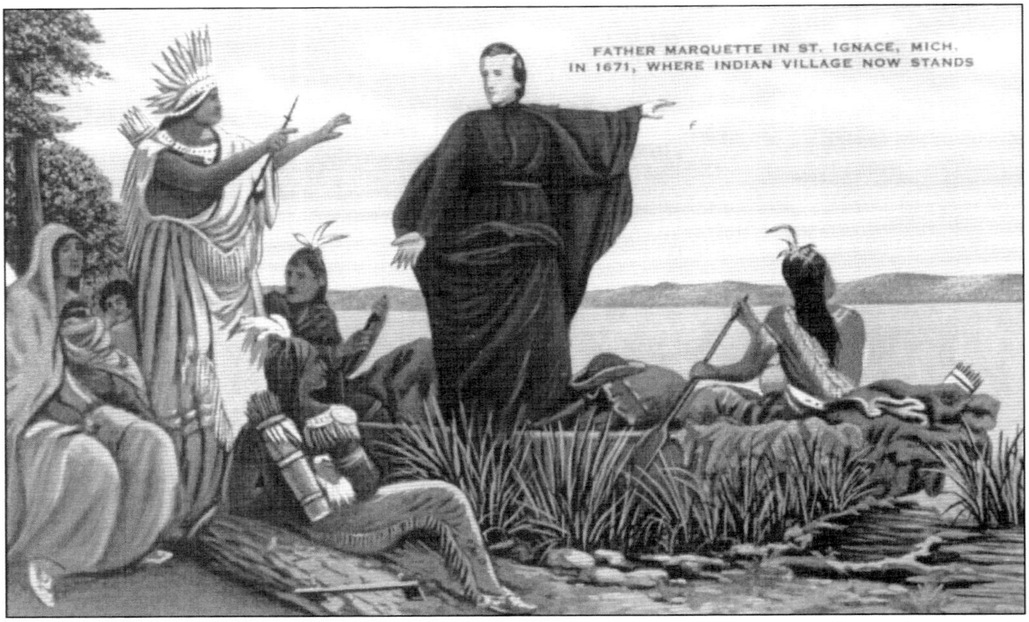

Among the first Europeans to visit the Straits of Mackinac area was French Jesuit priest Fr. Jacques Marquette. Born in 1637, Marquette first traveled to Canada, or New France, and arrived at present-day St. Ignace in 1671, where he established the mission of Saint Ignace de Missilimackinac. This postcard depicts a popular painting of Father Marquette ministering to his new neighbors in his continued attempt to convert them to Christianity.

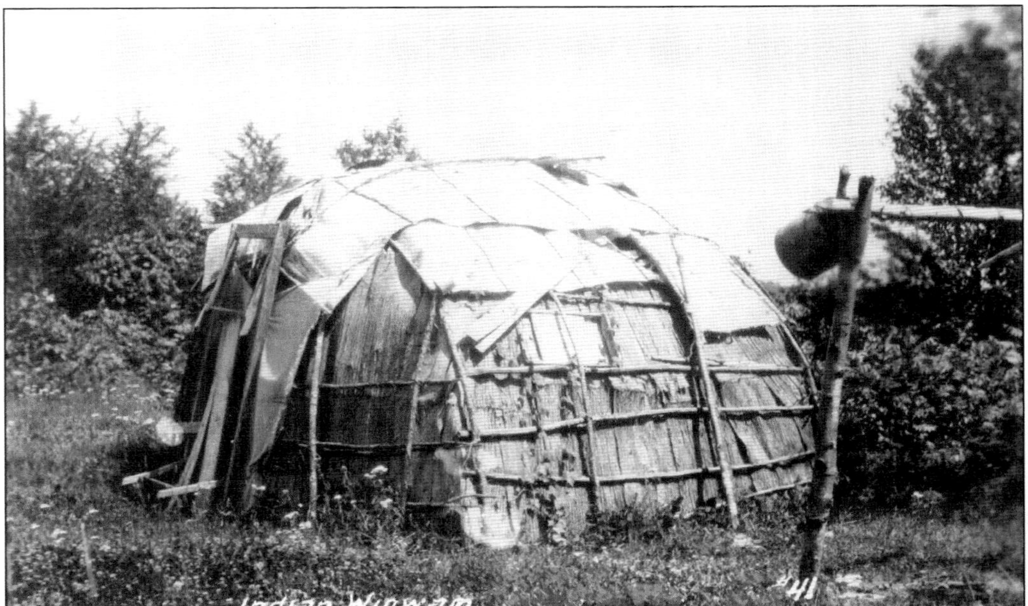

Father Marquette constructed a missionary bark chapel on a quiet inlet on the shores of East Moran Bay in St. Ignace similar to the reconstructed wigwam shown in this postcard. Using humble buildings like these as their churches, the devout French priests, called black robes, were determined to bring "civilization" to this primitive wilderness.

This statuesque monument located near his St. Ignace mission marks the final resting place of Father Marquette. His missionary life was cut short at the age of 38, when he contracted a fatal illness during a 1675 exploration trip along the Mississippi River. Originally buried in Ludington, Marquette was reburied at St. Ignace two years later. A historical marker at the site explains that the monument was erected by the citizens of St. Ignace in 1882.

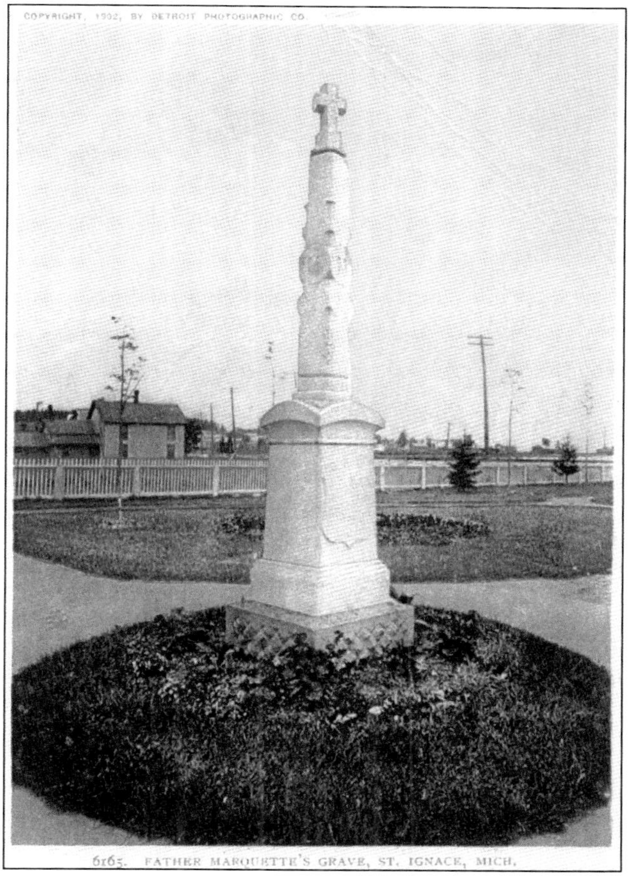

This 1913 view looks out over East Moran Bay. The Marquette monument graces Marquette Park located on North State Street adjacent to the Museum of Ojibwa Culture. An Ottawa settlement and a Huron village were located nearby. The native people living there reportedly loved their Jesuit priest and did their utmost to preserve his memory.

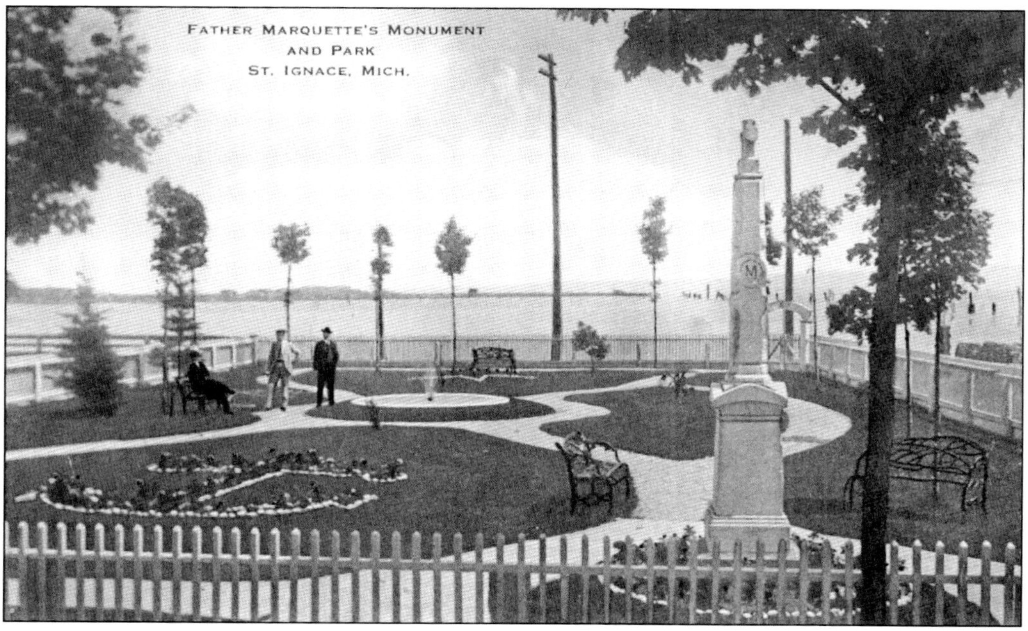

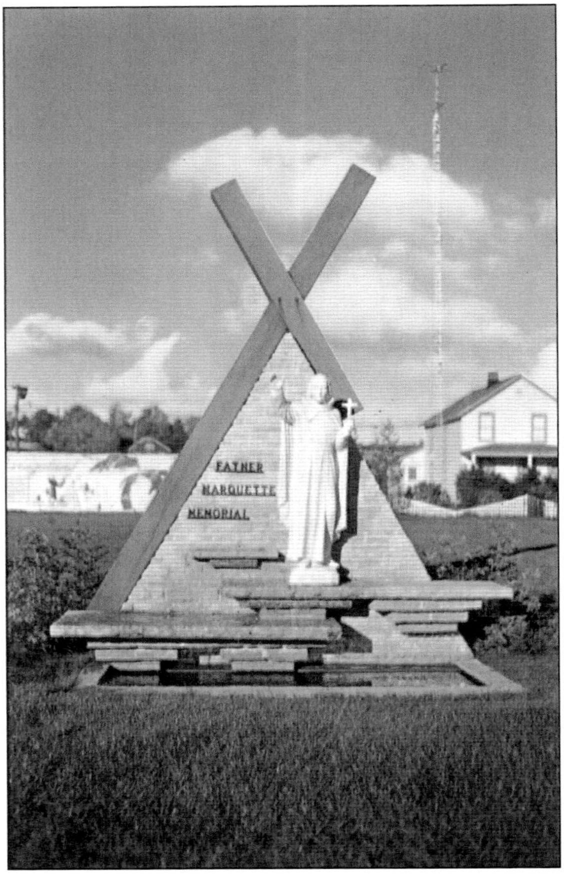

This 1959 postcard shows the St. Ignace Father Marquette Shrine, which was dedicated by the Marquette Diocese in 1957. Notice the wooden cross providing a special backdrop to Marquette's statue. Father Marquette continually wrote letters back to France, eventually published in the *Relations des Jesuits*, exclaiming the magnificence of his new life and explorations.

The description on the back of this vintage postcard states that on the second Sunday in August an annual Field Mass was held at Father Marquette's shrine. Here, an Indian choir chants Mass songs in native language from Bishop Frederick Baraga's translation. Bishop Baraga, another Jesuit black robe, was nicknamed "the snowshoe priest" and concentrated most of his missionary work in Michigan's Upper Peninsula.

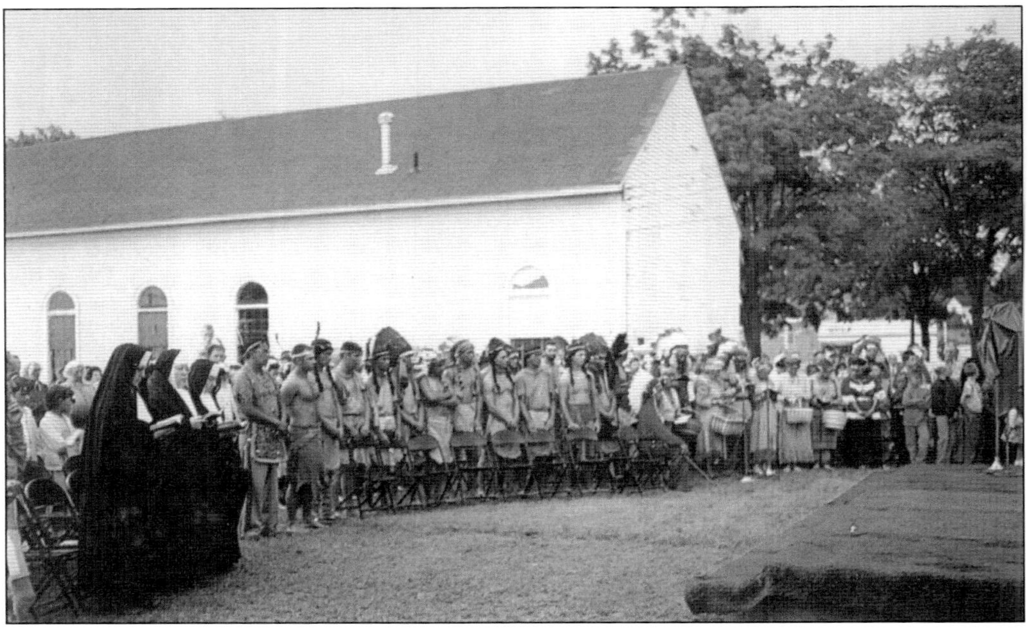

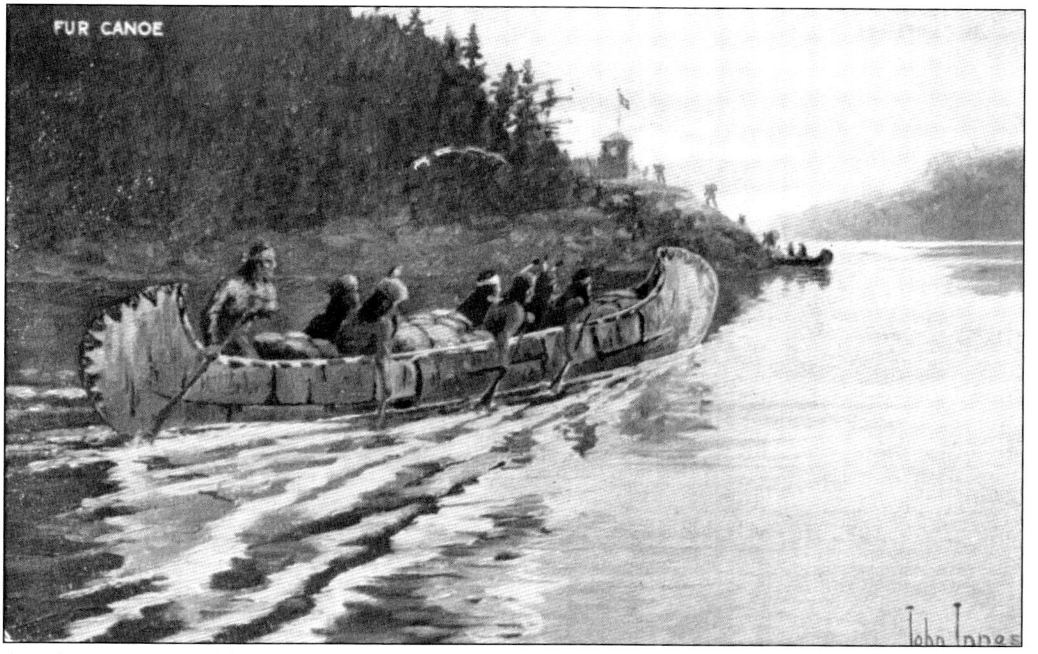

Another segment of the Michilimackinac population was the hardy French fur trader, voyageur, and explorer, often called coureurs de bois—"runners of the woods." Accompanied in huge birch bark canoes by Native American guides who trapped the animals, the fur traders were on hand with trinkets, blankets, and beads for exchange. Furs were sent back to France, where demand was high for hats and clothing attire. Too often, brandy was the medium of exchange, which caused frequent instances of unbalanced trade and extra aggravation for the Jesuit priests, as noted in their chronicles. The early fur trader left little account of his dealings, but ledgers of early fur-trade companies show that beaver pelts, or *amik*, were the main prize. There were also shipments of foxes, wolves, bears, otters, mink, deer, muskrats, and raccoons.

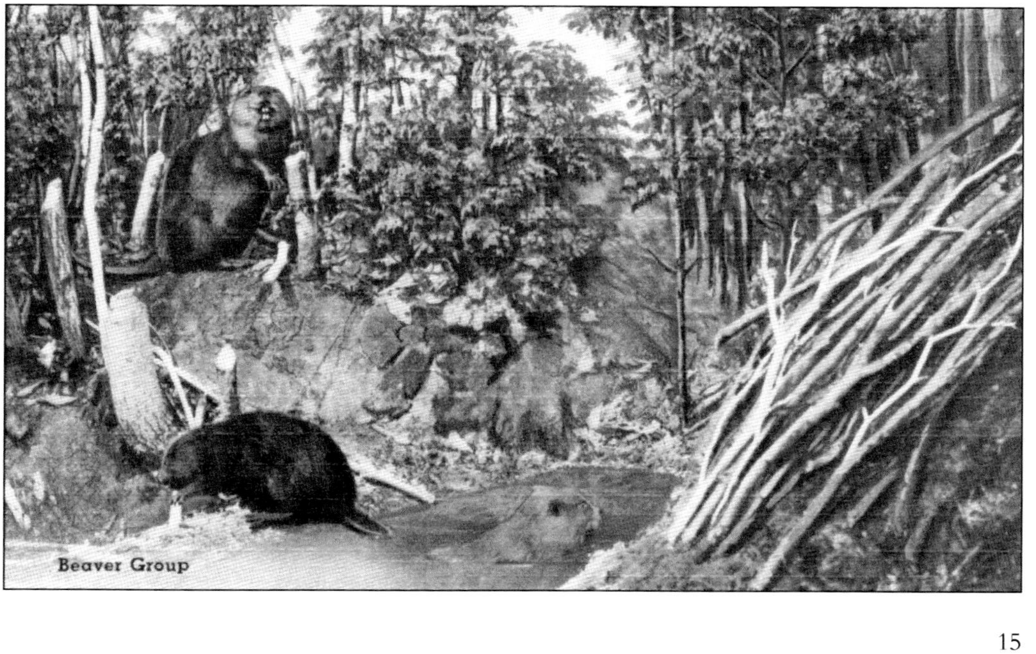

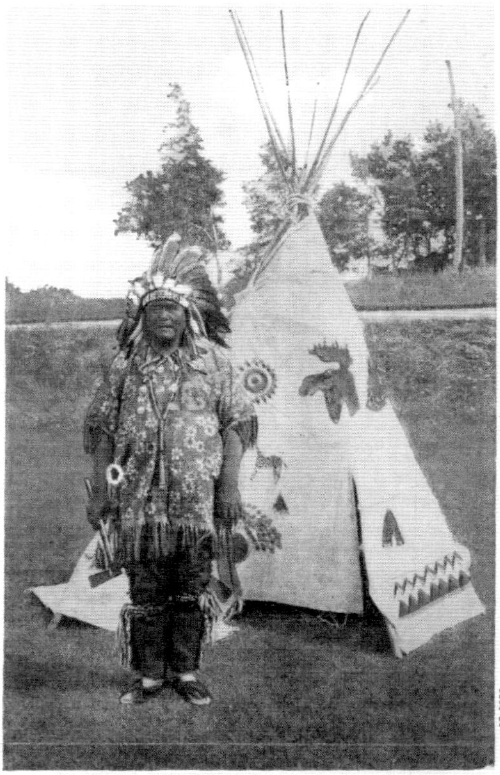

25 Big Joe of the Ottawa Tribe in Northern Michigan

To the Anishinabe, every person was valued. Elders were respected for their wisdom and experience, and even though men and women had different roles in the village, their tasks were equally important to survival. Native people also respected nature and everything that was part of it. Their survival depended on hunting animals, gathering plants, and fishing in the lakes, rivers, and streams, but they never took more than they needed nor did they waste any part of an animal or plant. Plants were used for food and medicine, animal bones for tools, animal skin for clothing, and meat for food. These 1940s postcards show elders Big Joe (left) of the Ottawa tribe, and Chief Jake Gim-me-won of the Chippewa, both dressed in full regalia.

CHIEF JAKE GIM-ME-WON, CHIPPEWA LEADER

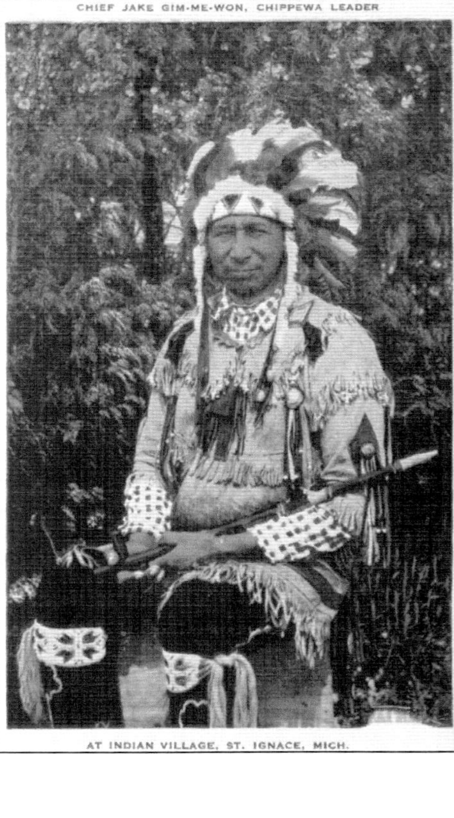

AT INDIAN VILLAGE, ST. IGNACE, MICH.

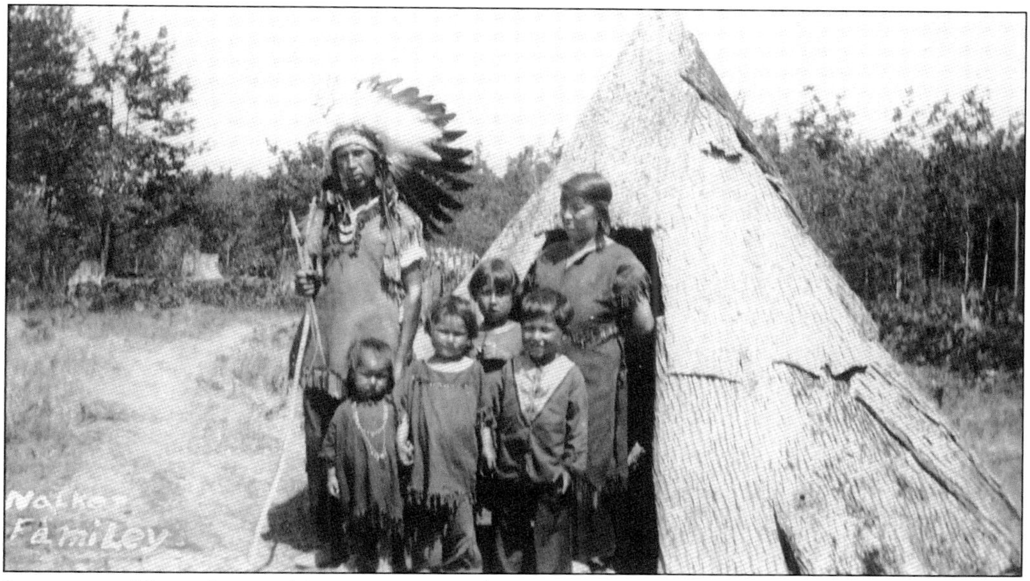

In a postcard from the Mackinaw City area, these Native Americans are identified as the Walker family. An important feature in Anishinabe culture was the treatment of children, who were bestowed with great affection and concern for their comfort and welfare. Families belonged to clans, and the spirit of each clan belonged to a respected animal ancestor, such as bear, deer, moose, or eagle. (Courtesy of John Marsh.)

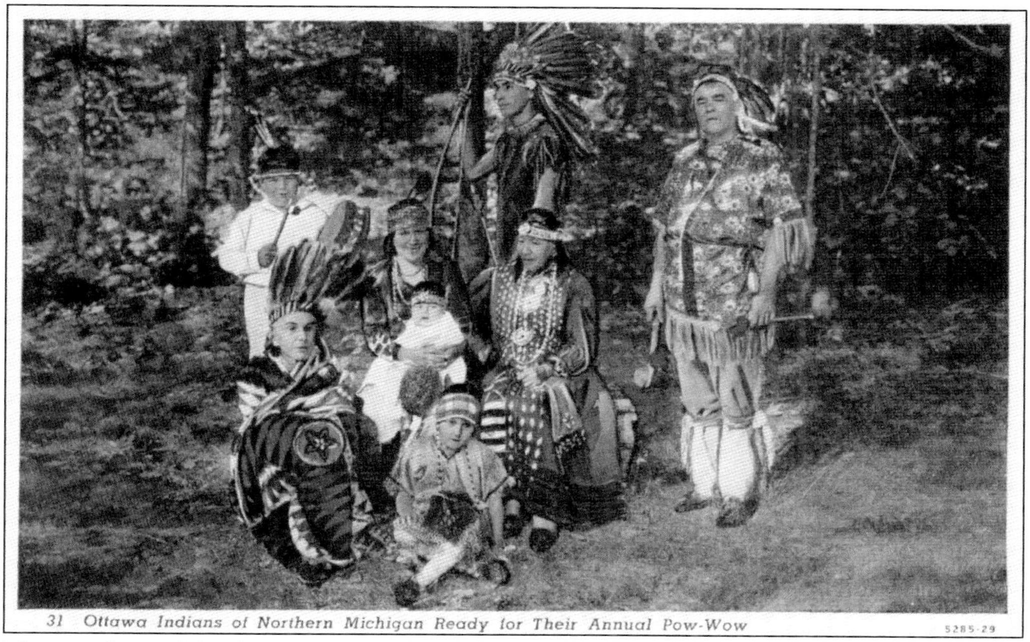

The members of this family are identified as "Ottawa Indians of Northern Michigan Ready for Their Annual Pow-Wow." Postmarked 1939 from Petoskey, Michigan, the message on this card relates that the temperature was 85 degrees in September. In its towns and villages, Michigan has preserved the names of well-known native peoples, such as Chief Ignatius Pe-to-se-ga, Odawa for "where the light shines through," from which Petoskey is derived.

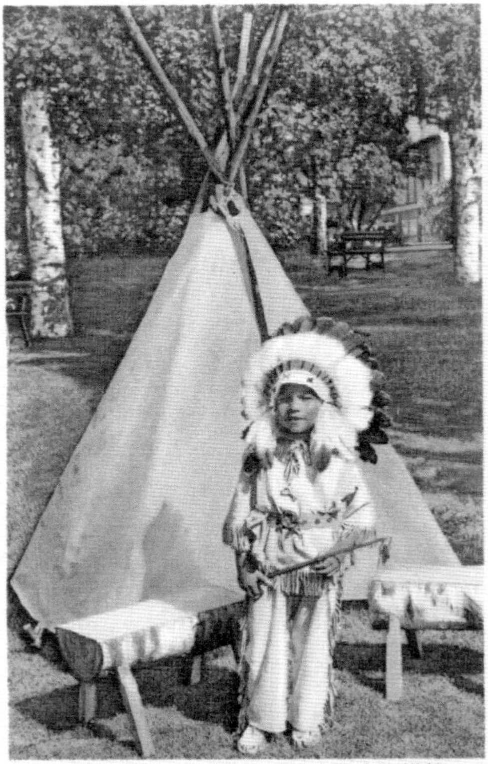

99—Little Indian Brave, (Ga-mu-na-neese), Northern Michigan

Young Native American boys had much to do to help their families, including catching and cleaning fish and bringing them back to the village. There were arrows to make, small game to shoot, snares to check, and wood to cut and haul. Young girls helped with grinding corn, skinning animals, drying food, making clothing, learning decorative quillwork, and weaving baskets. Children, or *abbinochi*, also helped with berry picking and making maple sugar. Care of the young was of utmost importance, and a child's naming was an important life event with special preparations. Personal names were not usually given at birth but after some incident occurred or if a characteristic suggested an appropriate name. Names could be changed with new circumstances related to dreams, omens, or the adventures of the individual. Early Anishinabe did not have surnames.

"ABSOLUTELY INDIAN MADE" INDIAN VILLAGE, ST. IGNACE, MICH.

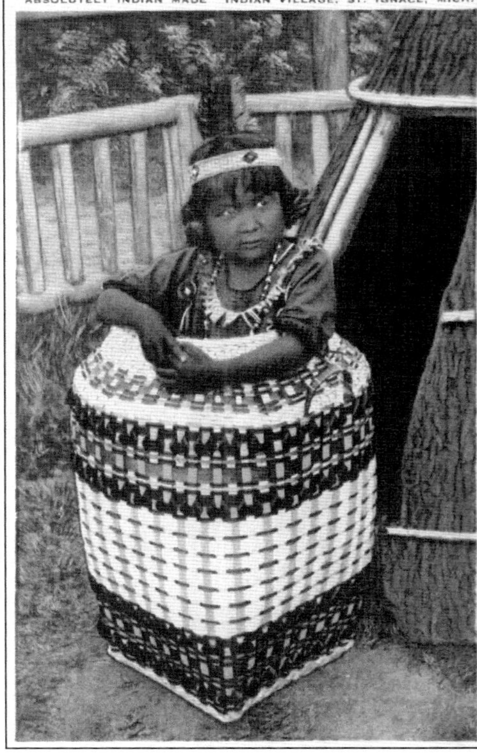

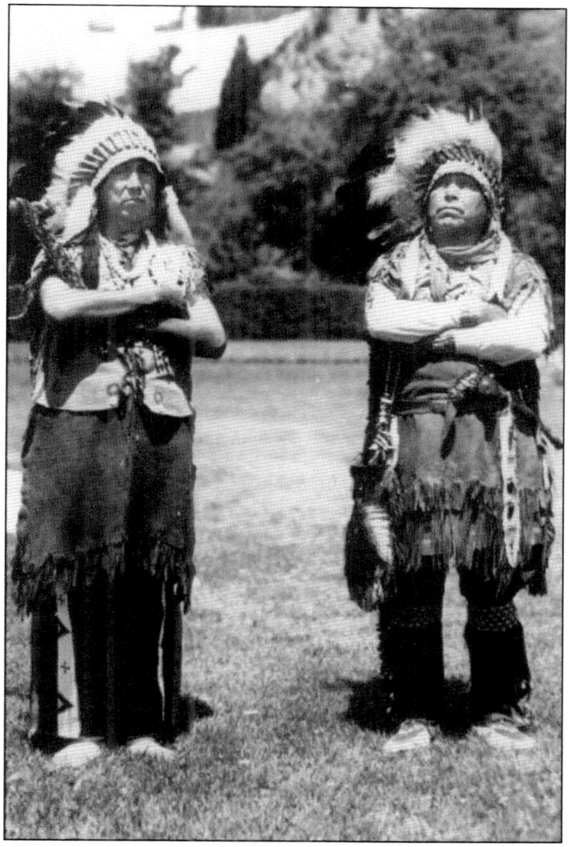

The Ojibwa word for chief was spelled in several ways, including *ogima*, *ogema*, and *ogemaw*, many of which are used in Michigan place names, such as Ogemaw County, Ogemaw State Forest, and Ogima, a mining settlement in the Upper Peninsula. The two unidentified chiefs to the right appear only mildly interested in having their picture taken. The word "squaw," for an Indian woman, actually originated with the Narraganset tribe in the eastern United States around 1643. White men heard the term and applied it to all Native American women, and from this misuse, it became a derogatory term. Chief White Wolf and Happy Day Woman, members of the Chippewa Tribe at Totem Village near St. Ignace, are pictured below. Interestingly, "papoose," the white man's corrupted name for a Native infant, also originated with the Narraganset.

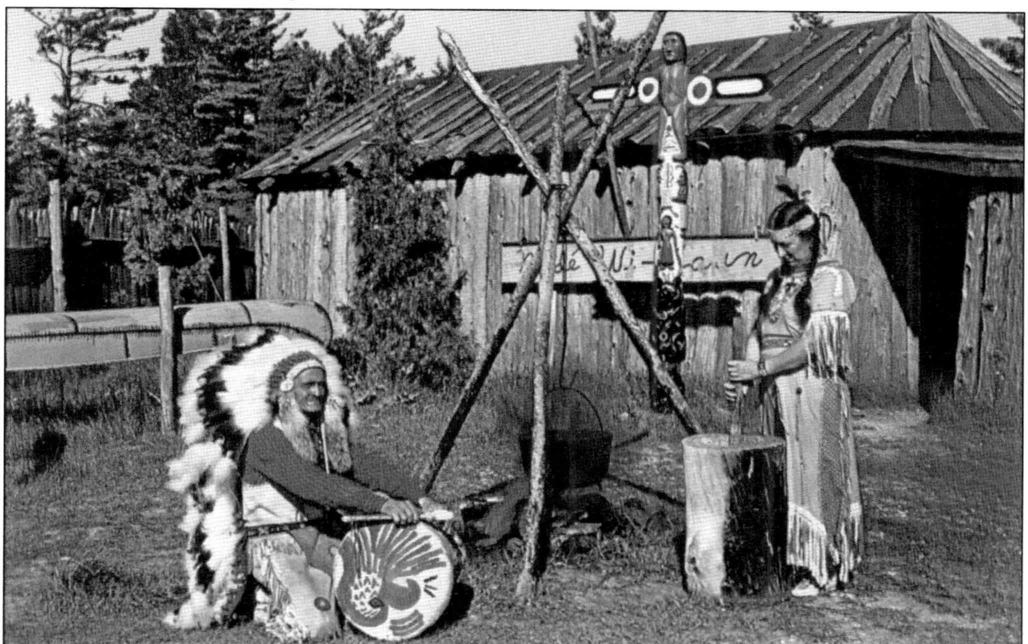

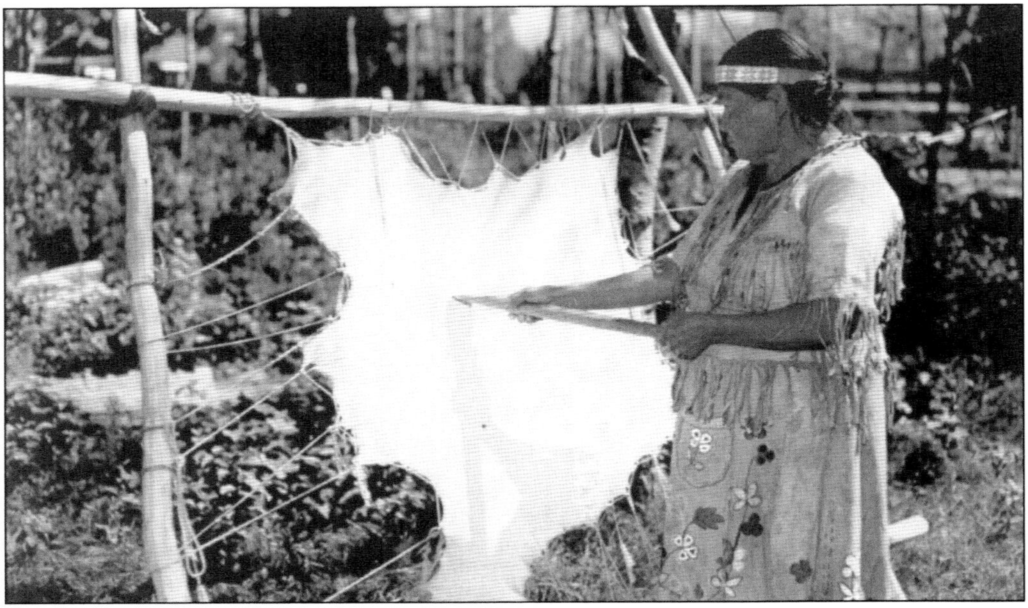

Early Ojibwa women had many duties and responsibilities all four seasons of the year. In the spring, maple sap was collected and boiled into maple sugar, a necessary food provision. One family might make from 500 to 800 pounds in four to six weeks. New birch bark canoes for hunting, fishing, and gathering wild rice were also made in the spring. Summertime brought garden planting, herb gathering, and berry picking. Gardens yielded squash, pumpkins, corn, beans, potatoes, and sunflowers. Berries and herbs were used for flavoring food as well as for medicinal purposes. In the fall, among other duties, women helped the men catch fish for smoking for later use. Wintertime was for making and decorating clothing. These contemporary postcards show an Ojibwa women tanning a deer hide and another making moccasins from buckskin.

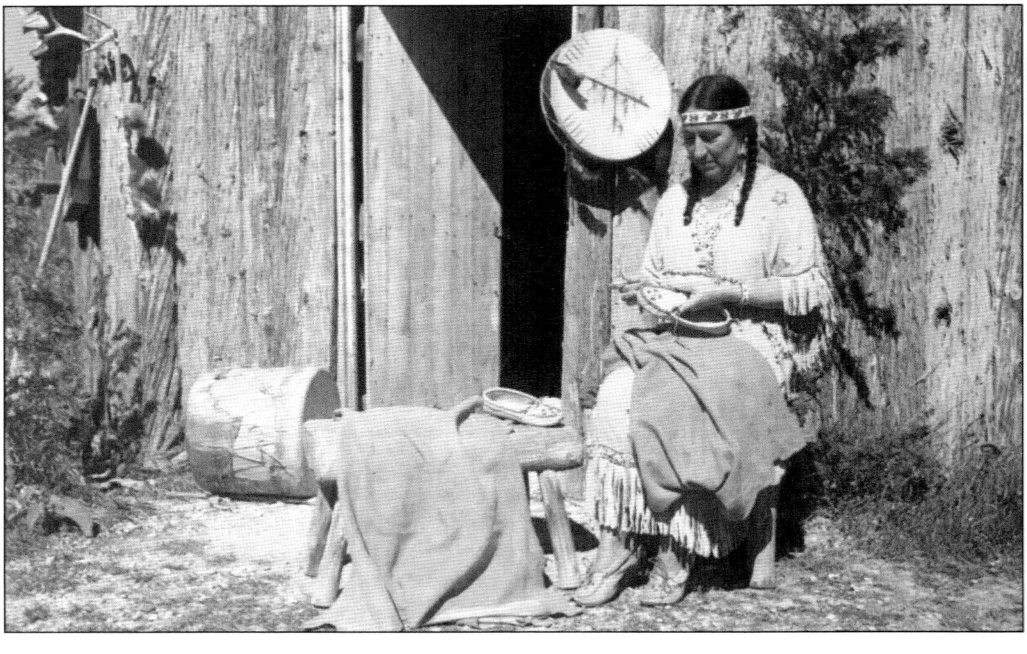

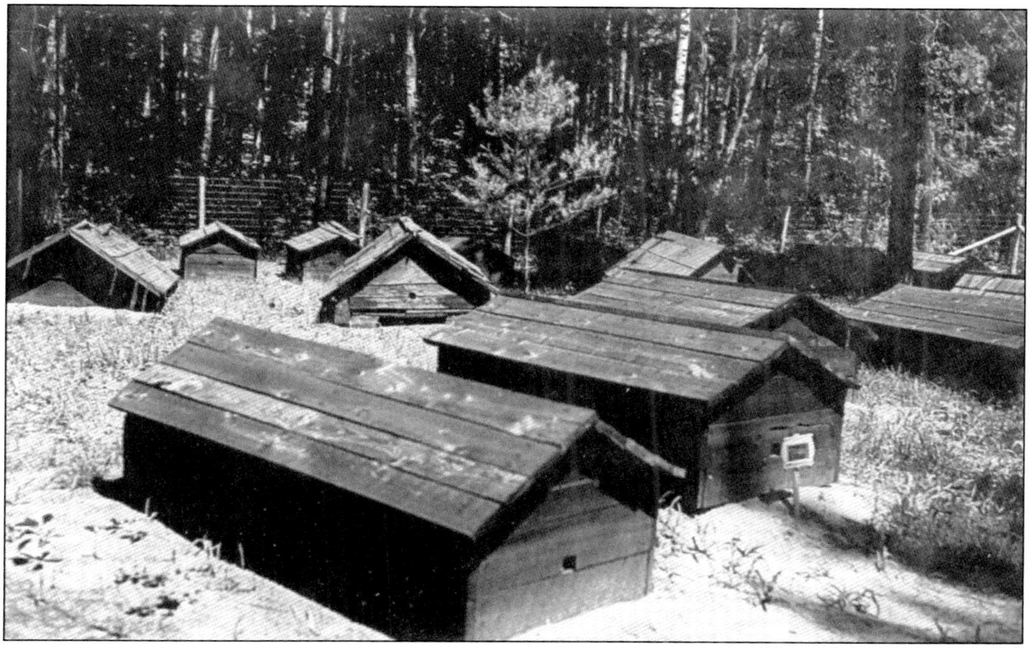

After the death of an Ojibwa, the body was placed upon a platform, usually in a wooded area, where it remained for several days. It was thought that the spirit would leave the body and travel to the afterlife. The remains were then wrapped in birch bark and buried in a shallow grave with the feet pointing westward. Personal possessions were placed with the deceased, usually a medicine bundle or a weapon. Small wooden "spirit houses" were erected over the grave, and family members mourned for one year. Each autumn, the Ojibwa observed the Feast of the Dead, a remembrance of all who had died in the past year. These postcards show Ojibwa burying sites located around the Straits of Mackinac.

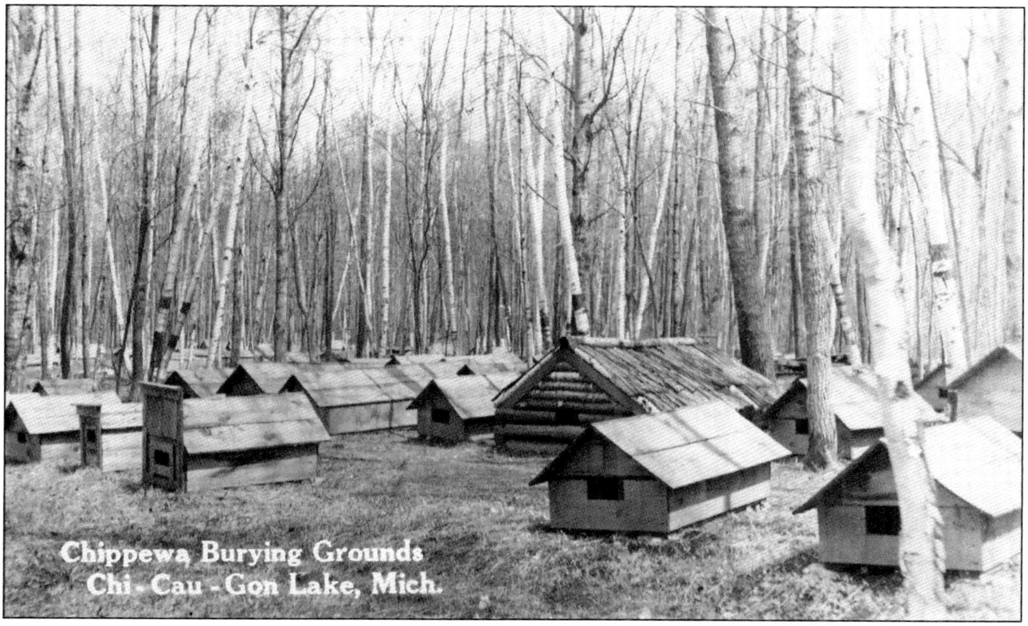

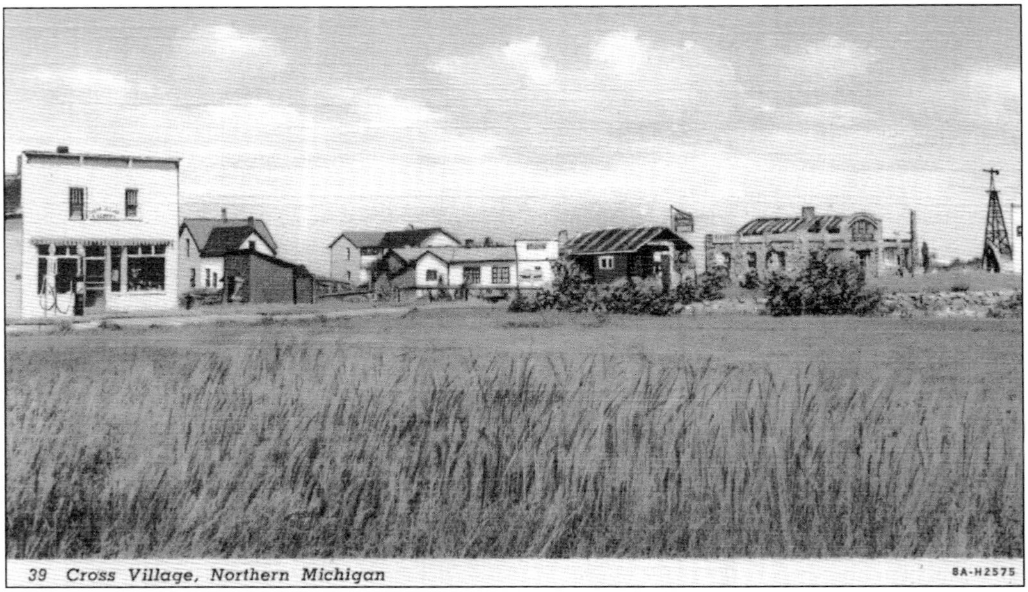

After the soil was nutrient-depleted and crops began to fail, Ottawa from Michilimackinac moved to the northeastern shore of Lake Michigan to an area they called Waw-gaw-naw-ke-zee ("the tree is crooked") marked by a large landmark pine tree high on the bluff near present-day Good Hart. Separate settlements were scattered all the way from Cross Village to Harbor Springs and Petoskey. The French called it L'Arbre Croche, meaning "crooked tree."

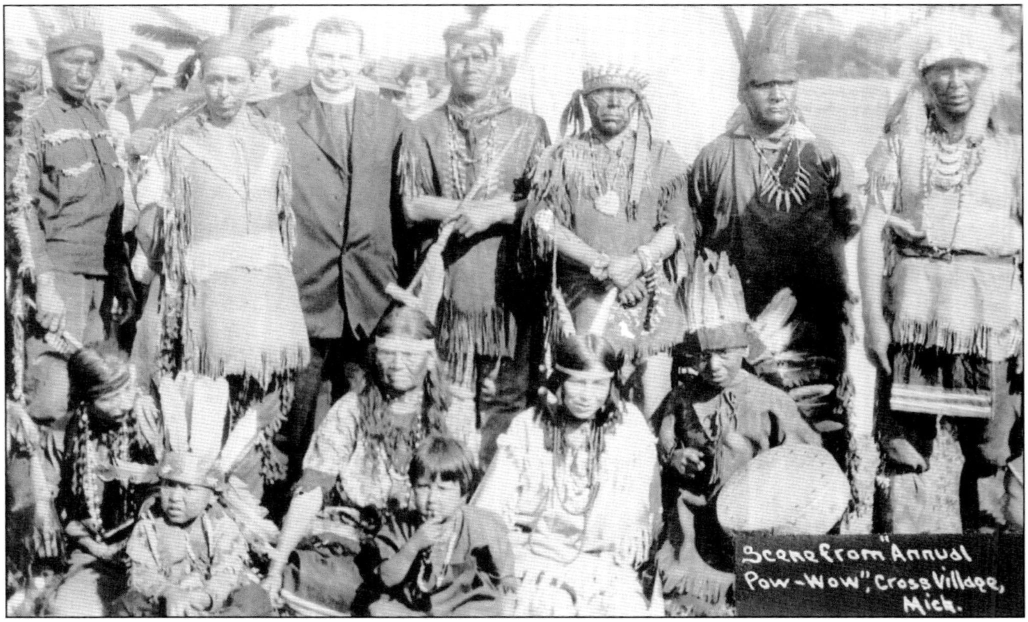

The Ottawa were known as At-a-wa-was. This name was pronounced and spelled in many different ways, including Adawe (meaning "to trade"), O-da-ways, and Odawa. It was French Jesuit missionary Pierre François Xavier de Charlevoix who called them Ottawas. The Ottawa and Odawa names are used interchangeably, but Odawa is preferred by the Little Traverse Bay bands of Odawa Indians. This postcard shows a scene from an annual powwow held at Cross Village.

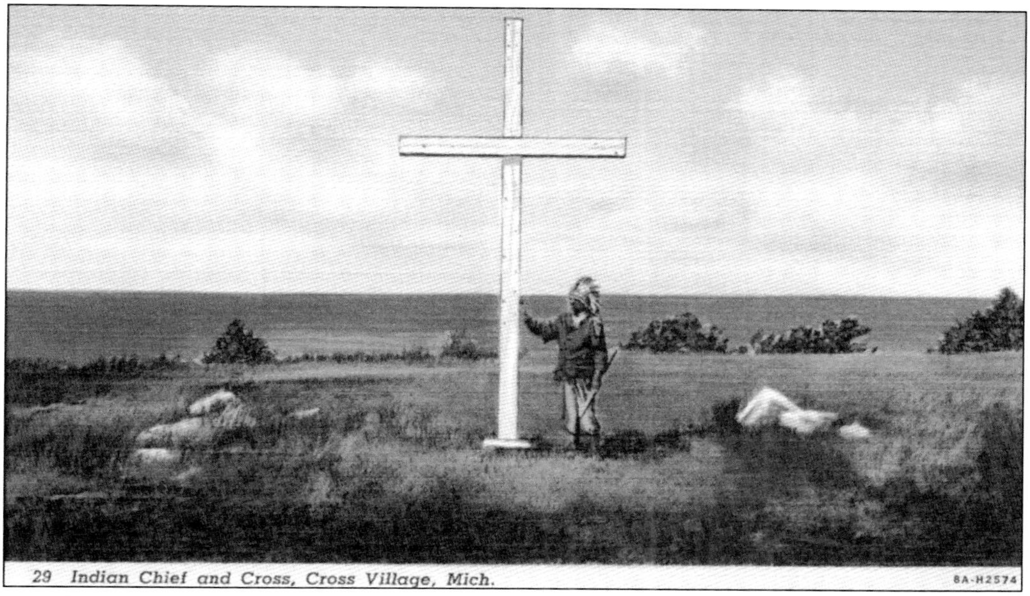

French Jesuit missionaries such as Charlevoix were busy establishing Catholic missions all throughout Michilimackinac and for the Odawa at L'Arbre Croche. A large religious cross was erected on the bluff at Cross Village. The original cross has been replaced many times over the years, and a replica remains there today. Anamiewatigoing is the native name for the village and means "at the tree of prayer."

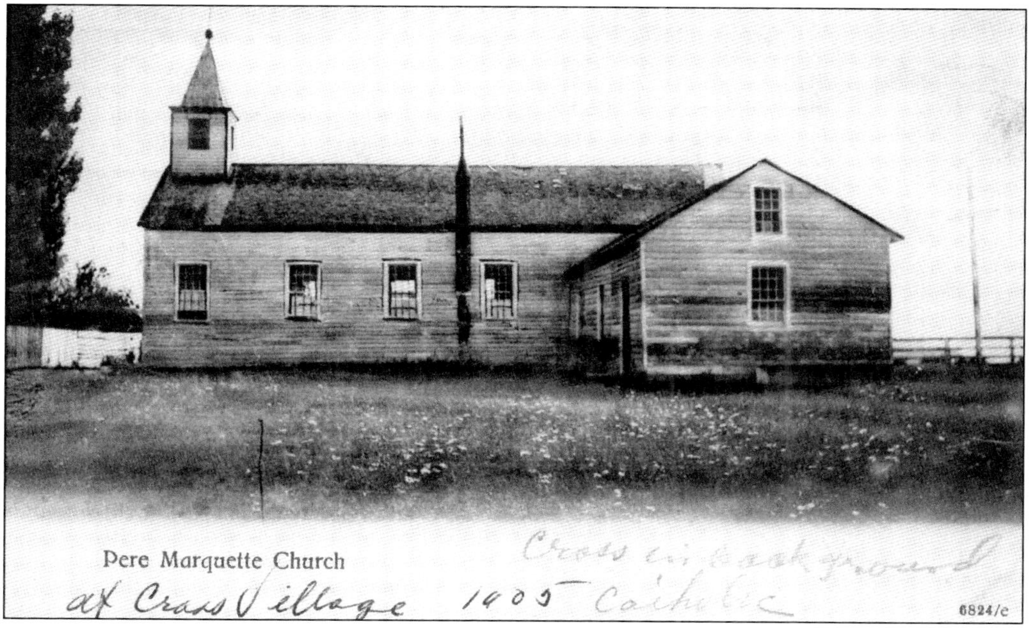

This 1905 postcard shows the primitive Pere Marquette Church at Cross Village with the landmark cross in the background. Connected to the Jesuit mission of Saint Ignace de Michilimackinac, this church saw many baptisms, marriages, and funerals as the area grew in population. Most of the records of the church are in Latin and Odawa and date back to 1847. The native settlement dates back to the late 1600s.

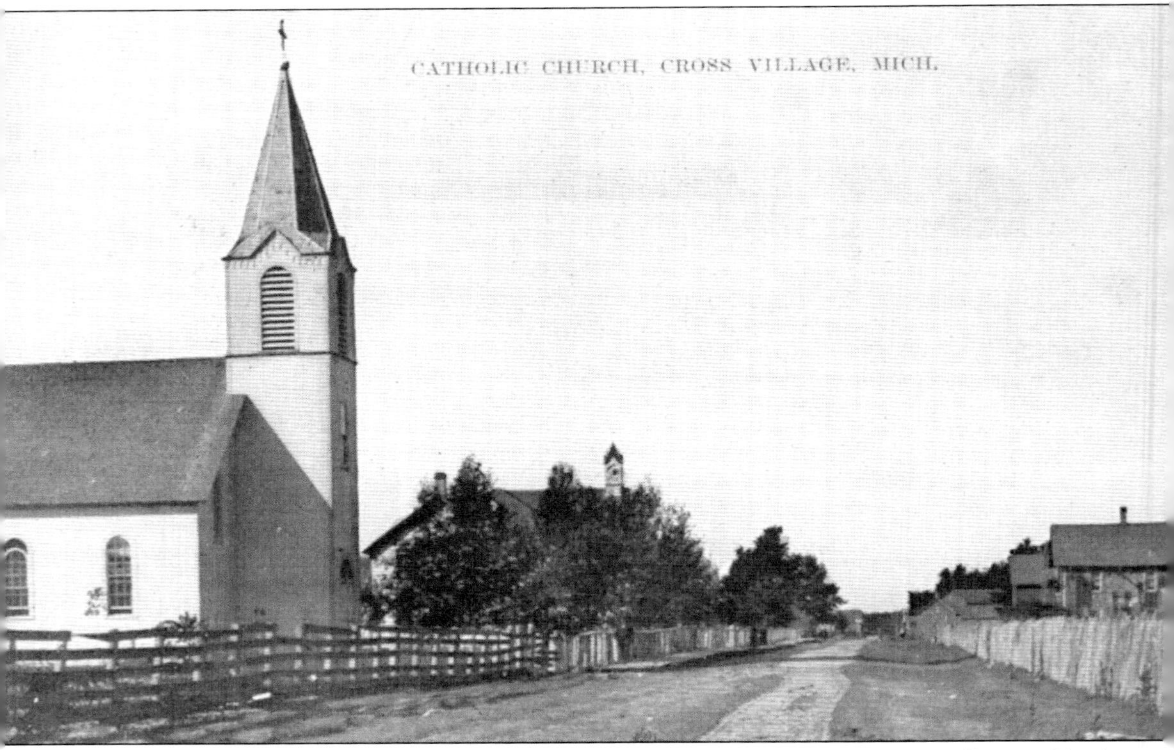

In 1855, Fr. John Bernard Weikamp, born in 1818 in Prussia, came to Cross Village and built a convent. A member of the Franciscan Order, Father Weikamp established what was called the Benevolent, Charitable, and Religious Society of St. Francis, which eventually owned 2,000 acres of land. A self-sufficient institution, the convent operated a gristmill, a carpenter shop, a sawmill, and a blacksmith shop. Even the wooden shoes worn by the nuns were made on-site, but its reputation was mainly for its famous currant wine. The convent closed in 1896. On the back of this early-1900s Cross Village postcard addressed to Rev. Father Opalatus Loeffler in Odanah, Wisconsin, Father Agaito writes, "Merry Christmas and Happy New Year to you and all the Fathers. Father Anton let me cut only one-half of the wood for the church and school. Mr. Samolewski wants $8.00 a ton for the hay. The Indian money did not arrive yet. Father Pranto thinks it will not come. That will be a hard blow. Raise Pranto's rent?"

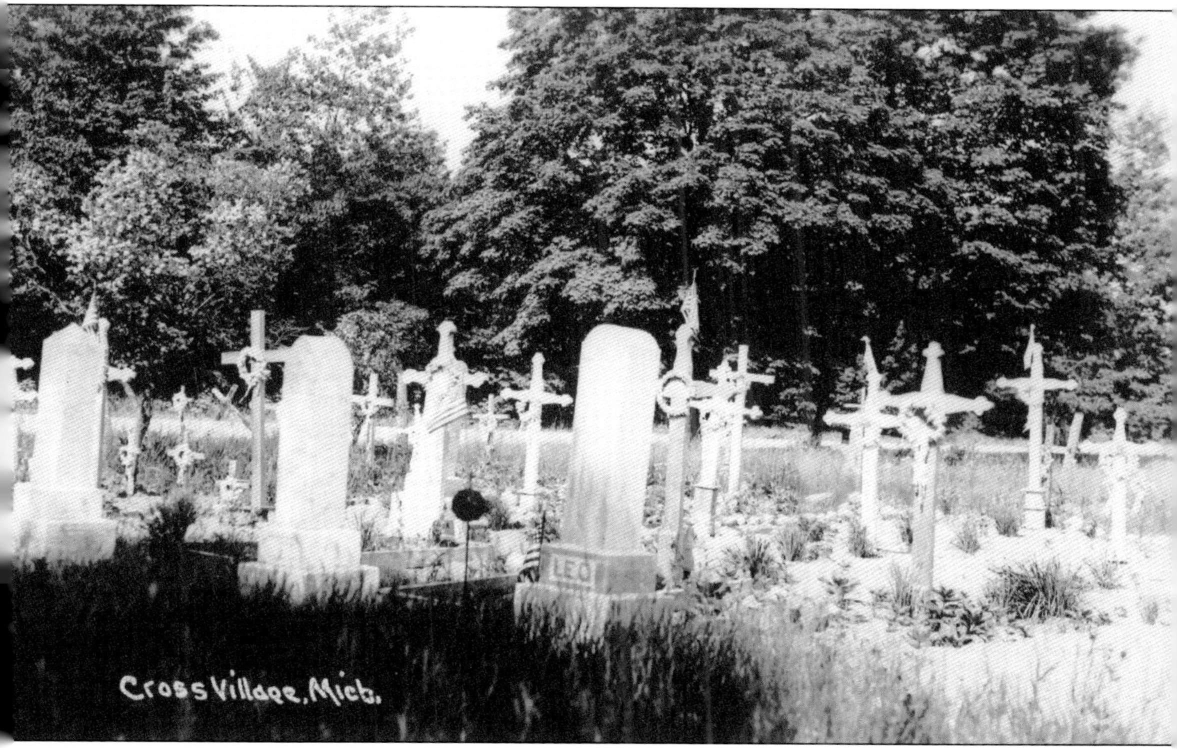

Gitche-ie-nay-gow-ge-cut-che-gah, or "they have put the sand over him," was a common expression among the native people to express that a man is dead and buried. When a parent died, a fast was observed for 10 days, during which time the mourner avoided long walks or trips in case he would be doomed to continuous walking. Only short morning walks were allowed for exercise. The person who lost a parent would not comb his own hair during the 10 days, for to do so would cause it to be thin. Sweets were avoided also to prevent tooth decay. Superstitions were a part of the Ottawa culture; for instance, the tapping of a woodpecker settling upon the roof was considered a very bad omen. Dead persons supposedly had power to remove disease or affliction from the living by rubbing the hand of the deceased over the afflicted body part. A mixture of interesting grave markers is shown in this postcard of an old settlement cemetery in Cross Village.

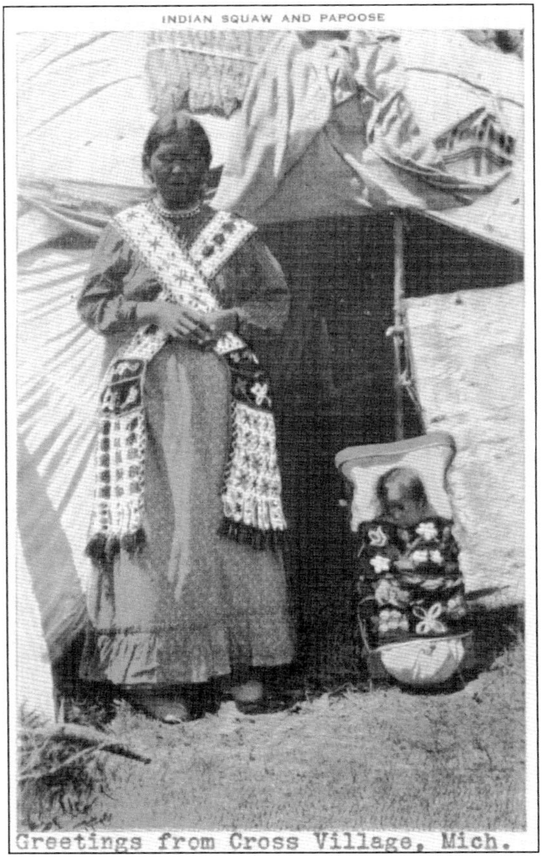

The two Michilimackinac postcards on this page, both from around 1940, show how Native American infants were kept in cradleboards. Considered a "third mother," after Mother Earth and the biological mother, these cradleboards kept babies feeling secure and protected and left mothers free to perform their work. Cradleboards were lined with soft fibers, such as dried moss or rabbit fur, and infants wore little clothing while inside. Mothers could hang the cradleboard from a tree, where it could swing like a hammock, or simply prop it up near their daily tasks. Ottawa and Chippewa cradleboards were usually rectangular planks with *U*-shaped footboards and a wooden arch over the head. The image to the left is entitled "Indian Squaw and Papoose," which would be improper terminology today.

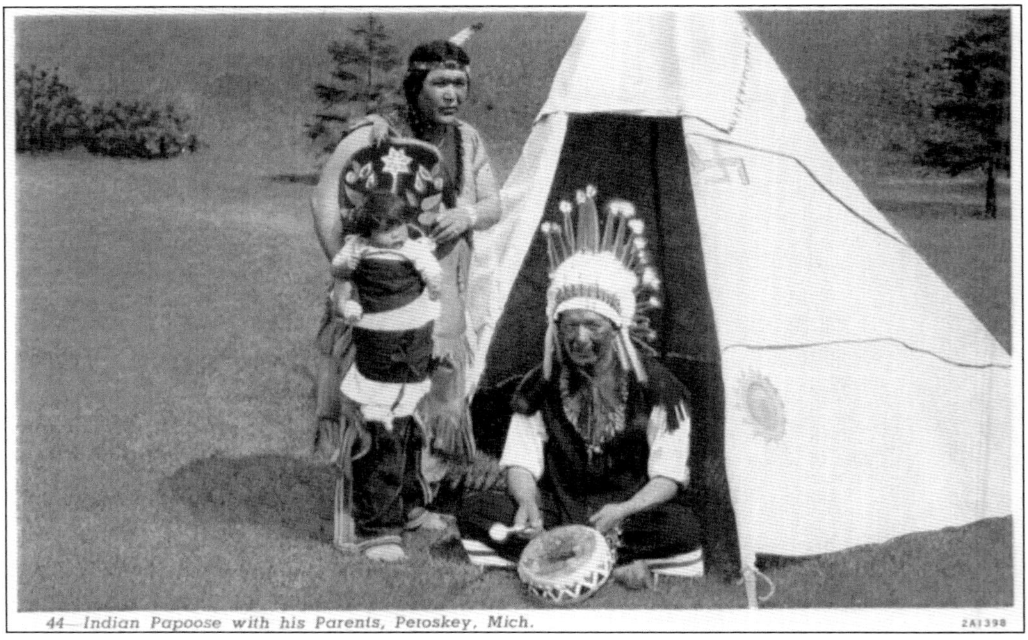

Also postmarked in the 1940s, these postcards show relatives of Chief Ignatius Pe-to-se-ga (1787–1885). To the right is "Princess" Ella Jane Petoskey (1880–1972), a granddaughter of Chief Petoskey who belonged to the Ottawa tribe. She is wearing a beautiful beaded headband and a fringed buckskin dress. Ella graduated from Carlisle College in Pennsylvania and traveled extensively, speaking and teaching at various Indian reservations. She is buried in Friendship Township Cemetery in Emmet County, Michigan. Below is Samson Keywaykondo, a nephew of Chief Petoskey, dressed with an elaborate cape and full headdress.

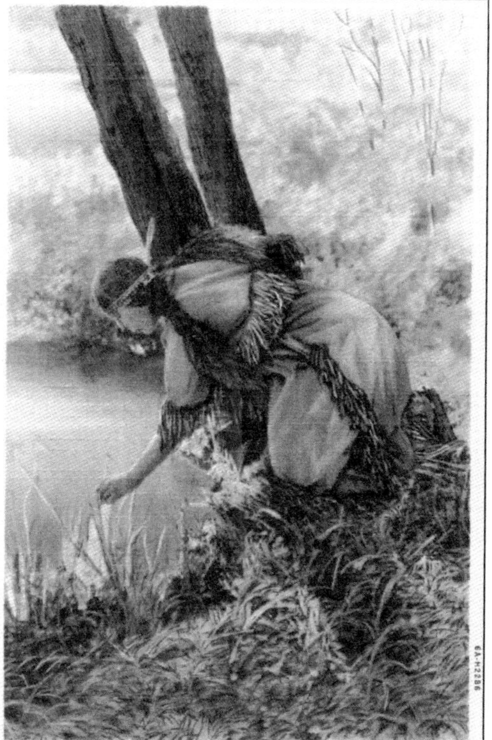

66A PRINCESS ELLA PETOSKEY

105 Samson Keywaykondo, Nephew of Chief Ignatious Petosega,

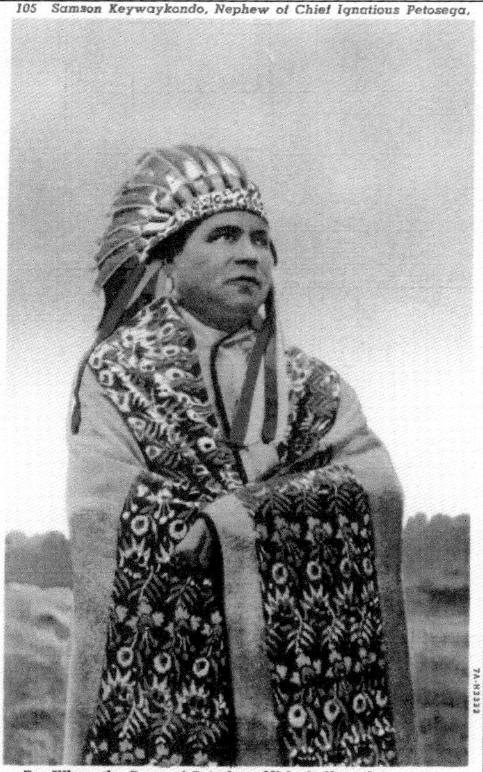

For Whom the Town of Petoskey, Mich. is Named

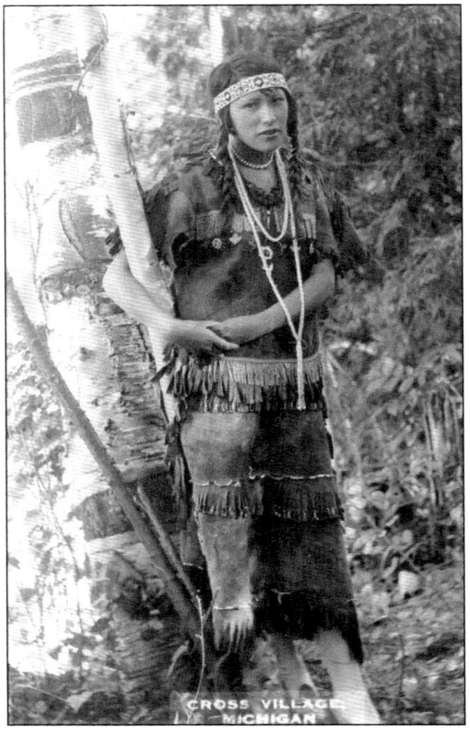

Odawa and Ojibwa beadwork and quillwork are beautiful and widely renowned. The women in these postcards are wearing magnificently beaded headbands and jewelry. Beadwork, both woven and embroidered, followed quillwork in the early decorations of moccasins, carrying bags, and other personal items made of animal skin. The Ojibwa used seed beads in a variety of colors, with much care in their selection and combination. Beads were strung and attached using animal sinew, usually of deer. Beaded work was also used on sacred drums and for saddle covers. Beaded band weavings were made on a simple loom. Intricate patterns are seen in the beadwork below. Authentic beadwork by Native American women is still available in the towns and villages surrounding the Straits of Mackinac.

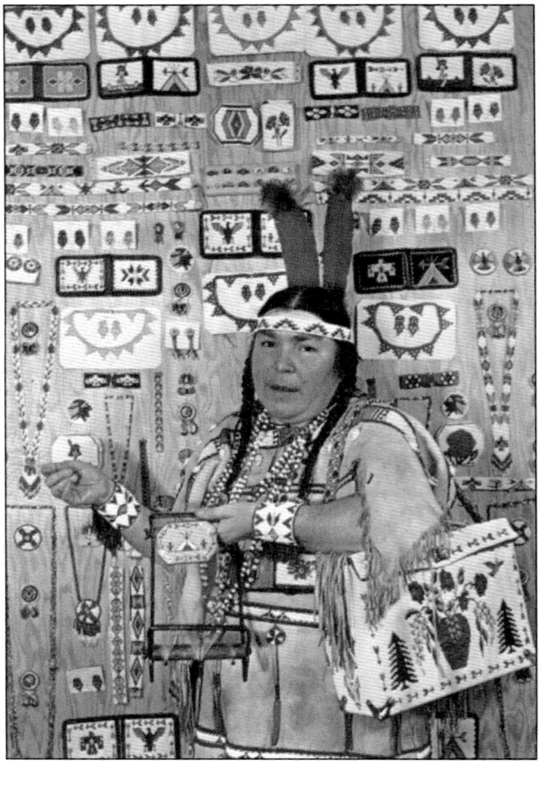

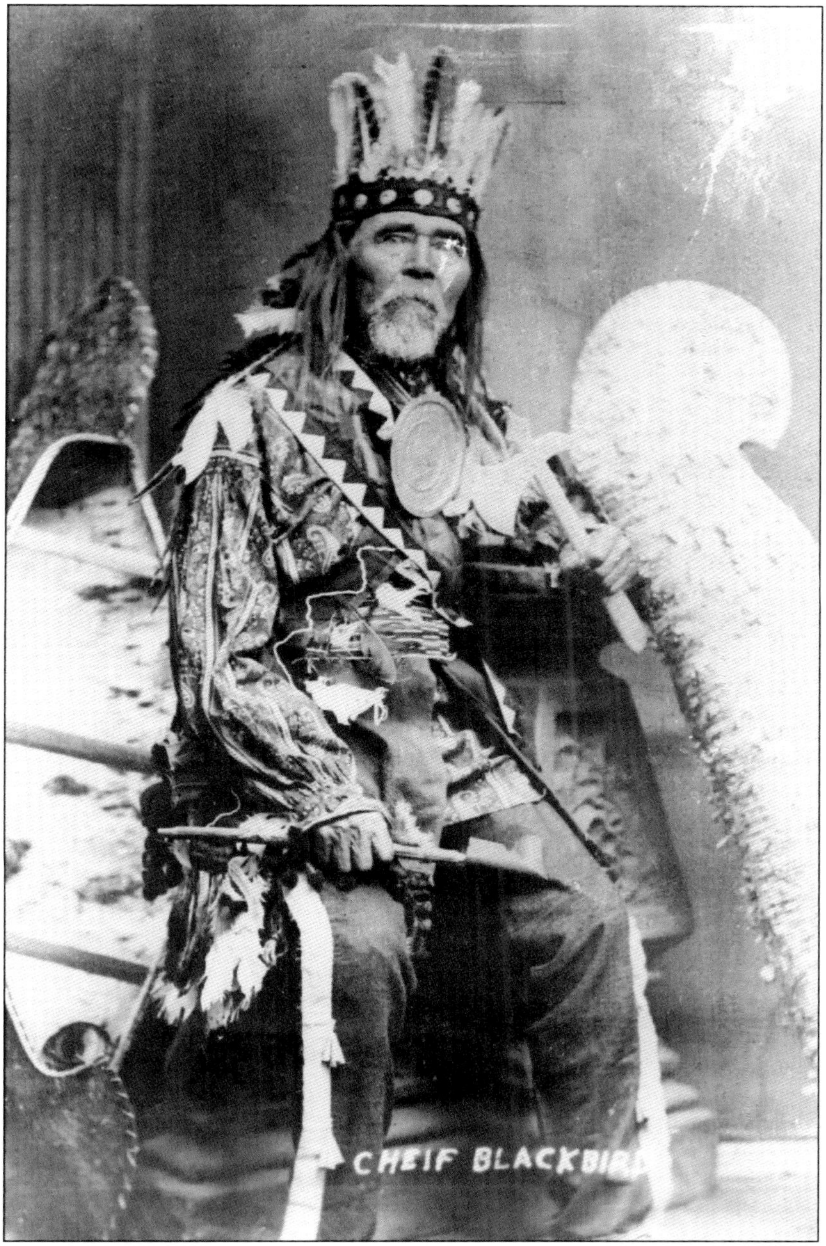

This postcard depicts a magnificent portrait of Chief Andrew Jackson Blackbird. Dressed in ornate garb and sitting next to a birch bark canoe, Chief Blackbird represents his Ottawa heritage proudly. Born in the L'Arbre Croche region around 1815, he was the son of Chief Mack-e-te-be-nessy, which translates to "black hawk." As with other native names, Makadebinesi was mistranslated to "black bird," and the name remained. In 1858, Andrew J. married Englishwoman Elizabeth Margaret Fish. In 1887, he published his *History of the Ottawa and Chippewa Indians of Michigan: A Grammar of Their Language, and Personal and Family History of the Author*, a fantastic historical account of facts and details of Ottawa and Ojibwa life. It also includes his sometimes-overlooked theory on the name origin of Mackinac.

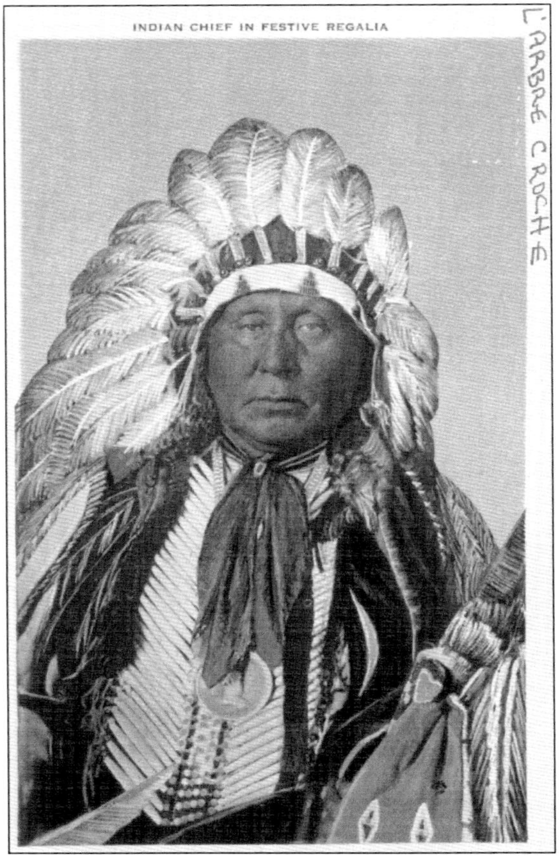

Anishinabe of the Three Fires (Odawa, Chippewa, and Potawatomi) and the Huron have contributed quite colorfully to the history of the Straits of Mackinac. History and legend were passed orally from father to son, as well as hunting skills and skill in battle. By mutual consent, warring tribes had to fit their battles between canoe-making time and harvest time. While it would seem strange in modern American culture, native wars would usually stop at pumpkin-gathering time. When the white man, or *wewaquonidjig*, brought diseases like smallpox to Michilimackinac natives—sometimes on purpose—thousands died and entire villages were wiped out. Relying more and more on European trade goods, succumbing to alcohol, and being cheated and pushed from their Mackinac homeland that Europeans claimed for themselves, Anishinabe lives were changed forever.

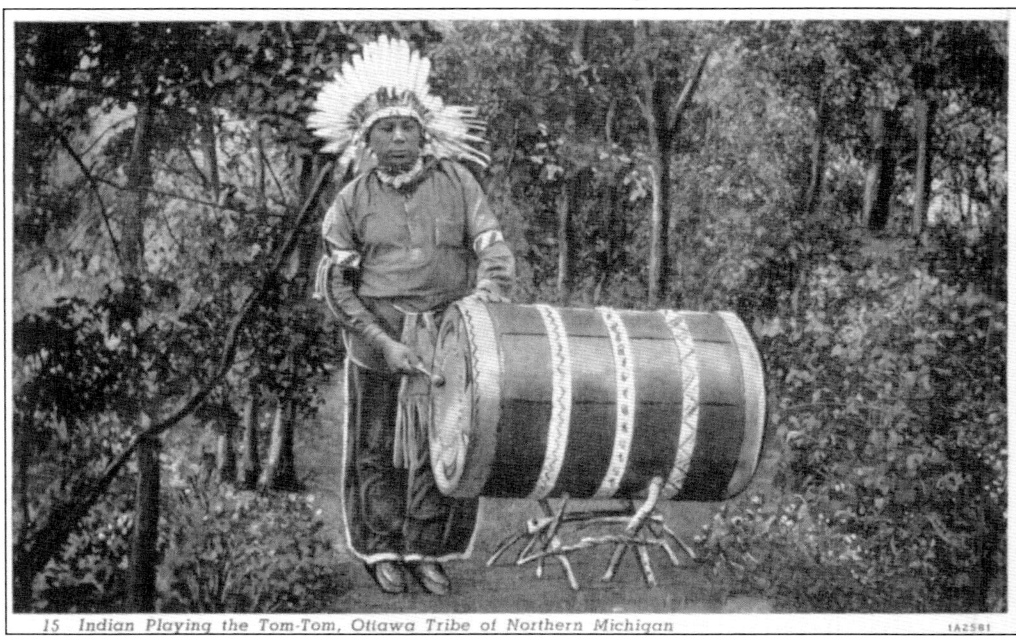

Two

St. Ignace

Naw-do-wa-qua-au-me-sheeng

Native Americans called the area Naw-do-wa-qua-au-me-sheeng, and when early French Canadians came to explore this busy settlement on the shore of the bay, they called it Nadowa-Wikweiamashong ("Bay of the Huron"). Today, it is St. Ignace and East Moran Bay, located on the north side of the Straits of Mackinac in Michigan's Upper Peninsula.

A prominent part of New France's territory of Michilimackinac, St. Ignace was home to the Ottawa, Chippewa, and Huron, French Jesuit priests, French Canadian fur trappers and traders, French residents, and eventually French military. It did not officially receive a nonnative name until 1671 when Fr. Jacques Marquette, a member of the Society of Jesus in France, arrived to establish a Catholic mission for native residents. He named his mission in honor of St. Ignatius of Loyola, the founder of his Jesuit order. Fortunately, Marquette wrote a great deal about this exciting part of Michilimackinac in letters and documents back to France, which were published in the *Jesuit Relations*. In French records, it was listed officially as St. Ignace de Michilimackinac.

What is known as Mackinac Island today, across the bay from St. Ignace, was not settled during Marquette's time, as it was a sacred Native American site and burial ground. The only activity on the south side of The Straits was a few migratory native encampments, so St. Ignace de Michilimackinac became the first developed city on the Straits of Mackinac. The second-oldest city in Michigan after Sault Ste. Marie, St. Ignace has been called the gateway to Michigan's Upper Peninsula and anchors the northern end of the Mackinac Bridge.

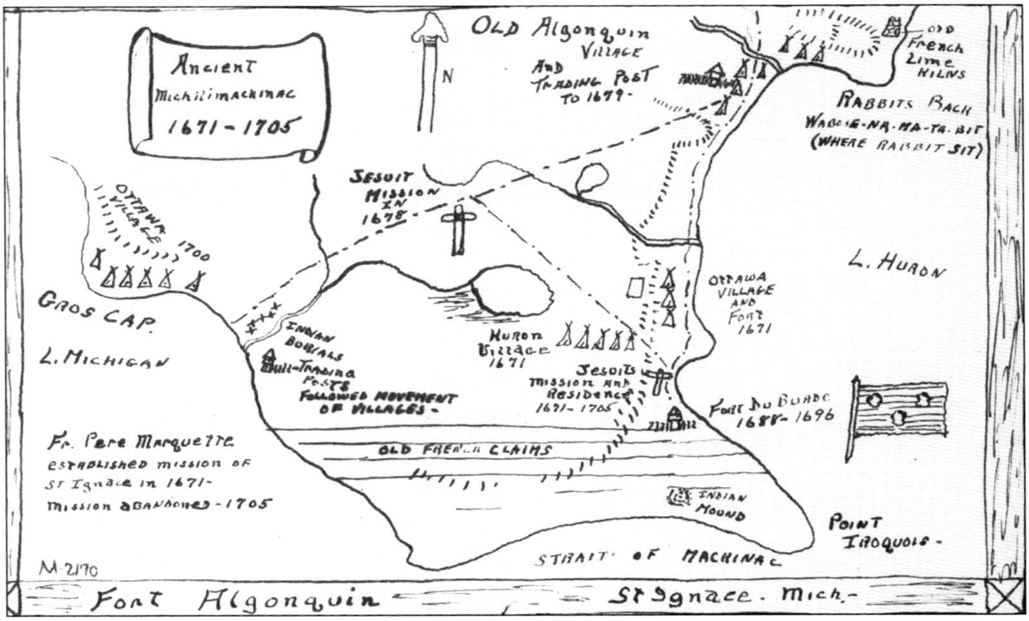

The hand-drawn map above is an artist's depiction of Michilimackinac between 1671 and 1705 and shows the land area of the Upper Peninsula jutting into the northern side of the Straits of Mackinac. On the left is Gros Cap, or "big cape/large place," situated just north of West Moran Bay where an Ottawa village was located in 1700. North of Point Iroquois on the right lies a Huron village. Another Ottawa village on the shore of East Moran Bay is adjacent to where Marquette's Jesuit mission began. At the top right of the map is Rabbit's Back, or Wabose-na-ma-ta-bit ("Where Rabbit Sit"), one of the famous sea stacks in The Straits area. Below is a greeting postcard, postmarked 1907 from St. Ignace (Naw-Do-Wa-Qua-Au-Me-Sheeng).

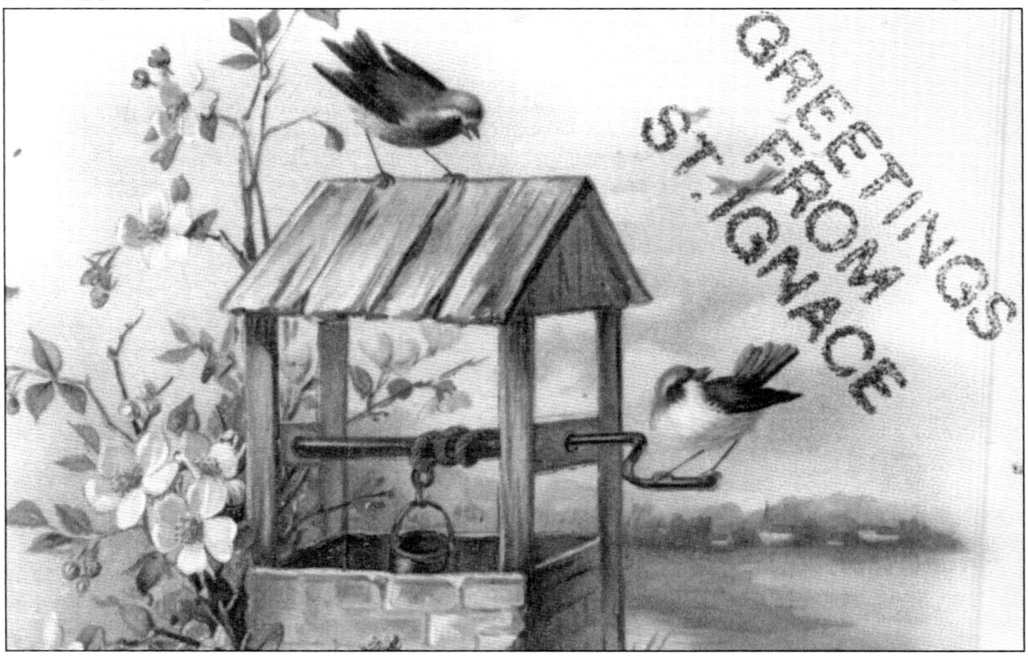

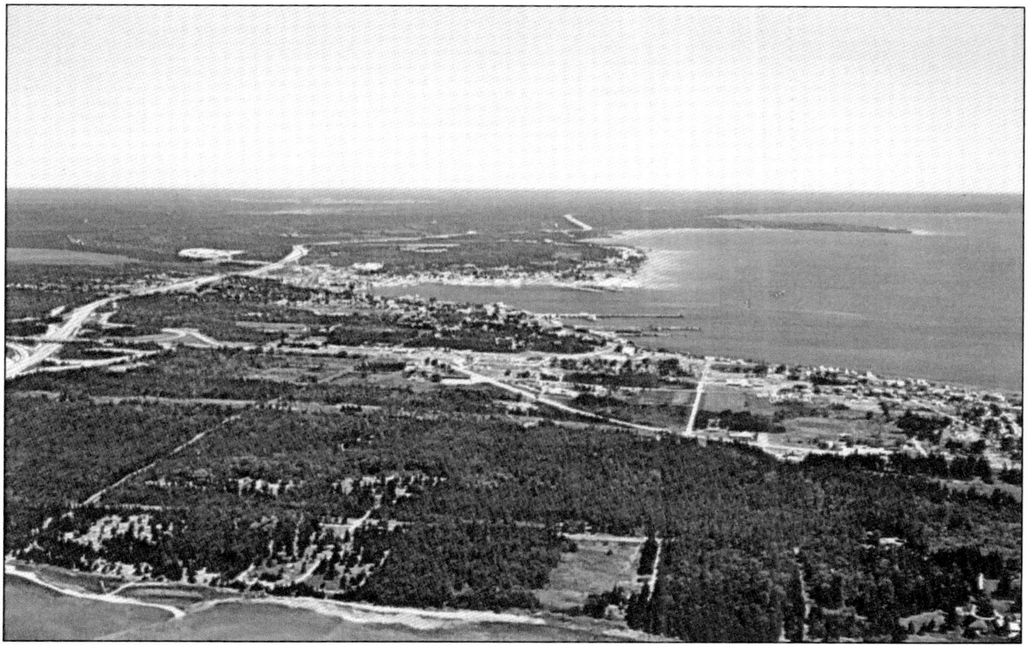

These aerial views from around 1975 give a bird's-eye view of the historical St. Ignace area. The top image shows Interstate 75 pushing north between Chain Lake on the left and East Moran Bay and the downtown St. Ignace business district on the right. Below is a close-up view of East Moran Bay and the long and picturesque main street that winds its way around the harbor. In the lower right is the State Ferry Dock, a once-busy site of railcar ferries and passenger boats. Mother Nature certainly bestowed a wealth of beauty and scenery on St. Ignace, and it has become an increasingly popular summer resort area.

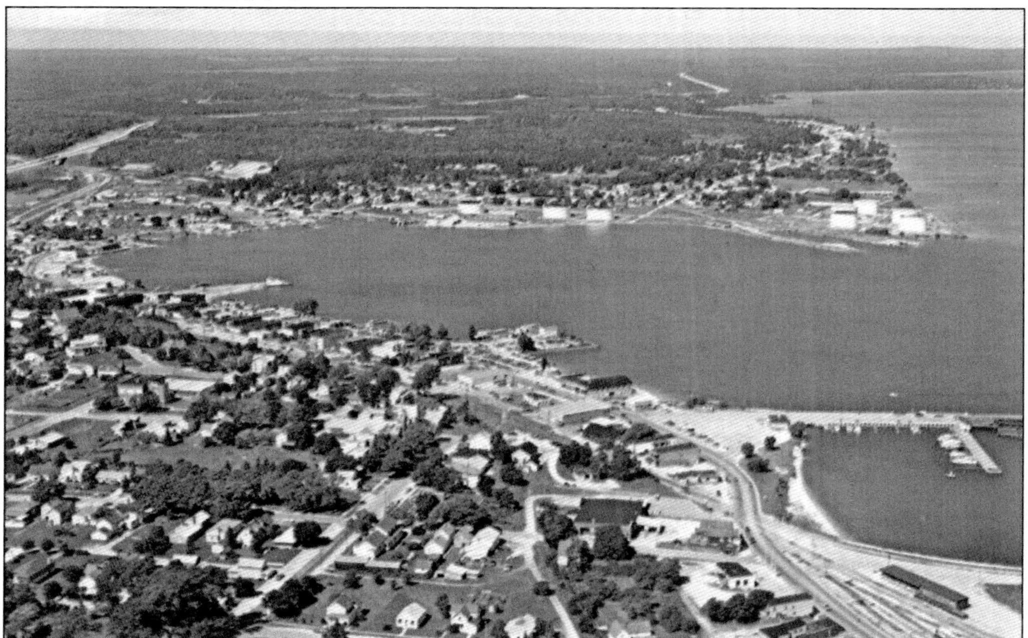

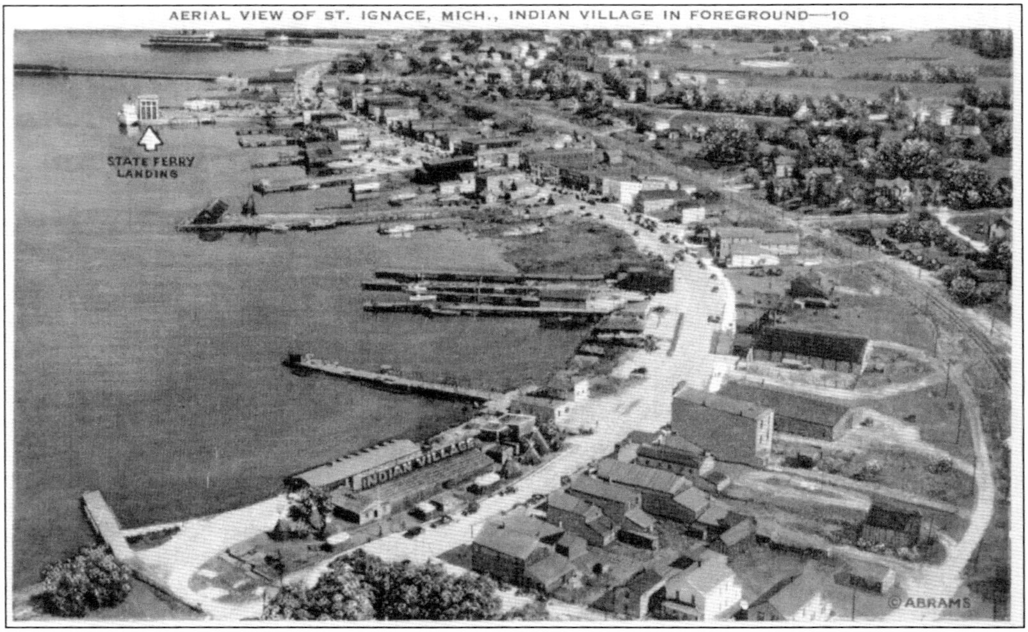

The view from this postcard, postmarked 1948 from St. Ignace, looks down at East Moran Bay from a slightly different angle. Halfway through the historical business district is a roadside tourist attraction and curiosity shop called Indian Village, which reportedly sits on the spot where Father Marquette first landed to begin his missionary work with the native residents.

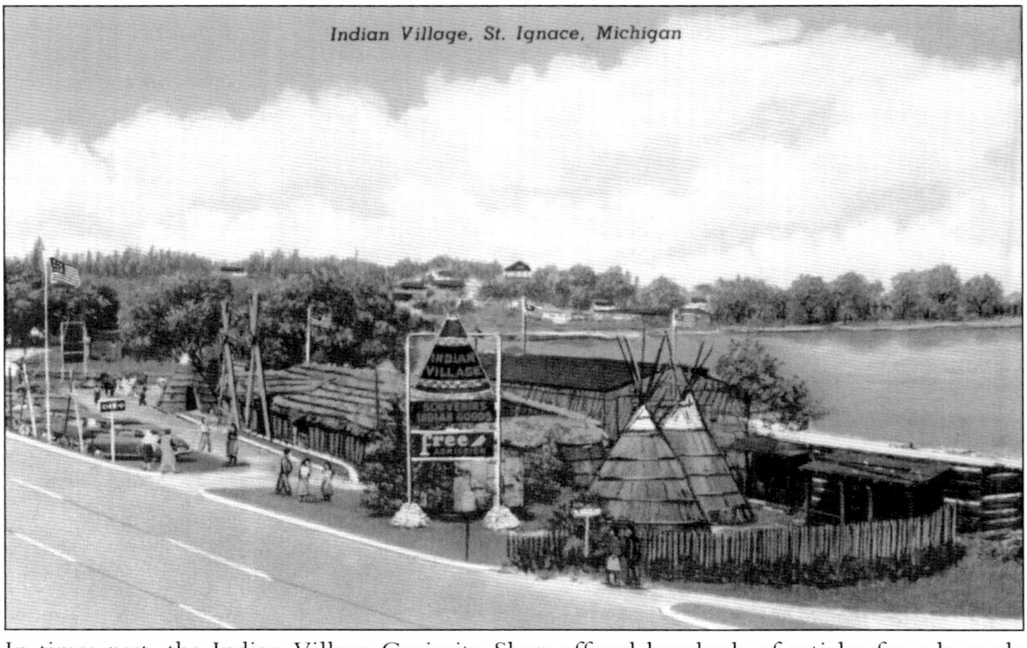

In times past, the Indian Village Curiosity Shop offered hundreds of articles for sale made by the skilled hands of descendants of the Native Americans who lived there. Today, Indian Village is still an interesting shop with many specialty items for visitors to purchase. Historical artifacts and photographs are also on display.

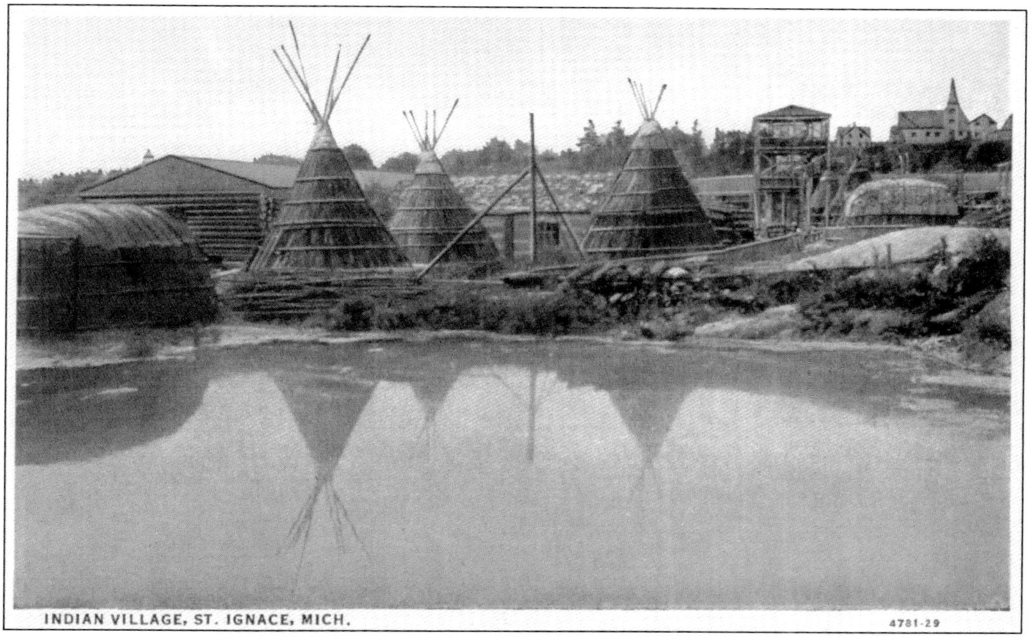

This postcard shows several Native American teepees and a birch bark wigwam among other buildings located on the grounds of Indian Village. The original owner of Indian Village was Clarence Eby who, in 1927, realized the potential of the tourist industry and created a special place for visitors to stop.

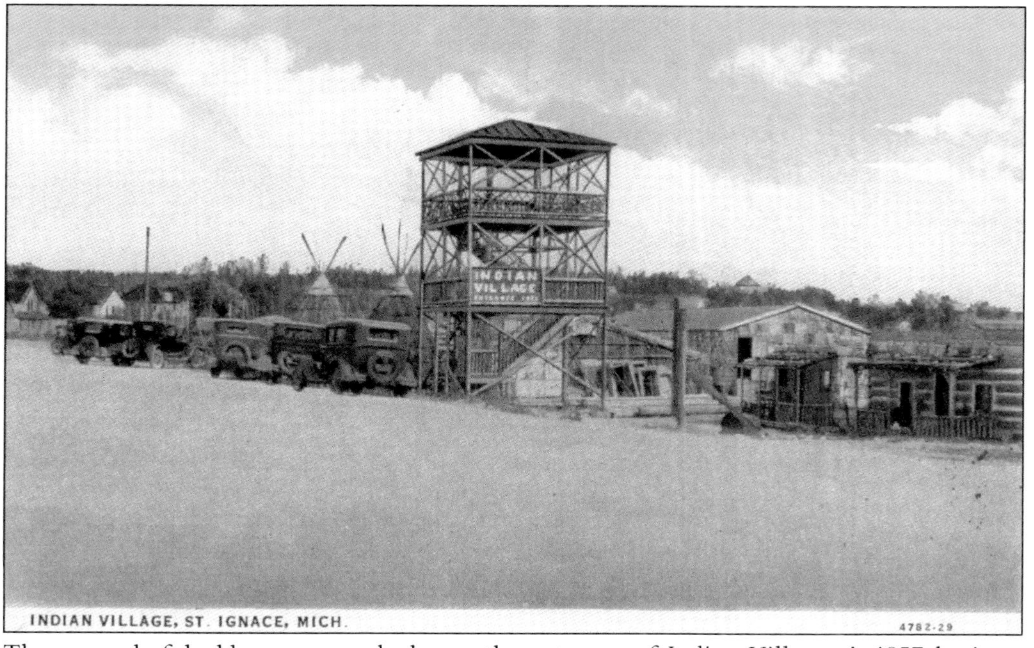

These wonderful old cars are parked near the entrance of Indian Village. A 1957 business directory of St. Ignace lists C.C. Eby and his wife, Helen K. Eby, living on Spring Street, owners of Eby & Co. and operating Indian Village as well as Castle Rock and Curio Fair, two other tourist attractions in St. Ignace. Mr. Eby excelled as an early St. Ignace entrepreneur.

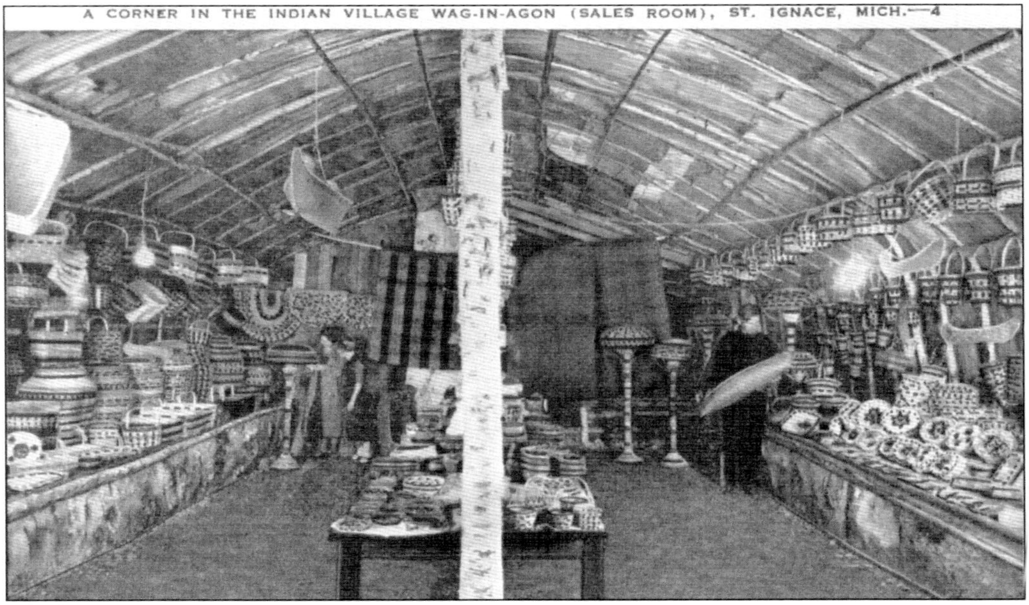

On the reverse side of this postcard showing the interior of the original Indian Village, advertising boasts, "Mere words cannot adequately describe and photographs cannot portray the colorful blaze of Indian creations displayed at Indian Village. The lingering aroma of sweet grass mingles with the sweet pine and balsam, used extensively, cannot but please anyone with its contact. There is no admission charge."

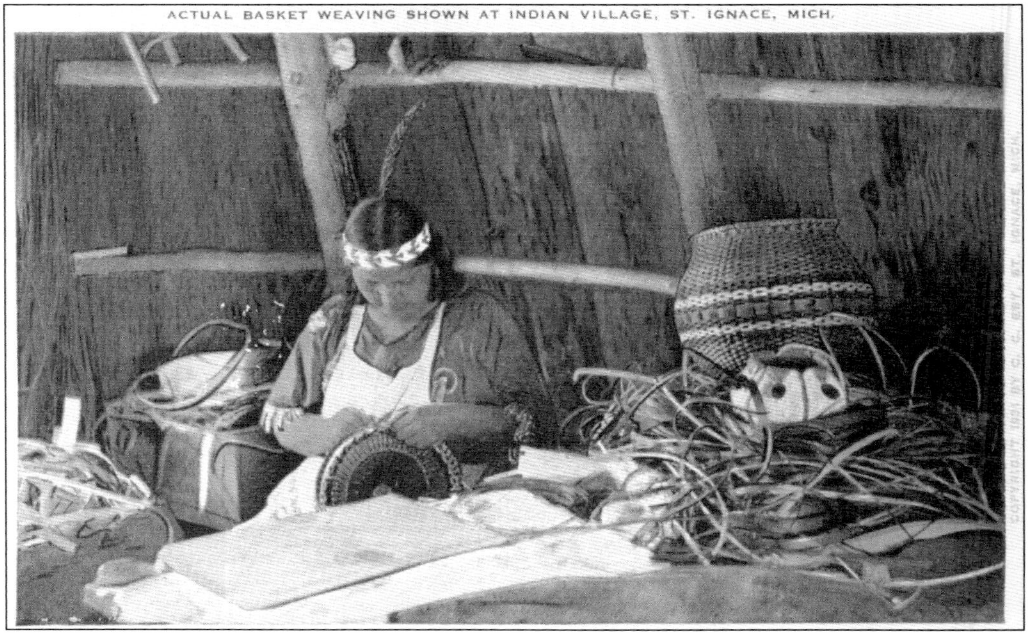

Native American baskets at that time were made of Ash splints created by pounding selected logs to separate wood layers or grain. The back of this card reads, "Indian Village employs only the best basket makers obtainable." Any of these baskets in collections today would be quite valuable.

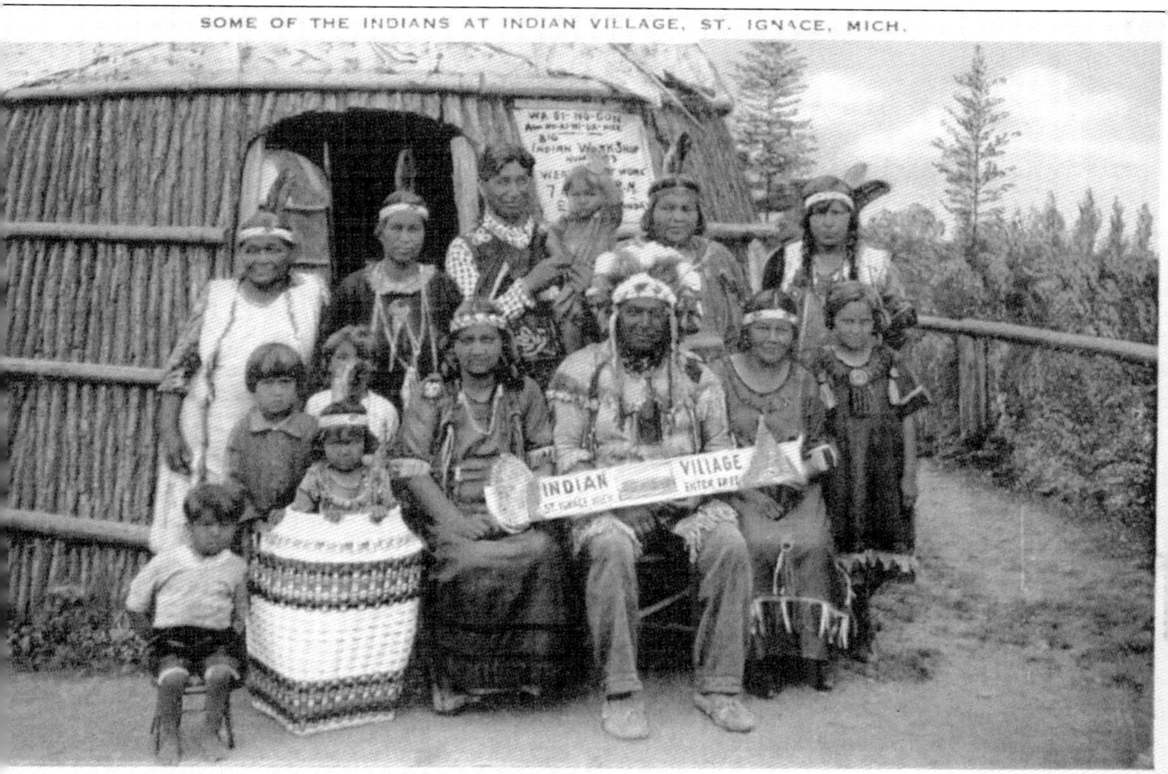

This vintage postcard depicts a group of Native Americans in colorful attire at Indian Village. Notice the small child in the back row waving to the photographer. The sign on the log wigwam behind the group reads, "WA-GI-NO-GON" on the top line and underneath, "Big Indian Workshop." As old ways were no longer possible, many native people earned money by selling their handicrafts to tourists; many of those handicrafts are a lost art today. Hand-beaded items, hand-dyed boxes decorated with porcupine quills, and specialty baskets are among the most desirable. Fortunately, there are a few descendents of these early artisans showing pride in their history by preserving the culture as well as the skills of their ancestors' early craft making. This postcard was originally produced in 1931 by Indian Village owner Clarence Eby.

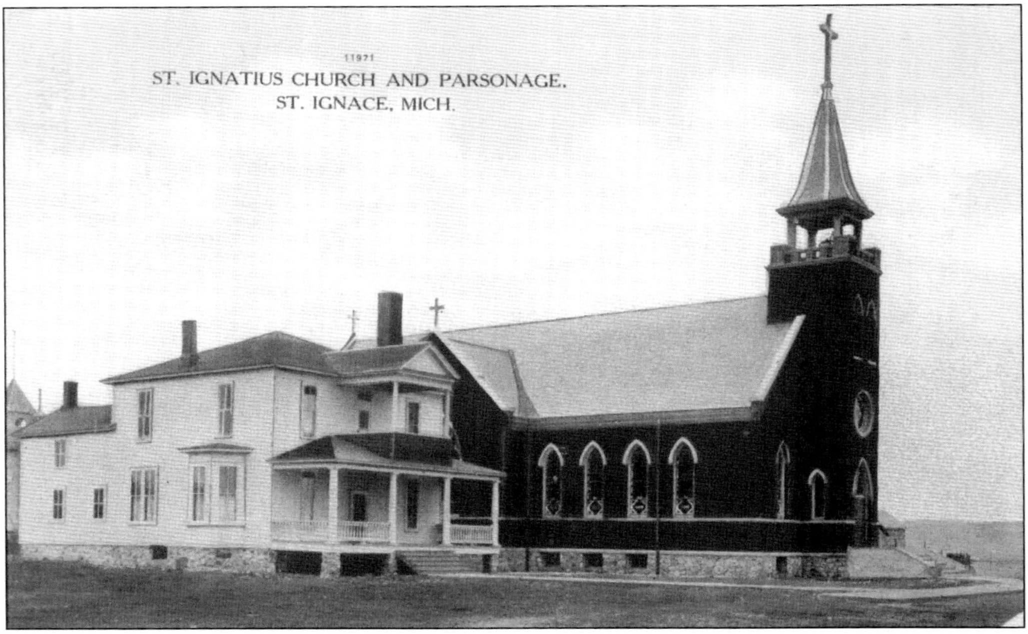

Postmarked 1909, this image shows the St. Ignatius Parish Church with the adjacent parsonage. Built in 1904 and located on Spring Street, this church was a magnificent addition to the community. Father Marquette would have been proud to see the modern development of the religious community that stemmed from his humble birch bark chapel near the rear of this property.

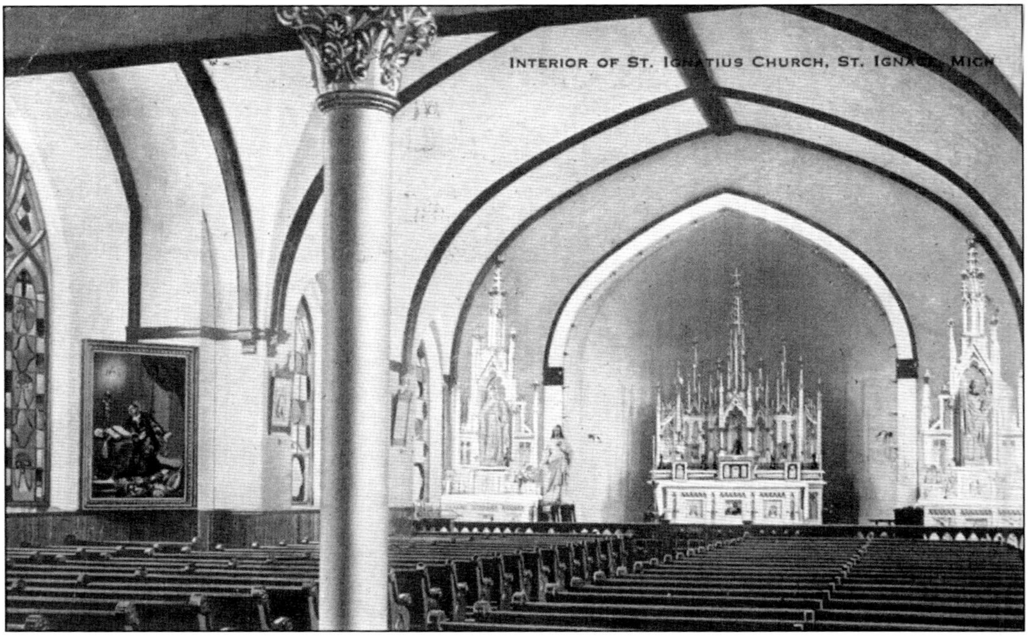

The St. Ignatius Church was given an ornate interior, as shown in this 1913 postcard taken nine years after the church was built. Notice the painting of Loyola on the side wall. St. Ignatius was born in 1491 at the castle of Loyola in Spain and died in Rome in 1556. His Society of Jesus, founded in Paris, was officially recognized by Pope Paul III in 1540.

When Father Marquette named his original Catholic mission, he wanted to honor the founder of his order. This 1906 postcard shows a close-up of the painting depicting Loyola "renouncing the world." Legend says that Father Marquette brought this painting to the St. Ignace mission, where it was faithfully guarded by resident natives. Reportedly, a log building first stood on this site, where missionary priests held services and served the parish.

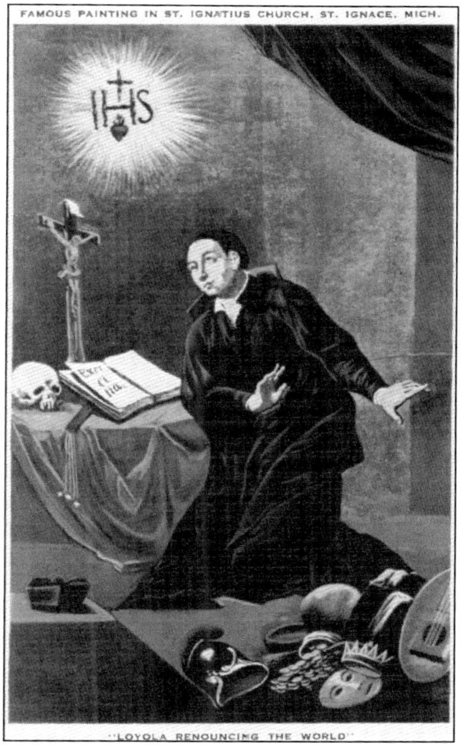

Built in 1837, the old Mission Church was a continuation of Father Marquette's humble beginnings. In the 1950s, this second mission church building was moved to the site of Marquette's grave in Marquette Mission Park overlooking East Moran Bay. It is now the Museum of Ojibwa Culture, a designated National Historic Landmark.

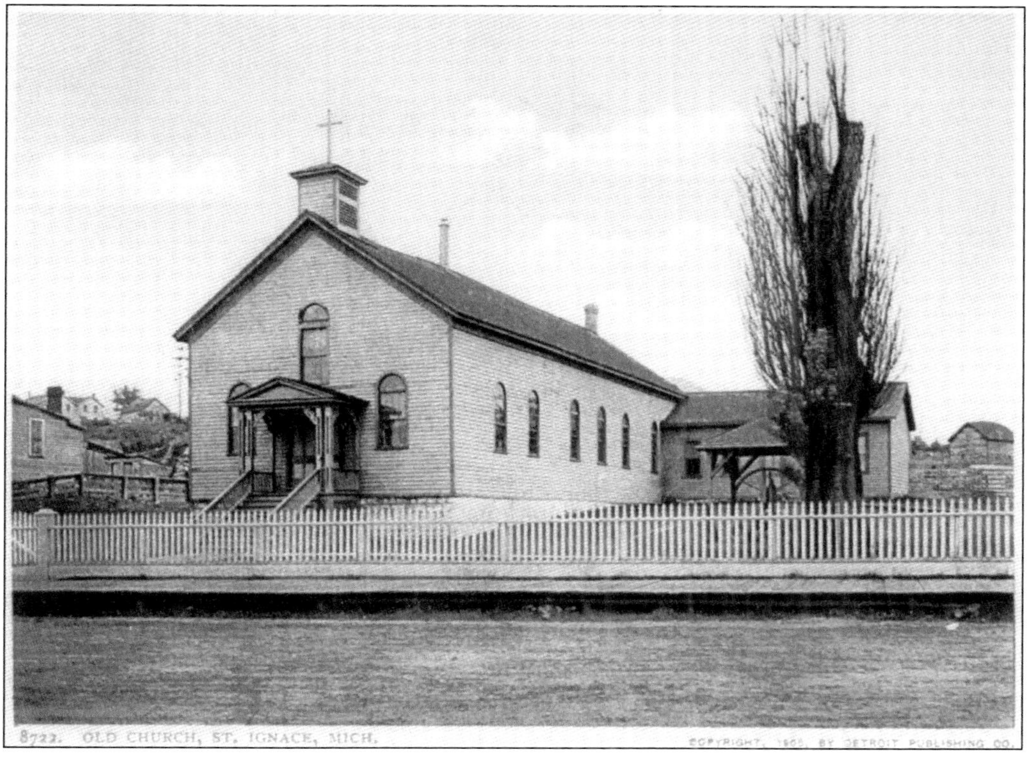

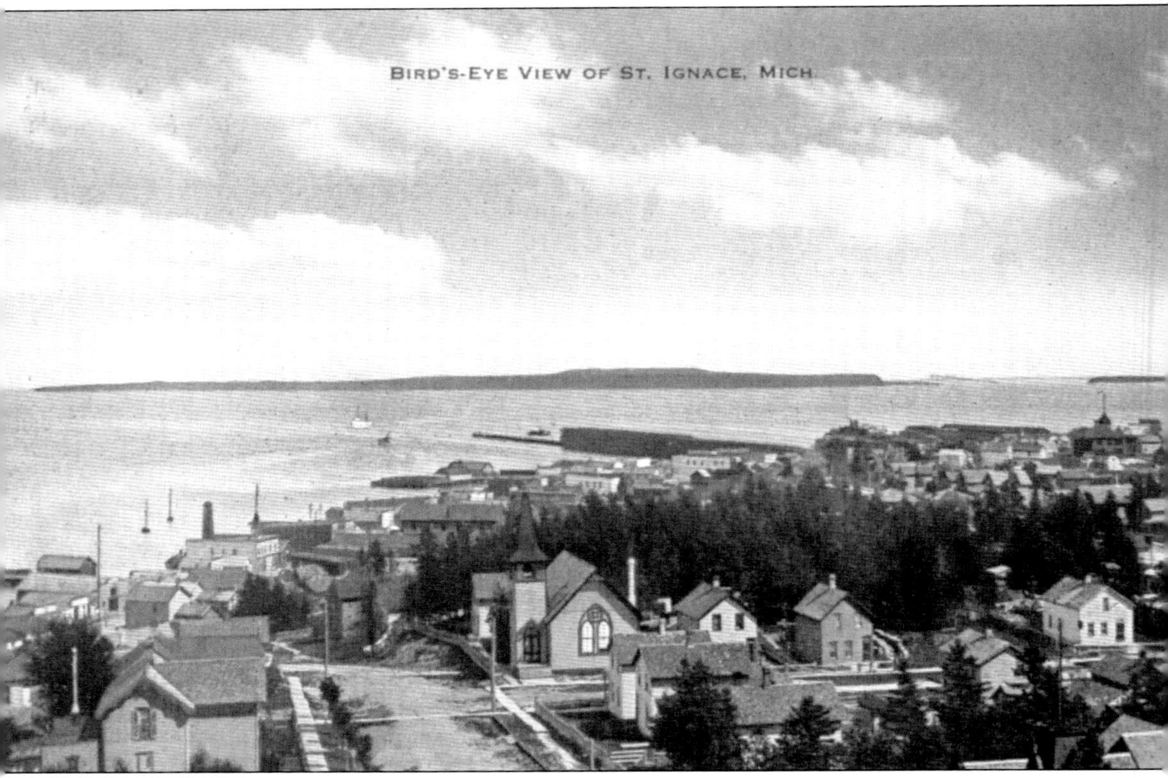

This 1922 postcard looks out over East Moran Bay in Lake Huron with Mackinac Island in the background. From certain vantage points in St. Ignace, Mackinac Island does resemble a sleeping turtle. Native Americans settled on this spot for several reasons. With abundant fish and game, it was a safe location with easy land access to the north and west and water barriers to the east and south, which gave the residents a sense of security. Many people who still reside here today are descendants of the French voyageurs, coureur de bois, soldiers, villagers, and Native Americans who once called this home. Higher elevations behind the main part of town make for scenic views for many St. Ignace residents. Part of the elevation was most likely used by Native Americans as a burial ground, as human remains and native relics have been found.

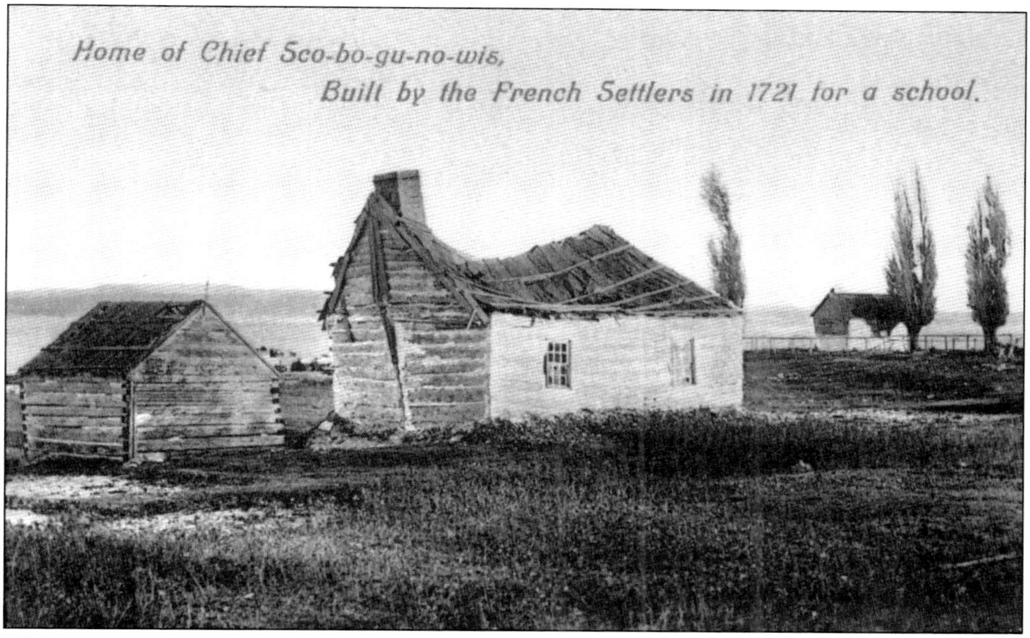

This early-1900s postcard reads, "Home of Chief Seo-bo-gu-no-wis, Built by the French Settlers in 1721 for a school." Another source states that French soldiers built the old log schoolhouse located on the north shore of East Moran Bay when they occupied Fort de Buade, the first palisaded fort in Michilimackinac.

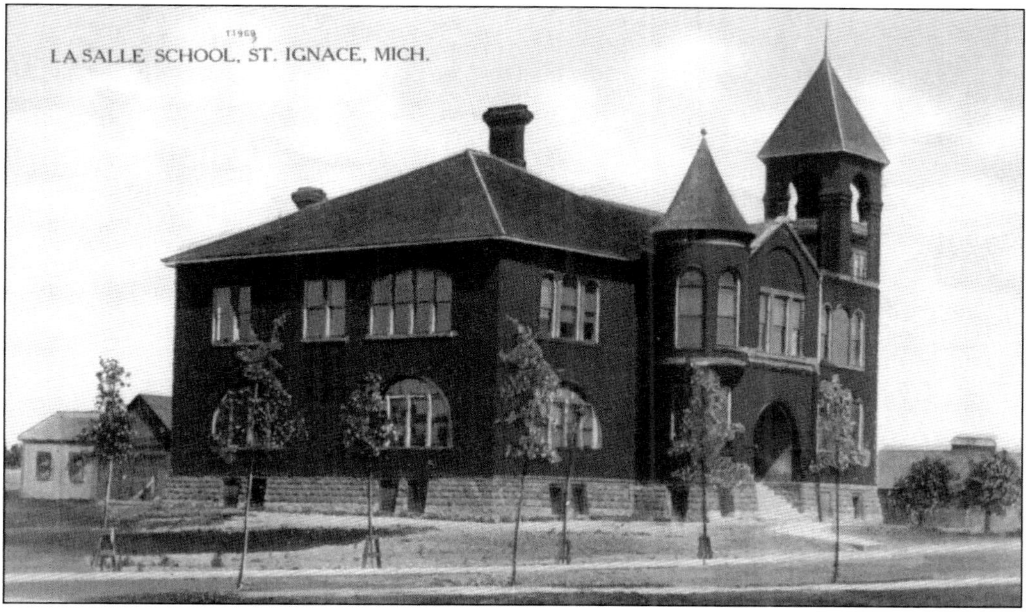

Located on Spring Street near the Catholic church, the LaSalle School was built in 1888 for approximately $10,000, replacing a smaller school in the center of town. There were no special features like a gymnasium, auditorium, or laboratory, and it supplied only a few books to its students. Today, LaSalle High School is a great facility and the proud home of the St. Ignace Saints.

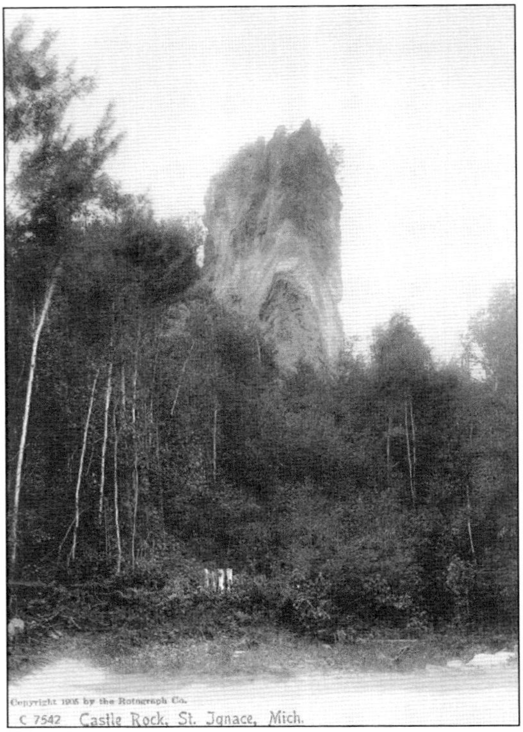

Prehistoric glaciers left many fossil-embedded limestone breccia sea stacks in the St. Ignace area and on Mackinac Island. One of the most famous is Castle Rock, located slightly north of St. Ignace near Interstate 75. It may have been an ancient Native American lookout and was often referred to as "Pontiac's Lookout," after the Ojibwa chief. An early advertisement called it a "scenic turret in the land of the sky blue waters, with the finest view in Michigan."

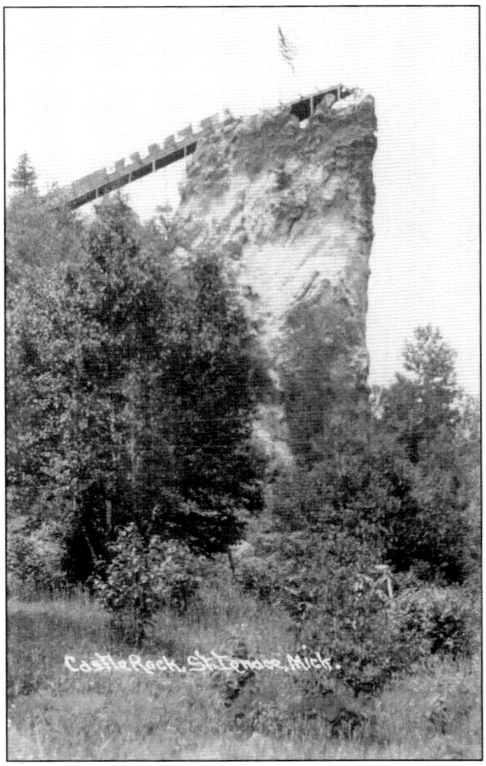

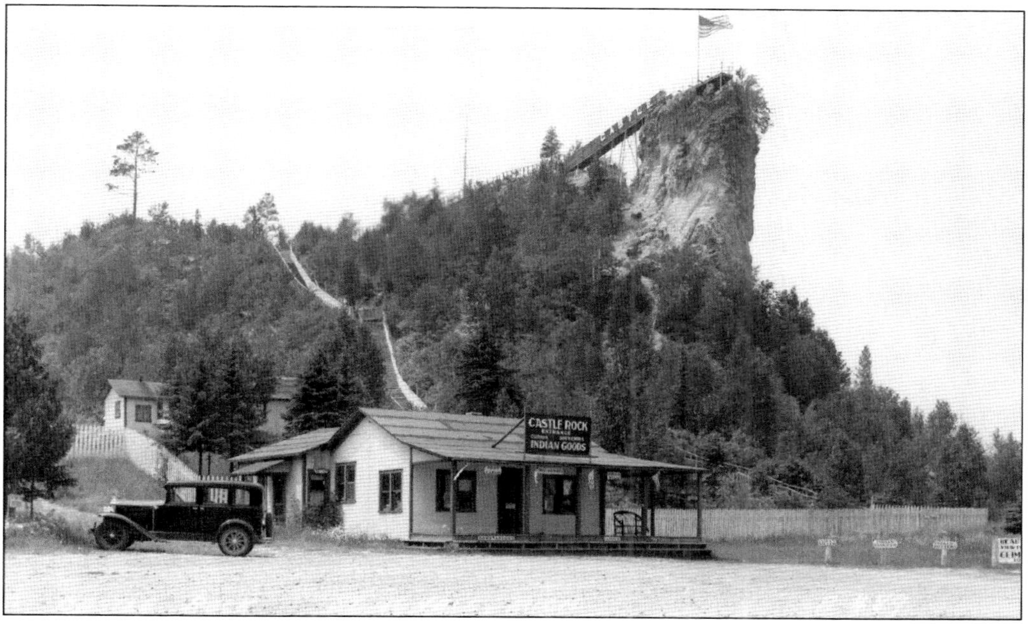

In the late 1920s, a stairway was built to the top of the sea stack, also called a sea chimney, and located below were tourist cabins and a souvenir shop. A few years later, Clarence Eby, owner of Indian Village in St. Ignace, purchased the site, expanded the gift shop, and continued it as a well-visited tourist attraction. There is an observation area at the top of the stack, but climbing to the top is not for the fainthearted, as it rises nearly 200 feet above road level. Today, statues of Paul Bunyan and Babe the Blue Ox welcome visitors to Castle Rock.

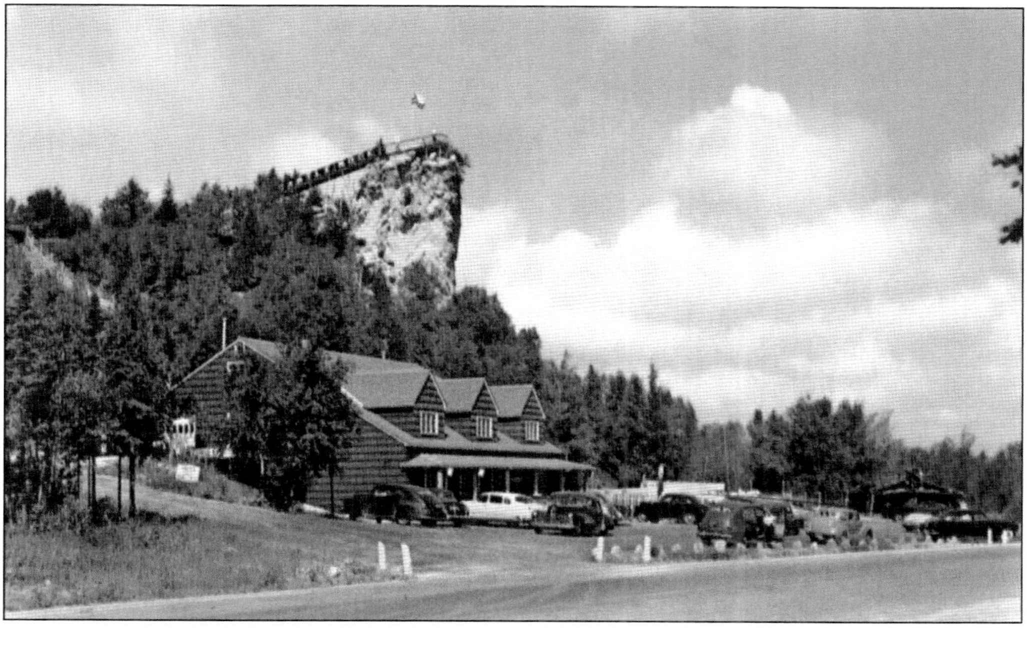

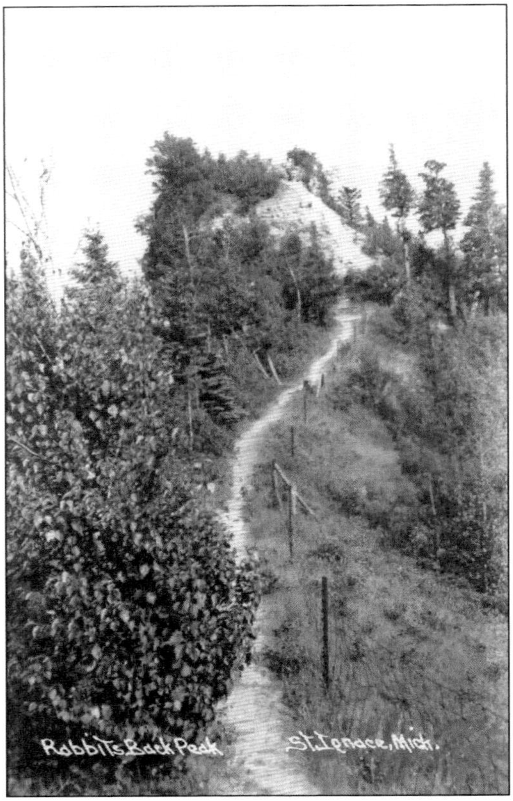

Another sea stack in St. Ignace is Rabbit's Back, or Wabose-na-ma-ta-bit. Located much closer to Lake Huron north of Evergreen Shores and south of Horseshoe Bay, this rock summit was a Native American lookout over the water. Rabbit's Back, or Rabbit Back, is now much narrower at the top than shown in this vintage postcard and is currently located on private property.

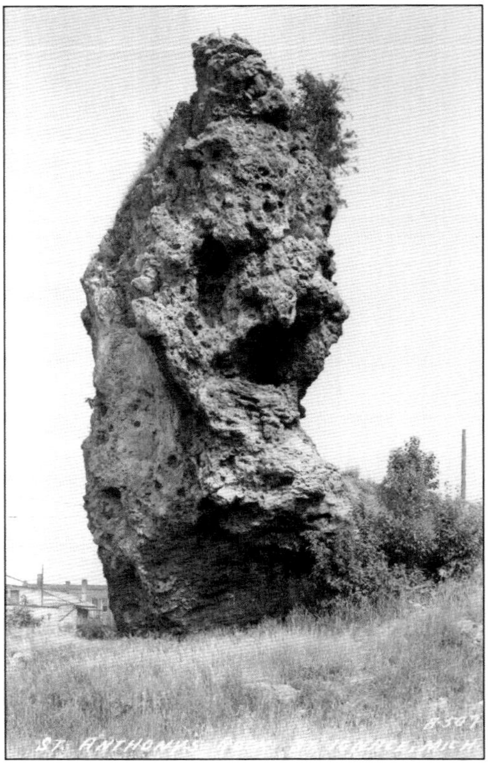

Called St. Anthony's Rock, this glacial formation, like the other sea stacks, is millions of years old. It is a bit hidden in St. Ignace near the downtown parking area behind State Street. Some say St. Anthony's profile can be seen in the rock, although earlier Native American legend believes it was a ceremonial rock revolving around a maiden's love and her eventual desire to leap to her death.

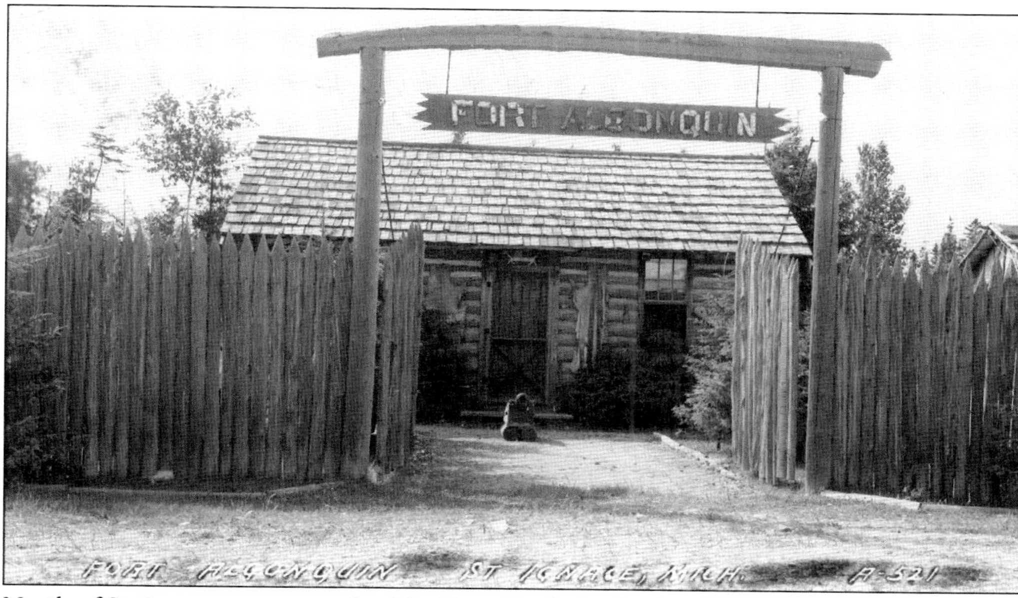

North of St. Ignace on present-day Mackinac Trail, this building was constructed to resemble an early fort. Built in the late 1920s and named Fort Algonquin, it was used to house the collection of Native American artifacts owned by Henry Norton. Currently, Fort Algonquin is a retail gift shop operated by Norton's descendents. Much of Norton's collection currently belongs to the Fort de Buade Museum in downtown St. Ignace.

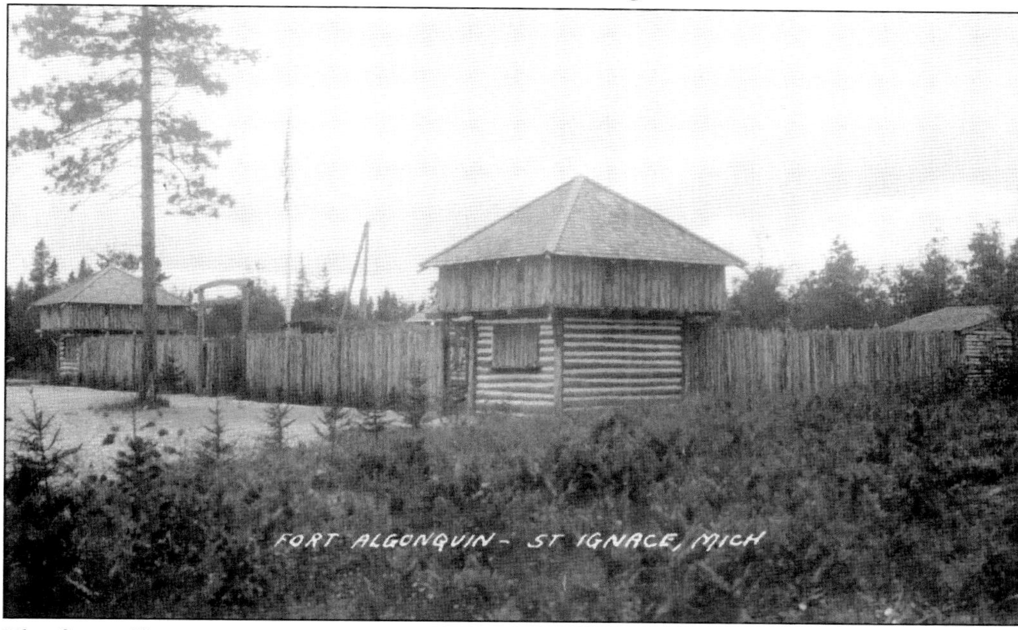

The first military post in St. Ignace, originally called Fort de Buade, looked similar to Fort Algonquin. Named in honor of the French governor for North America, Fort de Buade was built in the 1670s after Father Marquette established his mission. The fort was eventually abandoned and its exact location in St. Ignace remains a topic of conversation. It was also known as the first Fort Michilimackinac.

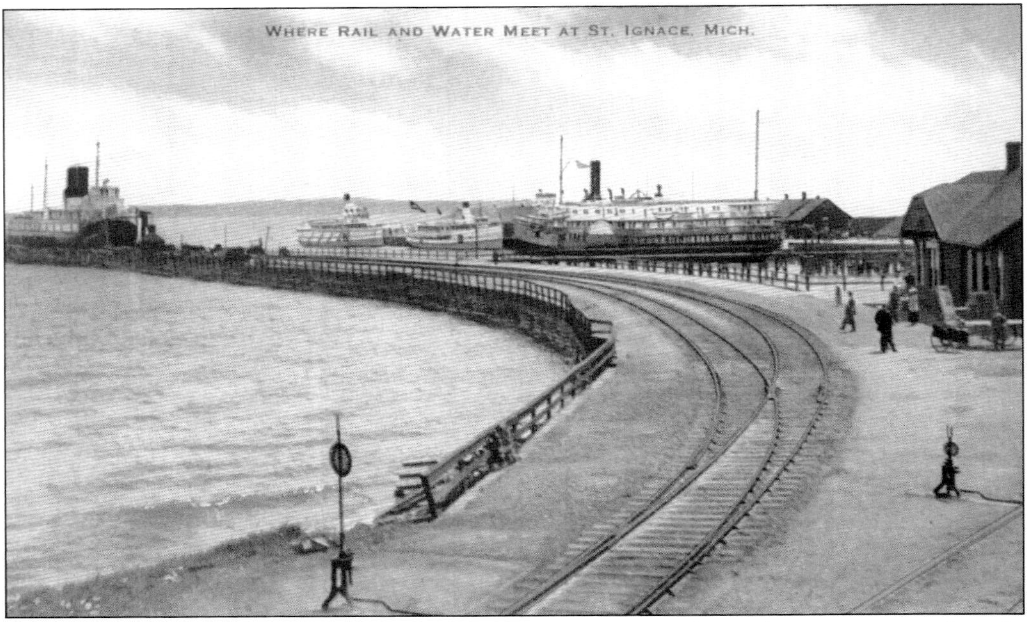

St. Ignace became a bustling municipality relatively quickly. This early-1900s postcard reads, "Where Rail and Water Meet." Railroad cars were loaded on special rail ferries, and passenger steamships were constantly arriving and departing. The St. Ignace "port" on the Straits of Mackinac brought a new migration of people to the North Country. The railroad connection between Michigan's two peninsulas was established in 1881.

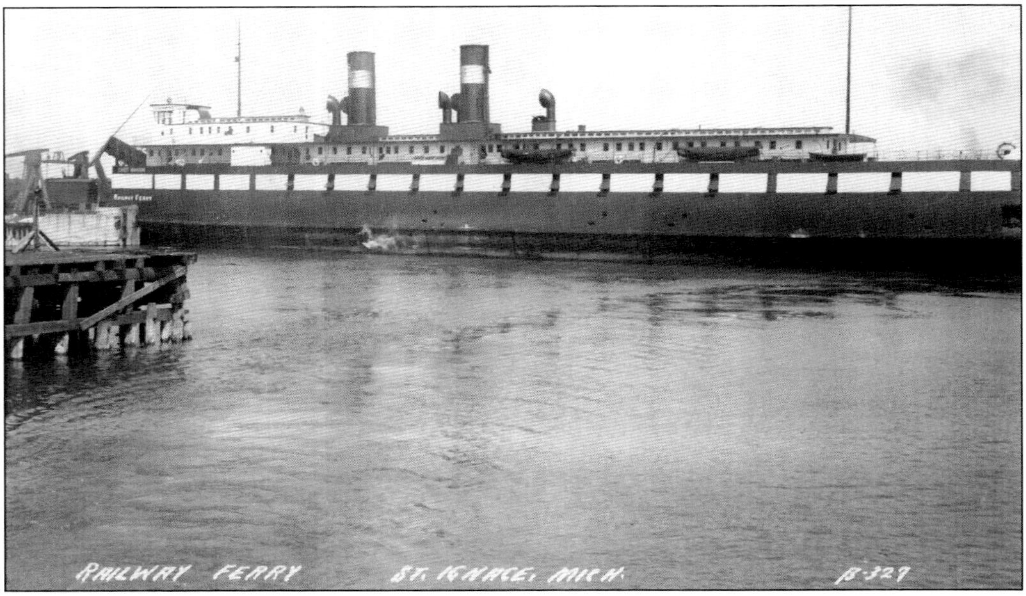

Railroad ferries plied the waters to and from St. Ignace and around the Straits of Mackinac, including *Sainte Marie I* and *Sainte Marie II*, the *St. Ignace*, and the SS *Chief Wawatam*. The rail ferries were also used as icebreakers, opening up shipping lanes in The Straits. The *Chief* and the *Sainte Marie* looked almost identical from a distance. The markings on this boat only read, "Railway Ferry."

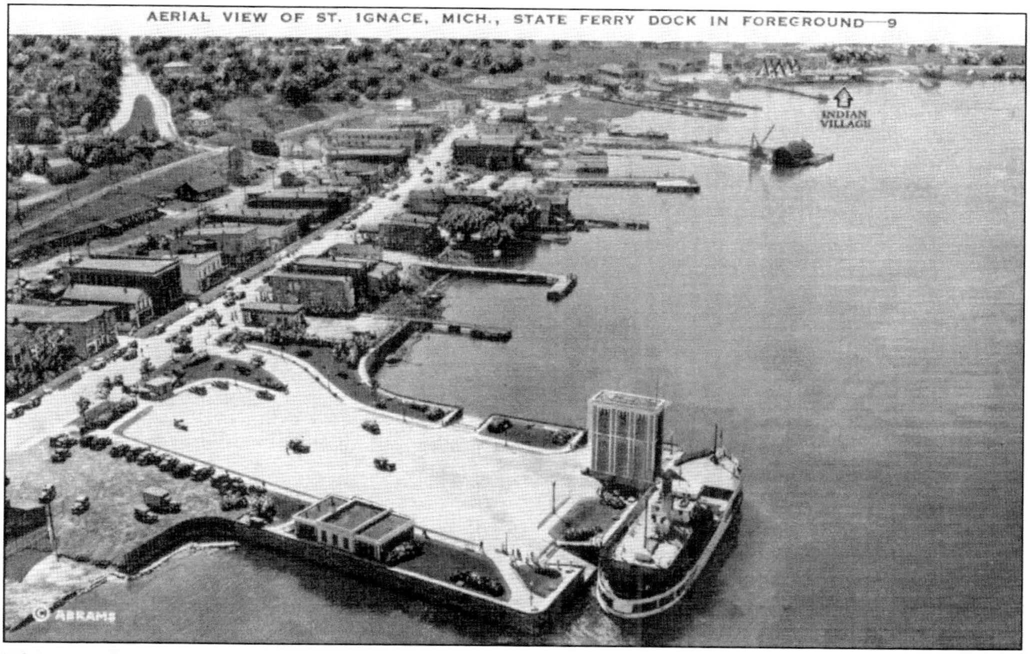

This aerial view of the State Ferry Dock in St. Ignace shows its large-capacity loading area for outbound vehicles to Mackinac City and the Lower Peninsula. In 1923, the State of Michigan created the first state ferry system in the United States. The earliest ferries were coal-fired with wooden propellers. Later, larger ferries could carry heavier loads, and a new industry was born.

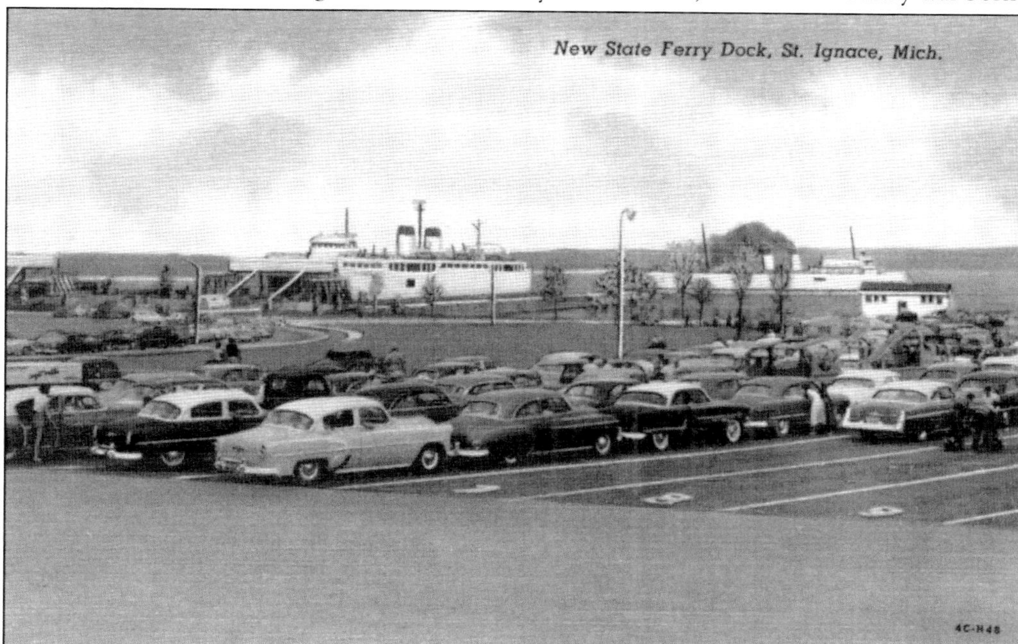

Automobiles wait in line to load a car ferry at the State Ferry Dock in St. Ignace. Famous car ferries of this era included *City of Munising*, *City of Petoskey*, *City of Cheboygan*, the *Straits of Mackinac*, *Sainte Ignace*, *Mackinaw City*, and the *Vacationland*.

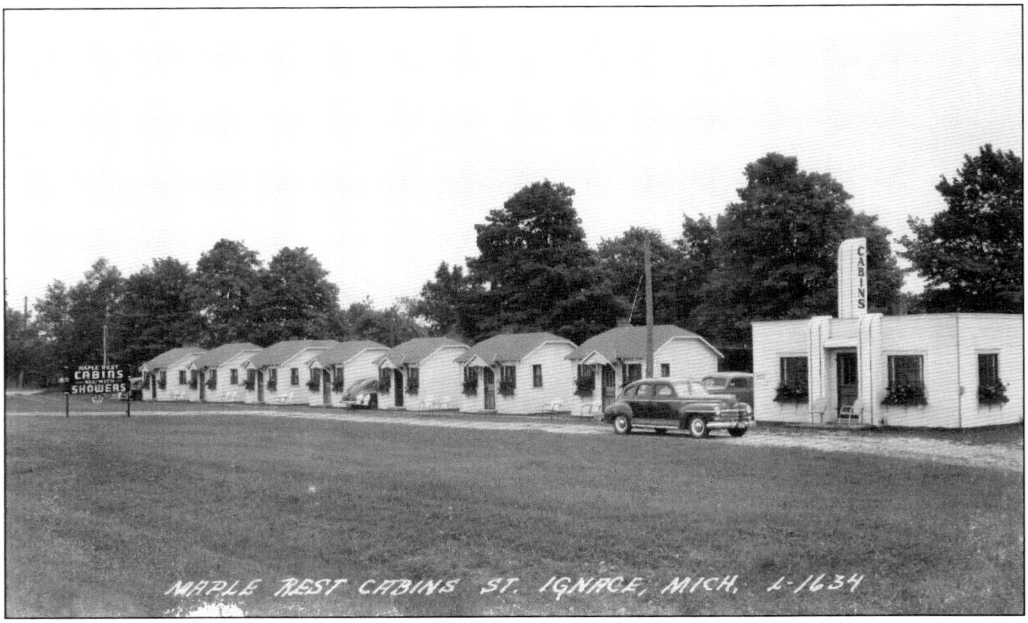

When tourists came to visit St. Ignace, they were greeted with stately hotels downtown and cozy cabins near the water, such as Maple Crest Cabins, seen here with a sign out front reading "All with Showers." An AAA-approved facility, this resort welcomed visitors year after year. The most competitive proprietors advertised, "Electric lights, hot and cold running water, gas cooking and tiled bathrooms."

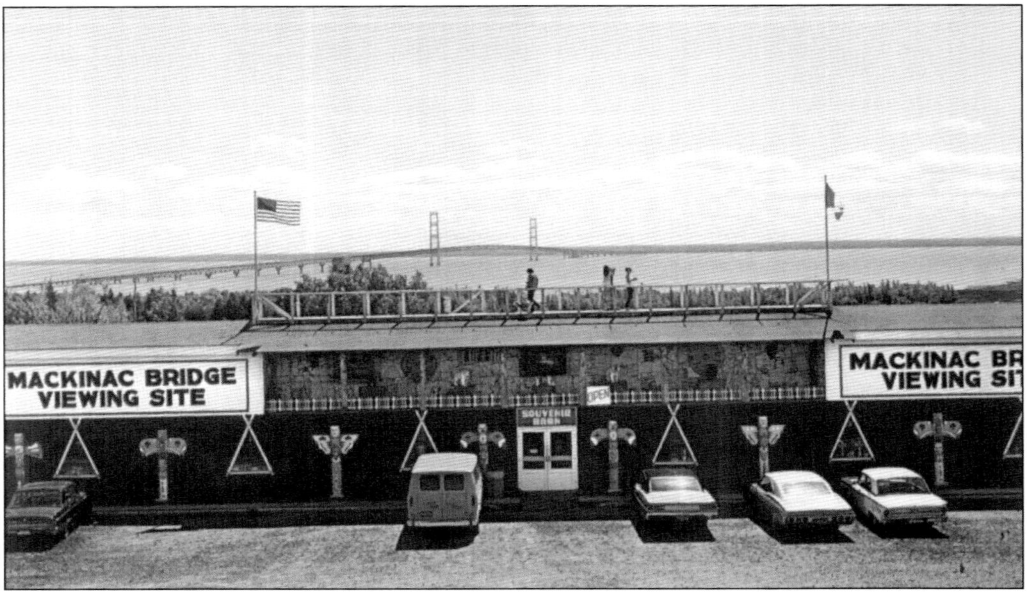

A dream came true for St. Ignace when plans for the Mackinac Bridge were unveiled, allowing automobile traffic to be directly connected between Michigan's two peninsulas. Opened to the public in 1957, Michigan's Mighty Mac was called an engineering marvel. Pictured in the background of this postcard, the bridge stretches across the Straits of Mackinac, dividing Lake Huron on the left from Lake Michigan on the right.

Three

Mackinac Island
Mich-inni-maki-nong

They called it Mi-shi-ne-mack-nong, but when the French heard the native people say it, the French pronunciation and spelling ended up as Mich-Inni-Maki-Nong, which later evolved to Michilimackinac. The most popular theory as to the origin of the name is that Michilimackinac means "large turtle," "great turtle," or "land of the turtle spirits" due to a relatively similar word in native language, *mi-she-mi-ki-nock. Mi-she* in the Chippewa language means "tremendous in size," and *mikinock* is the name of a mud turtle.

According to Andrew J. Blackbird, an 1880s author, grammarian, and member of the Ottawa tribe, the name has quite a different origin. Blackbird tells us that when Mackinac Island was first discovered by the Ottawa, there was a small tribe, a "remnant race" as he called it, already living on the island, the Mi-shi-ne-mack-naw-go, and like other tribes, they lived in constant fear of the warring Iroquois tribes from New York. When the Iroquois did attack, two members from the Mackinac Island tribe survived to tell the tale according to Blackbird. In honor of the decimated tribe, the Ottawa named the island after them as "place of the Mishinimaki." Departed descendents of the man and woman who survived were later named Paw-gwa-tchaw-nish-naw-boy, meaning "wild roaming supernatural being," perhaps giving meaning to another Mackinac Island nickname, the "Fairy Isle."

Many groups have called Mackinac Island home over the years: Ottawa, Chippewa, Huron, French, English, Irish, and American. Even a German immigrant, John Jacob Astor, made his fortune there. After two military forts declined, Mackinac Island became a tourist destination because of its scenic splendor and healthy climate. People escaped their allergies and smog-filled cities by booking passage on steamboats and hotel-like passenger ships for memorable excursions to Mackinac. This island, in the heart of The Straits, still welcomes thousands of tourists every year.

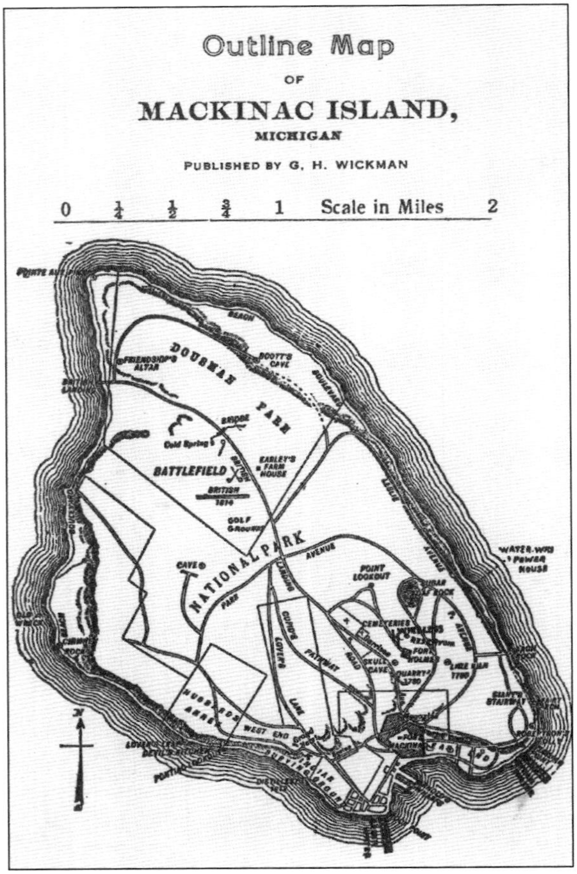

From this angle, the island does look somewhat like a turtle shell, and from certain places in St. Ignace, it looks like an elongated, sleeping turtle. This early postcard "map" shows many of the island's famous landmarks, including Skull Cave, Sugar Loaf, and the 1814 Battlefield.

In 1898, automobiles were banned on Mackinac Island because it was feared they might frighten the horses, which still have the right-of-way today. Cars are still not permitted, so bicycle rental companies do a good business, as many visitors choose that mode of exploration over walking. The eight-mile scenic bike ride around the island is a popular activity.

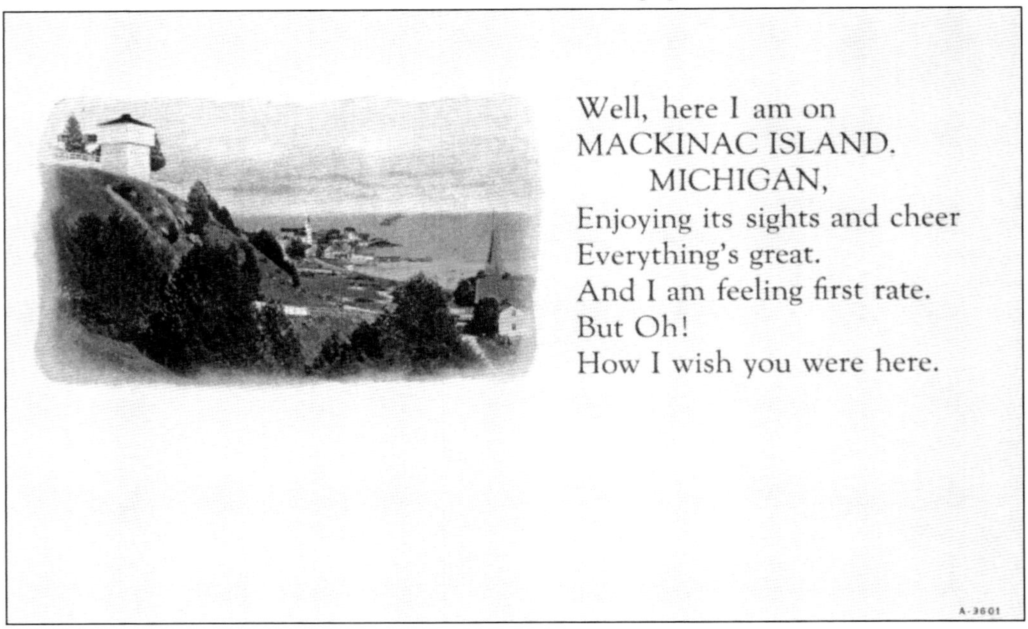

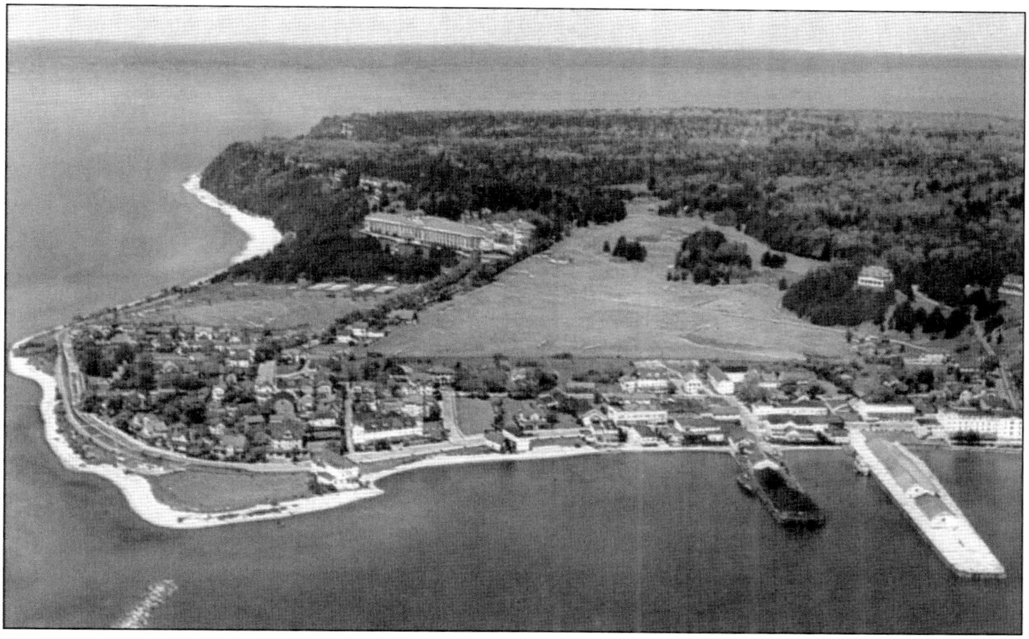

This aerial view was taken from above the village harbor looking northwest. Grand Hotel and adjoining golf course are noted landmarks in the center of the view, and boat docks for the passenger ferries are seen in the harbor. The Governor's Mansion is just above the covered boat dock.

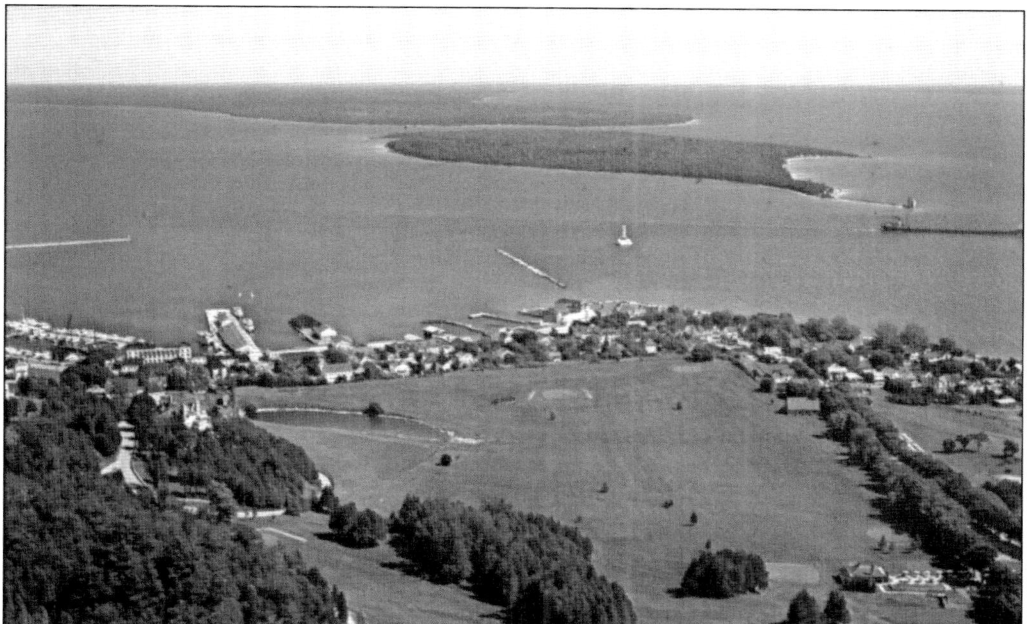

This is a bird's-eye view of a fairway on Grand Hotel's The Jewel golf course and the Mackinac Island village harbor below, looking southeast over Round Island and Bois Blanc Island, two other Native American special sites. A Great Lakes freighter is seen just passing Round Island Lighthouse, most likely on its way to the St. Mary's River and Sault Ste. Marie.

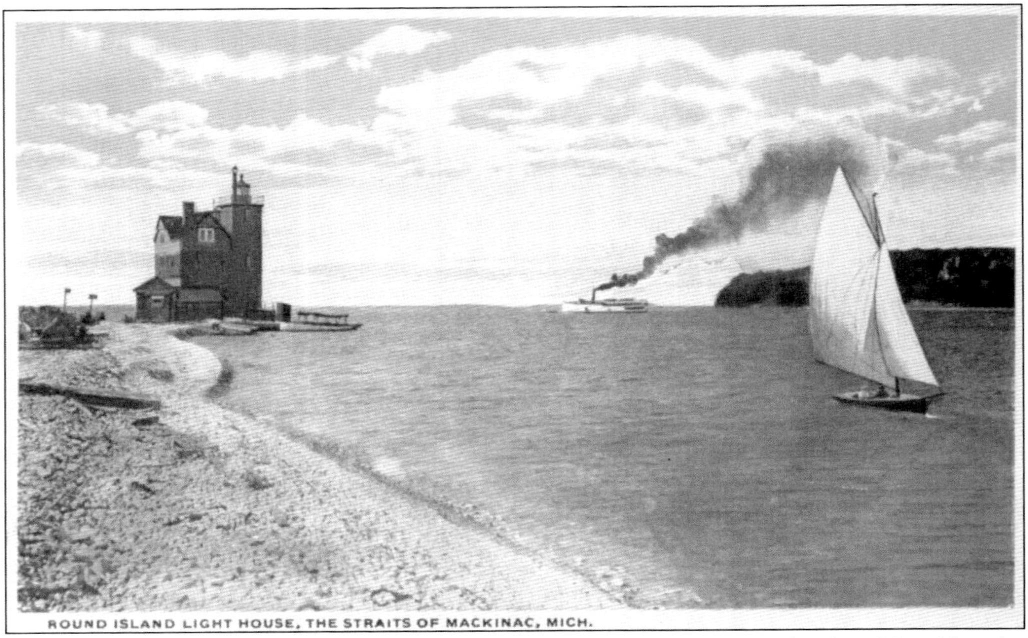

Round Island Light welcomes visitors arriving by ferry to Mackinac Island and is said to be one of the most photographed lighthouses in Michigan. Built in 1895, this light helps mark the narrow water passage between Mackinac Island and Round Island. Round Island Light was in a sad state of deterioration until it was featured in the movie *Somewhere in Time*, which brought it to the attention of preservations, who have magnificently restored it.

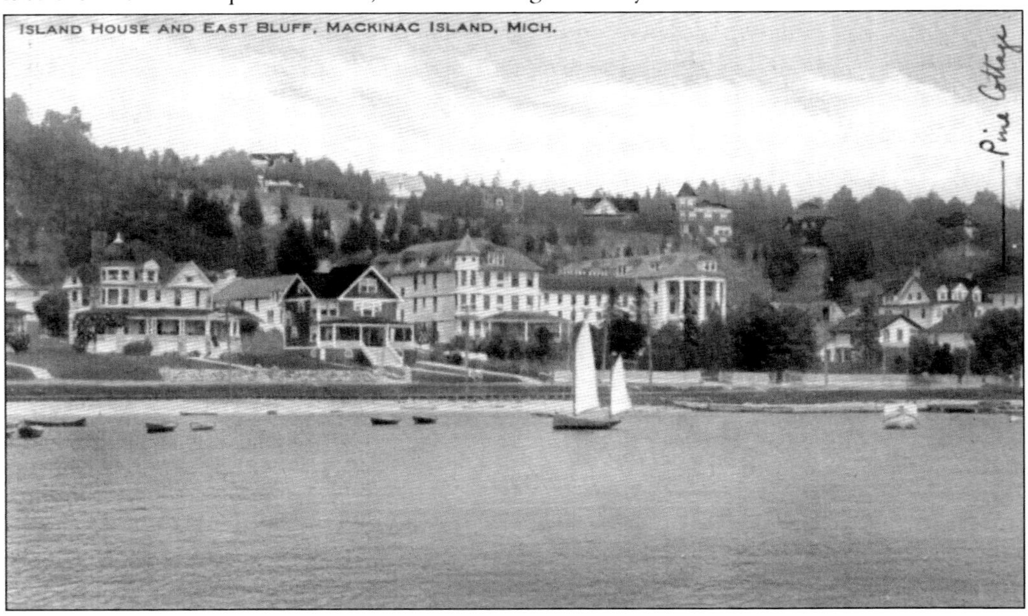

The ferry ride from St. Ignace or Mackinaw City to Mackinac Island is an experience in itself, and the approach to Haldimand Harbor is a site to behold. This 1912 postcard shows one of the many famous hotels, the Island House, which dates back to 1852, and behind it the limestone elevation known as East Bluff. Much of the architecture on the island is quaint, elegant, and inviting.

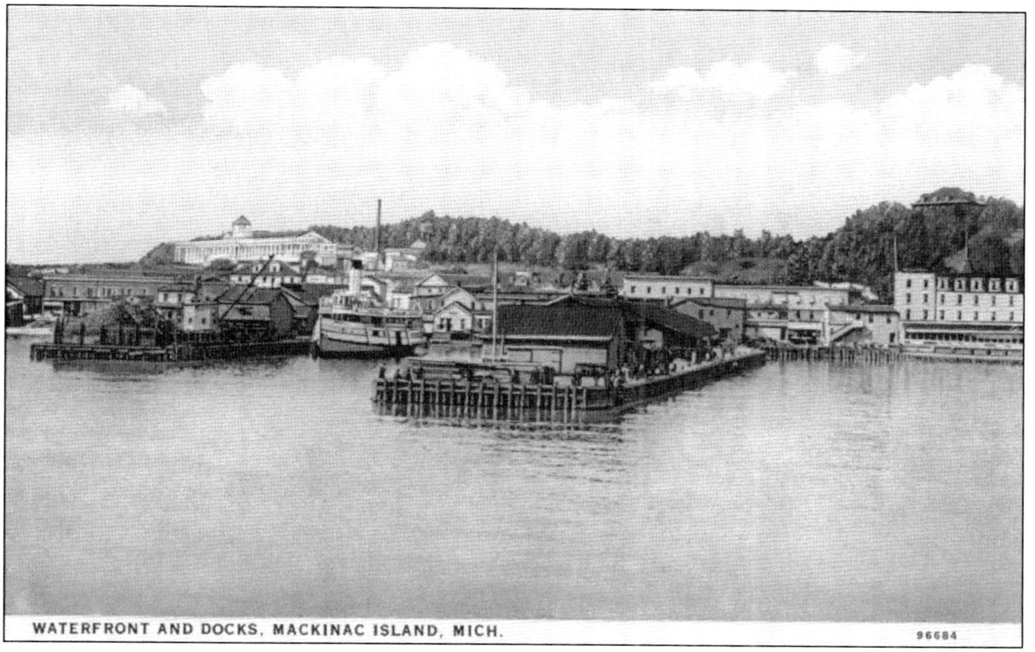

This 1929 postcard reveals the boat docks in the village harbor. Grand Hotel sits elegantly in the background. Fishing does not normally take place on these docks, as they are too busy with passengers and boats. Passengers continue to arrive here for grand adventures.

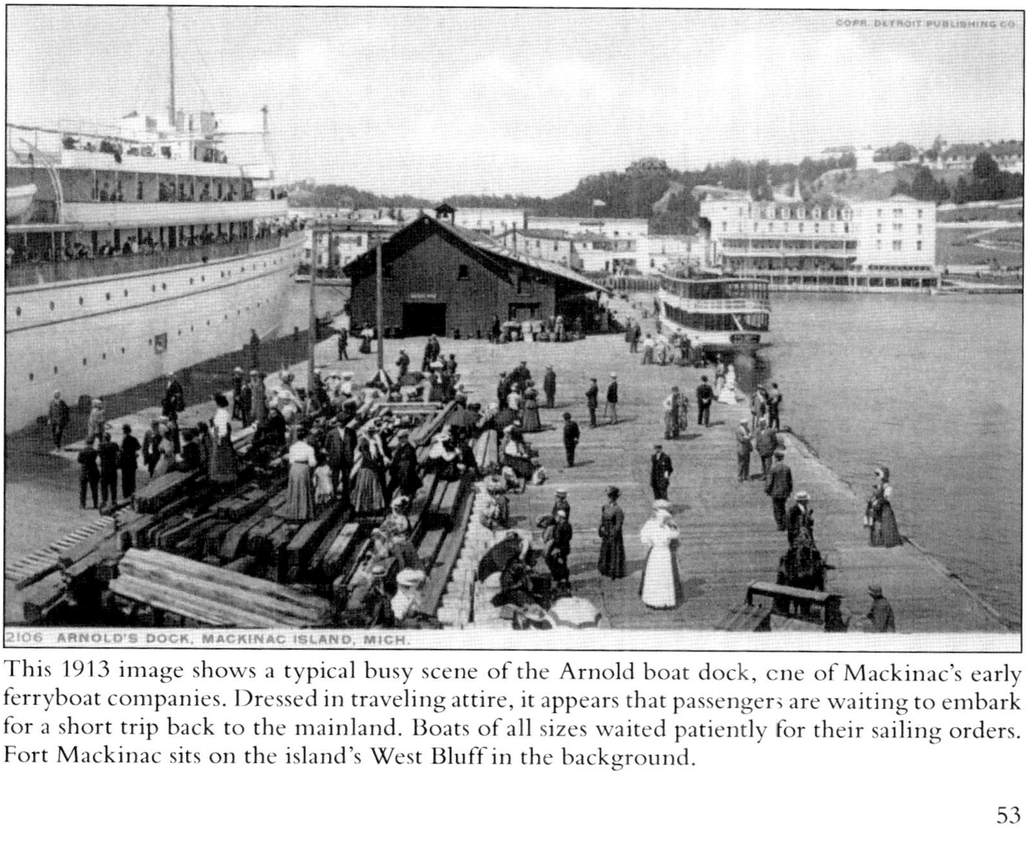

This 1913 image shows a typical busy scene of the Arnold boat dock, one of Mackinac's early ferryboat companies. Dressed in traveling attire, it appears that passengers are waiting to embark for a short trip back to the mainland. Boats of all sizes waited patiently for their sailing orders. Fort Mackinac sits on the island's West Bluff in the background.

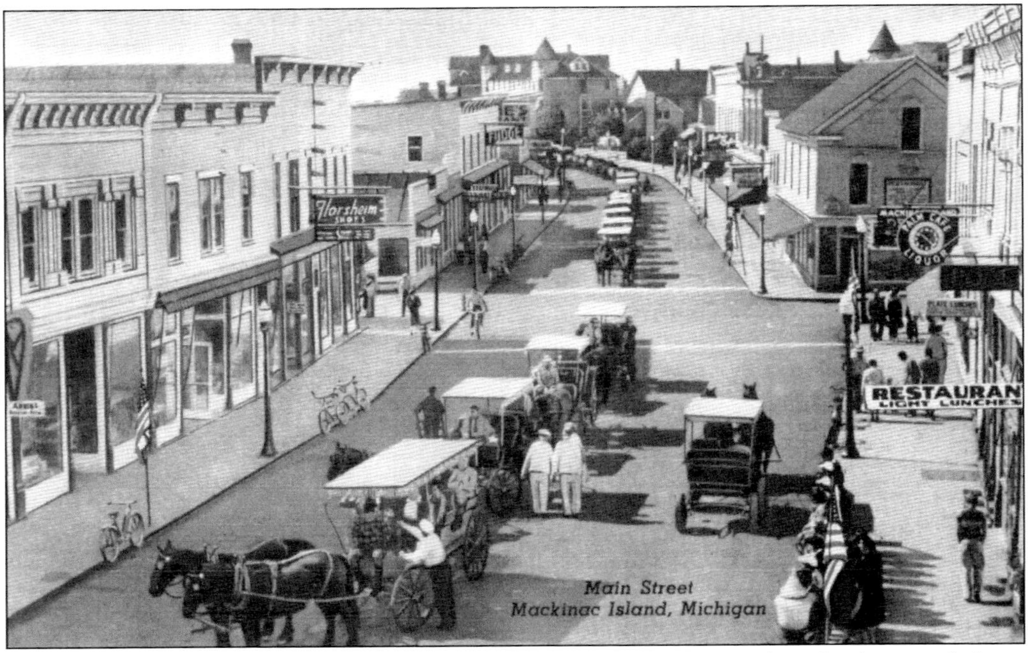

Visitors to Mackinac Island required hotels and restaurants. Later, gift and other retail shops were established. Because automobiles were left behind in St. Ignace or Mackinaw City, carriage rides were popular. This view of Main Street shows many more carriages than bicycles. Street cleaners were given the unpleasant job of following the carriages.

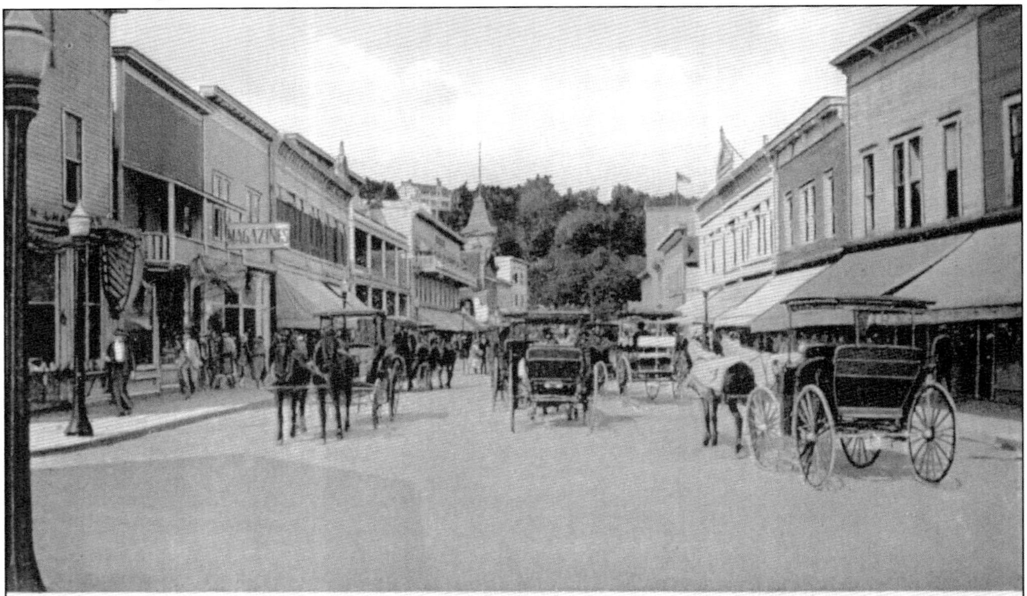

Tourists arrived by steamboat from cities like Buffalo, Cleveland, Port Huron, and Detroit on the Lake Huron side and Chicago and Milwaukee on the Lake Michigan side. Meeting distant relatives at Mackinac Island made for a splendid summer season. When the railroad came to Mackinaw City in 1881, visitors to Mackinac Island increased dramatically.

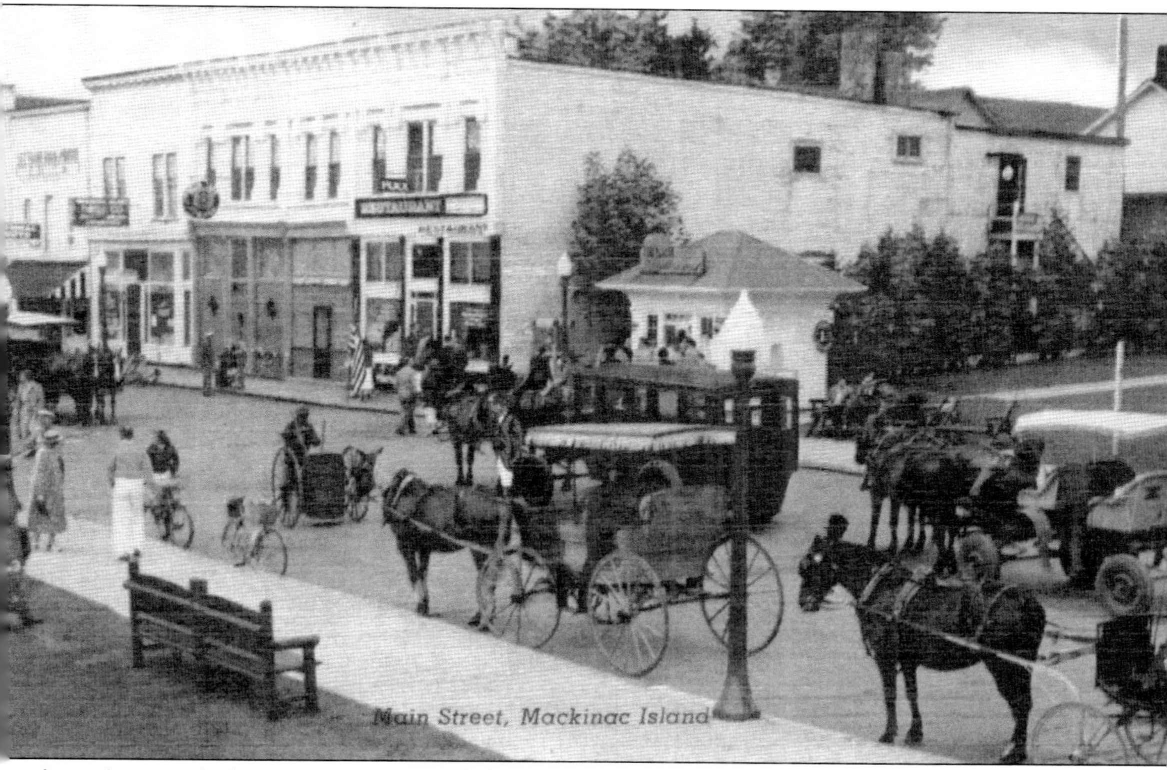

A carriage awaits its next passengers, while across the street gift shops compete for their share of the tourist trade. In 1875, one shop boasted, "Strangers and visitors, to this charming and romantic island, for ages the paradise of the Genii, so believed from time immemorial by the Indian tribes, wishing to procure a souvenir of their visit to the 'Fairy Isle,' the spiritual resting-place of the departed braves and renowned warriors of the West, will find a rare and splendid collection of genuine Indian curiosities of all descriptions at the Indian Bazaar. Fenton & Wendell, Proprietors." A competitor of Fenton and Wendell, Mr. S. Highstone, claimed that his "New Indian Curiosity Store has the largest, best assorted and cheapest stock of Indian curiosities ever opened on the Island of Mackinac, consisting of bark boxes, and baskets of every description, sweet grass in every variety, bead work, feathers, the assortment of which includes every description of fancy work made by Chippewa Indians. Also, photographic and stereoscopic views of all points of interest."

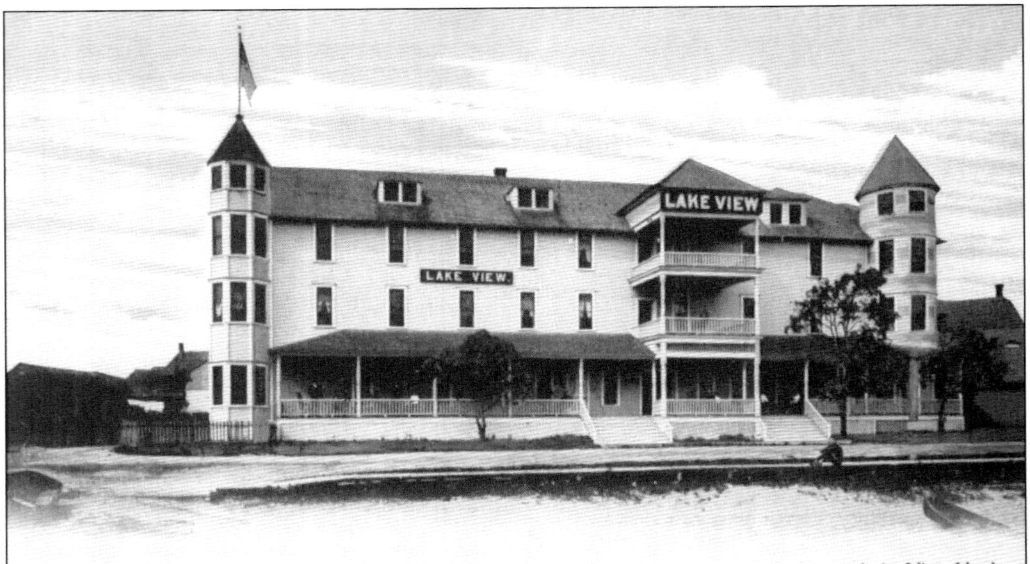

Mackinac Island, Mich. 253 Lake View Hotel

MANUFACTURED BY CURT TEICH & CO., CHICAGO, ILL.

These early-1900s postcards show two of the stately hotels for Mackinac Island guests: the Lake View Hotel and the Iroquois-on-the-Beach. In 1875, hotel prices varied from $2 to $3.50 per day, and the boardinghouse charged "$10 per week and upward." Rooms with water views were the most expensive. An 1875 Mackinac business directory listed these establishments: Dry Goods, Clothing, and Groceries; Druggist and General Merchandise; Steamboat Owner; County Clerk; Indian Curiosities; Steamboat Agent; Postmaster; Sheriff; General Merchandise and Fisherman's Supplies; and Billiard Saloon.

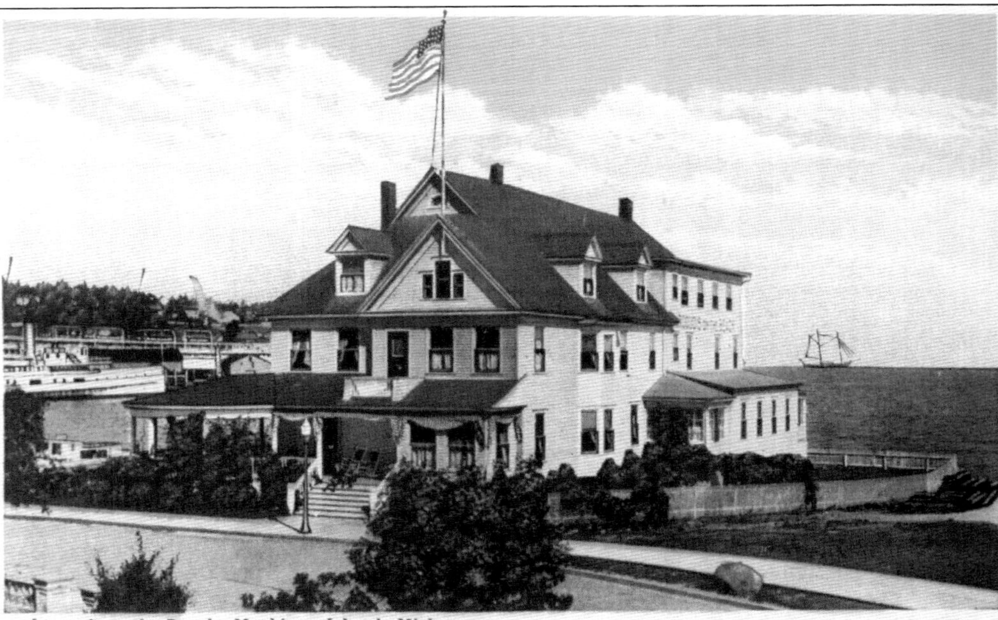

Iroquois-on-the-Beach, Mackinac Island, Mich. 96679

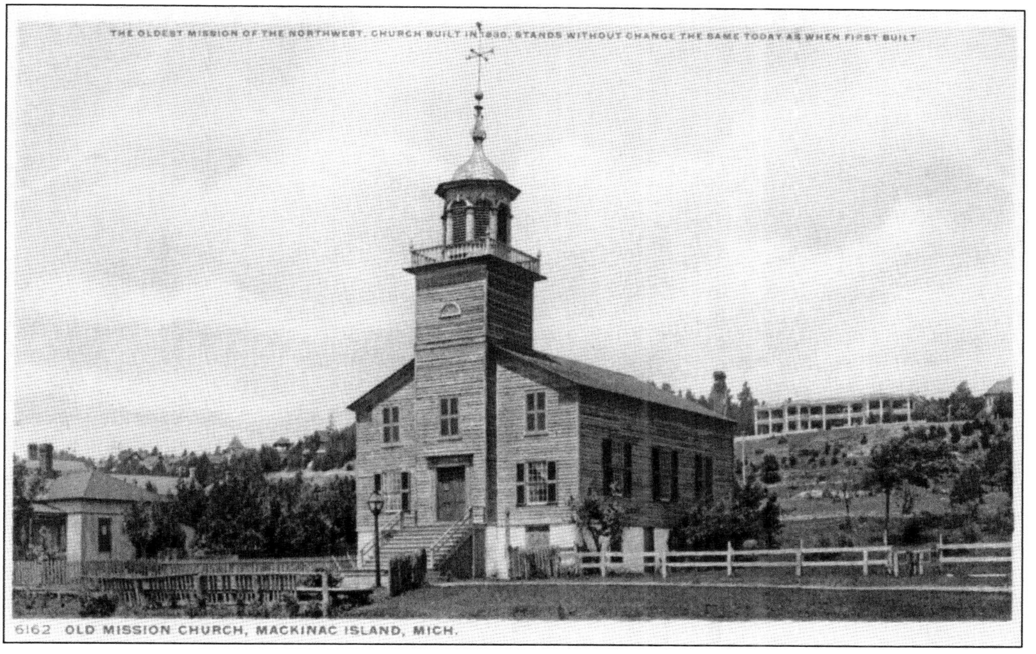

French Jesuit priests left a lasting impression on island residents regarding Christianity, which manifested itself in the building of two of the island's historic churches. Old Mission Church (above) was built in 1830 and was the first Protestant church on Mackinac Island. St. Anne's Church (right) was originally located in Fort Michilimackinac at Mackinaw City but was moved to Mackinac Island around 1781. This Catholic mission had the devout patronage of Magdelaine LaFramboise, the daughter of an Ottawa chief and the wife of a French fur trader. Raised in Ottawa tradition and baptized in her husband's faith, she became a community leader and millionaire. When her husband, Joseph, was killed, Magdelaine took over his business and became extremely successful at fur-trade transactions. She could negotiate in Ottawa, Ojibwe, French, and English.

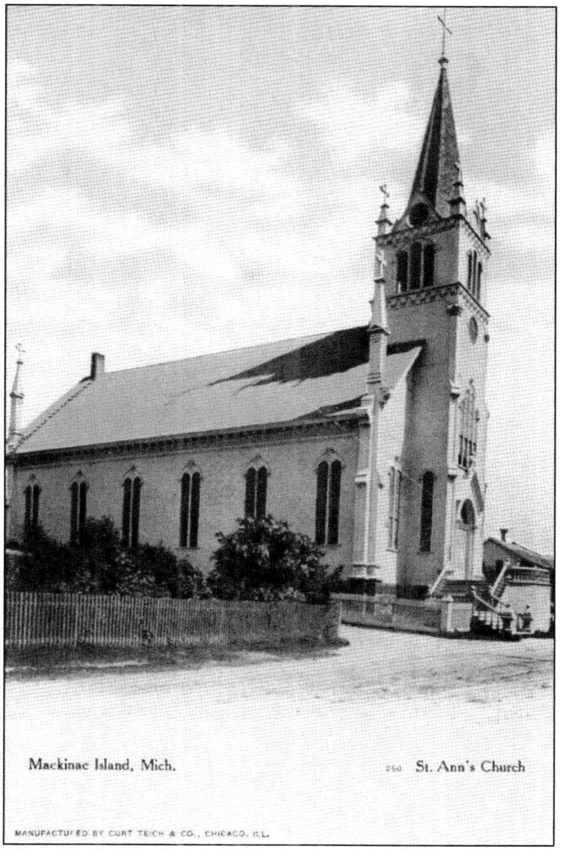

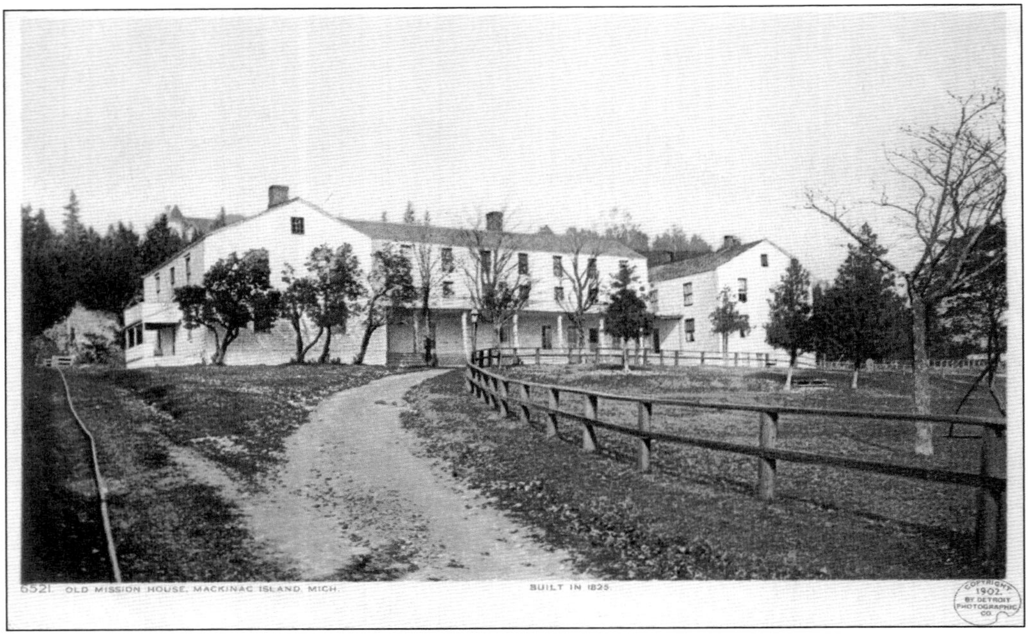

This early-1900s postcard shows Reverend Ferry's protestant mission, named the Old Mission House. It later became a hotel and, in the 1950s, housed the headquarters of the Moral Re-Armament (MRA), an international Christian moral and spiritual movement group. When the MRA relocated to Switzerland, it deeded its Mackinac Island property to Mackinac College, which operated there for just a short time before it closed.

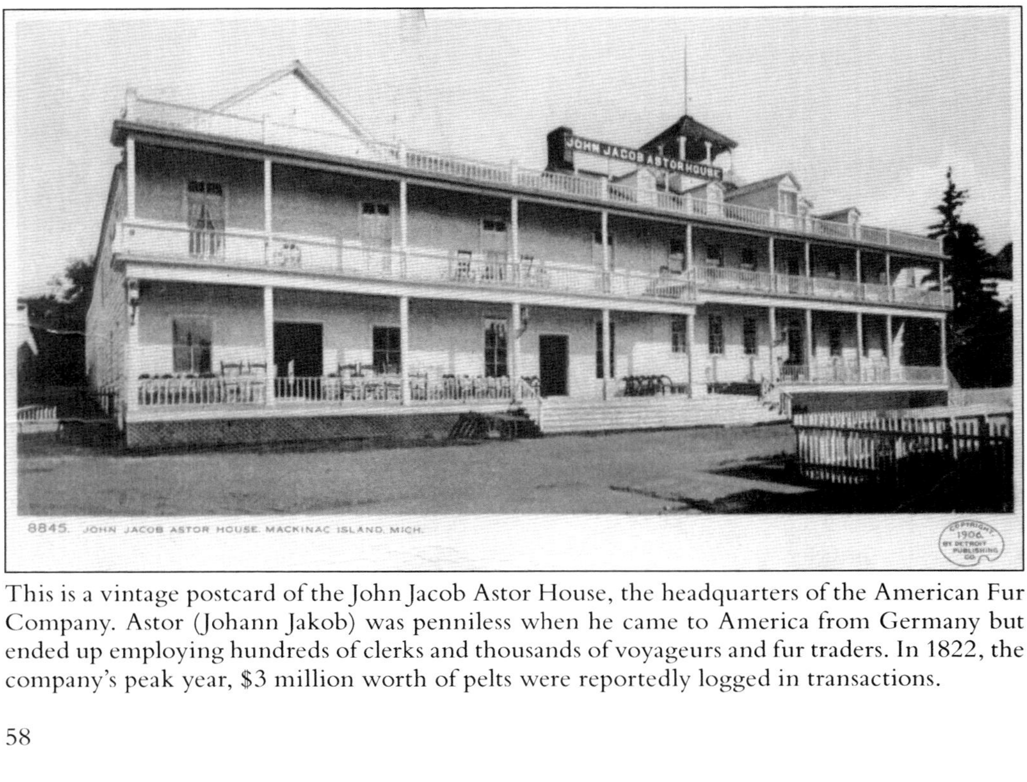

This is a vintage postcard of the John Jacob Astor House, the headquarters of the American Fur Company. Astor (Johann Jakob) was penniless when he came to America from Germany but ended up employing hundreds of clerks and thousands of voyageurs and fur traders. In 1822, the company's peak year, $3 million worth of pelts were reportedly logged in transactions.

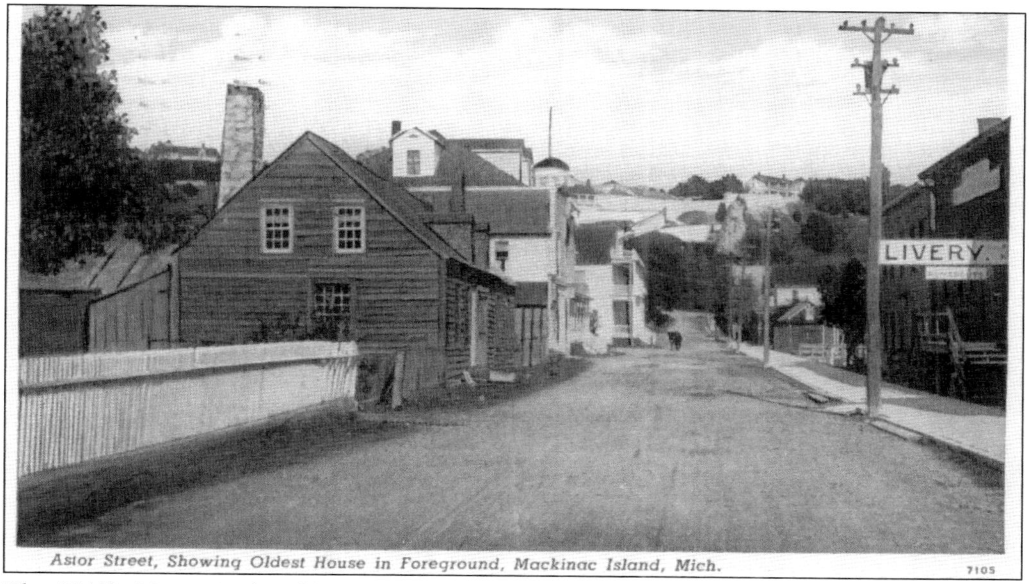

The Biddle House is the oldest existing house on Mackinac Island, but the street is Market Street not Astor Street as noted on the postcard. Probably constructed about 1780, the house was owned in the 1830s by Edward Biddle, a fur trader, and is a registered landmark with an accompanying historical marker. It has been restored and now belongs to the Mackinac Island State Park Commission. Fort Mackinac is on the bluff in the background.

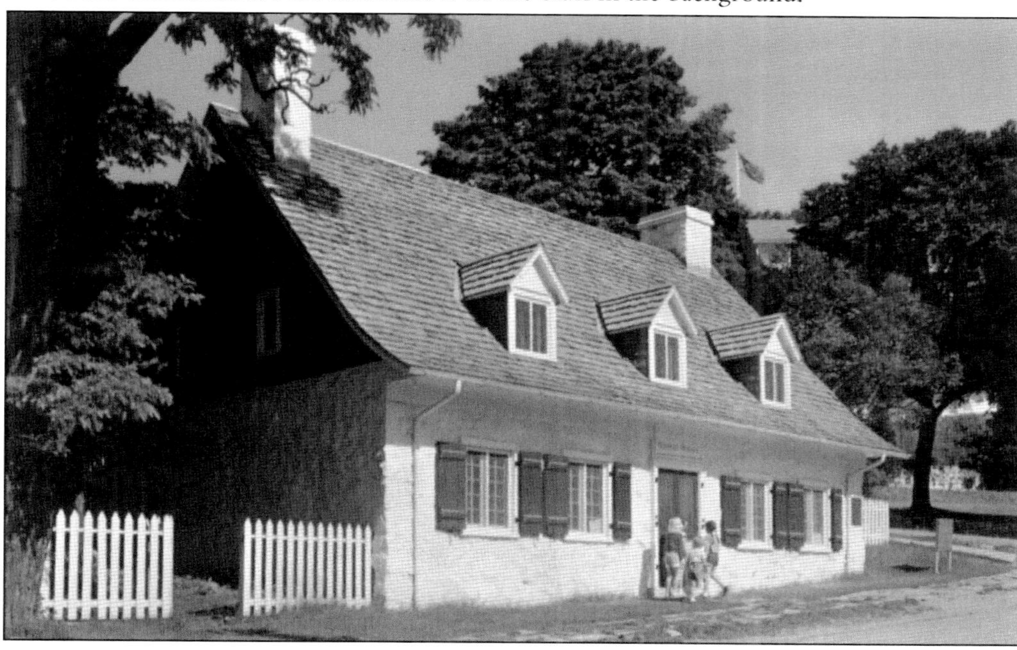

Another example of rustic architecture is the American Fur Company Store and Dr. Beaumont Museum. It was reconstructed from the original store, where Dr. Beaumont had studied the digestive process in the stomach of a soldier from Fort Mackinac who had been accidentally shot. In the 1930s, it operated as a boardinghouse, and it now belongs to the Mackinac Island State Park Commission.

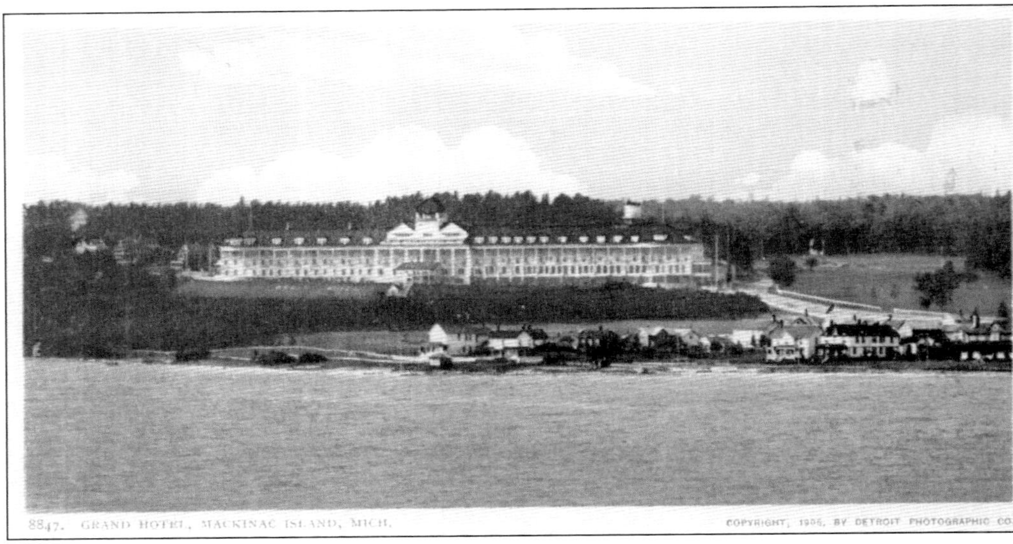

Grand Hotel is a stately landmark welcoming visitors to Mackinac Island. These early postcards show the hotel in its early years before it was expanded and remodeled. Built in 1887, John Oliver Plank was the first manager. It was called Plank's Grand Hotel, but when Plank fell out of favor with members of the transportation company that owned it, he left to develop other properties. Plank's name was dropped, and it became simply Grand Hotel, or as the locals call it, "The Grand." Names of noted Chicago guests in the early years included Gustavus Swift, Philip Armour, Marshall Field, and Potter Palmer. Others who enjoyed its ambiance were Mark Twain, George Pullman, and George Eastman. Room charges were $4 to $5 per day for the American plan, which included meals, a bit more expensive than other island hotels that were charging $2 to $3 a day.

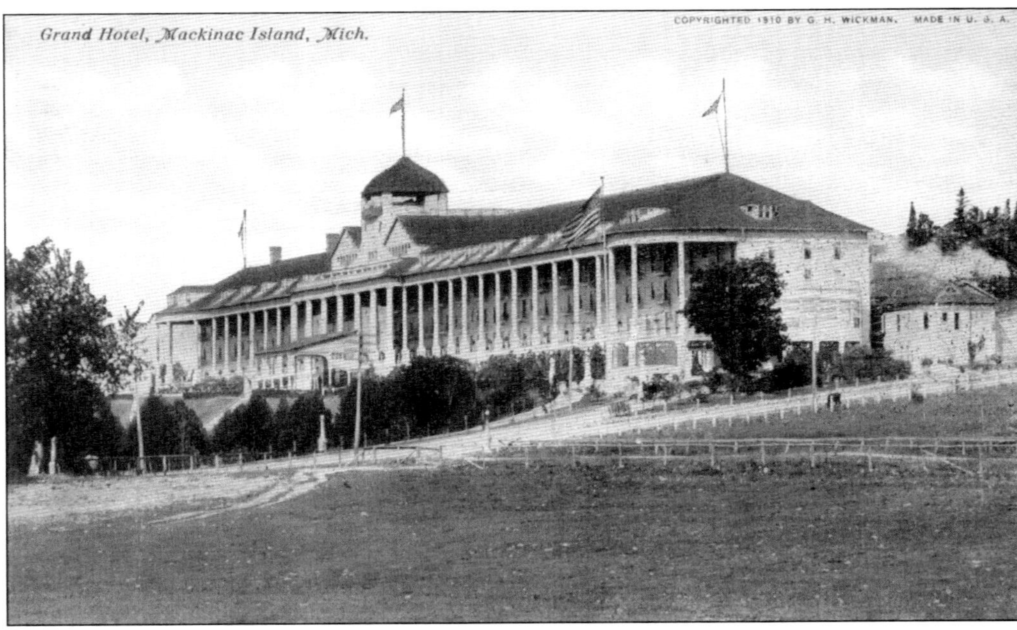

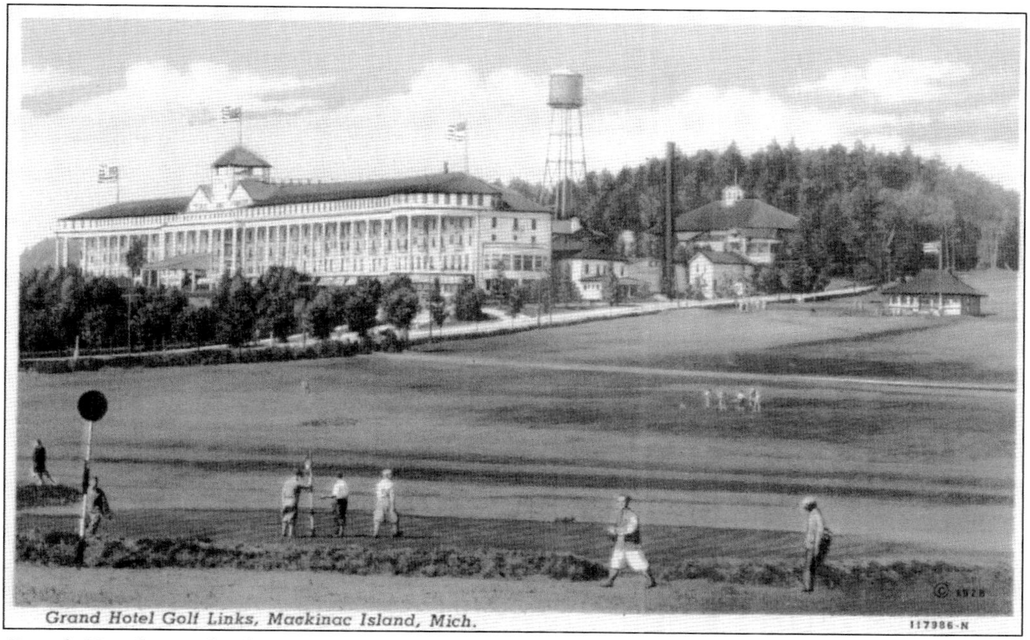

Grand Hotel was built and owned by two railroad companies and a steamship company. Originally, it had 200 rooms but grew to have over 300 rooms, all individually and tastefully decorated. William Stewart Woodfill became the general manager in the early 1920s, followed by Robert Daniel Musser Jr., who began his career at The Grand as a cashier and kitchen steward. In 1979, Woodfill sold the hotel to Musser and his wife, Amelia, who transformed the hotel with expansive restorations. Art, antiques, chandeliers, comfortable chairs, and colorful patterned carpeting added to the interior's charm. Guests still enjoy great hospitality and superb cuisine and can take part in recreational activities such as swimming, horseback riding, golf, croquet, and bocce ball.

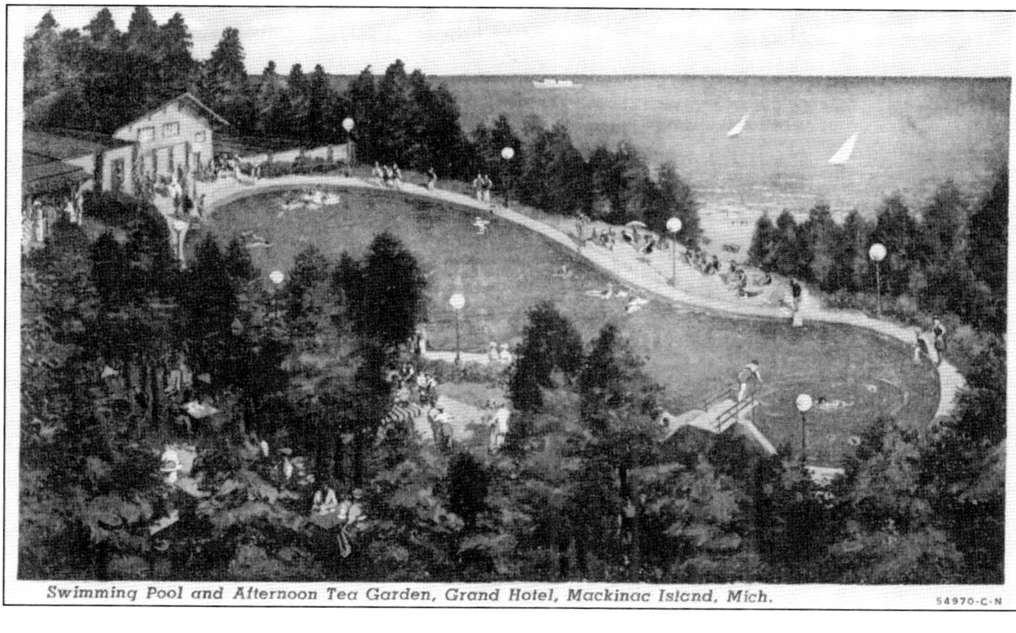

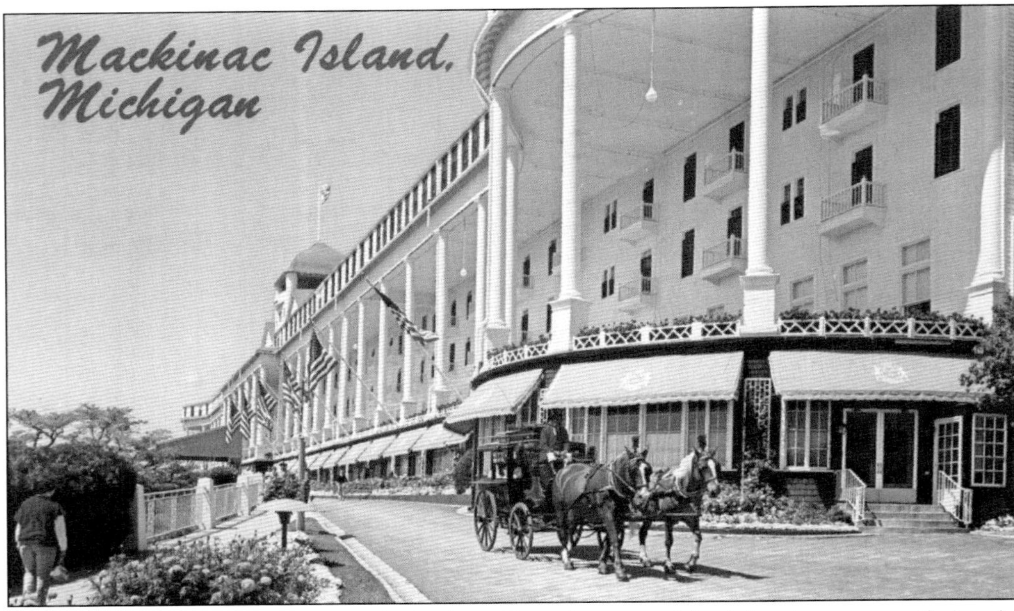

Before they were first remodeled, the high-ceilinged rooms with a lake view were called parlor suites and had carpet and bathrooms. The interior rooms, however, were rather austere, with a double bed, a cane-seat chair, a small dresser, and a closet to accommodate a large trunk. A bell-service cord hung from the ceiling. Further amenities included a kerosene lamp, a china washbasin, and a pitcher of water. Under the bed was a chamber pot with lid. The Grand's 600-foot-long porch was a splendid place to take a stroll, do some afternoon reading, write letters and postcards, or have tea with friends, as the view from the verandah is breathtaking. On a clear day, one could see the entrance to Lake Michigan on the west and down the Lake Huron shoreline to Cheboygan on the east.

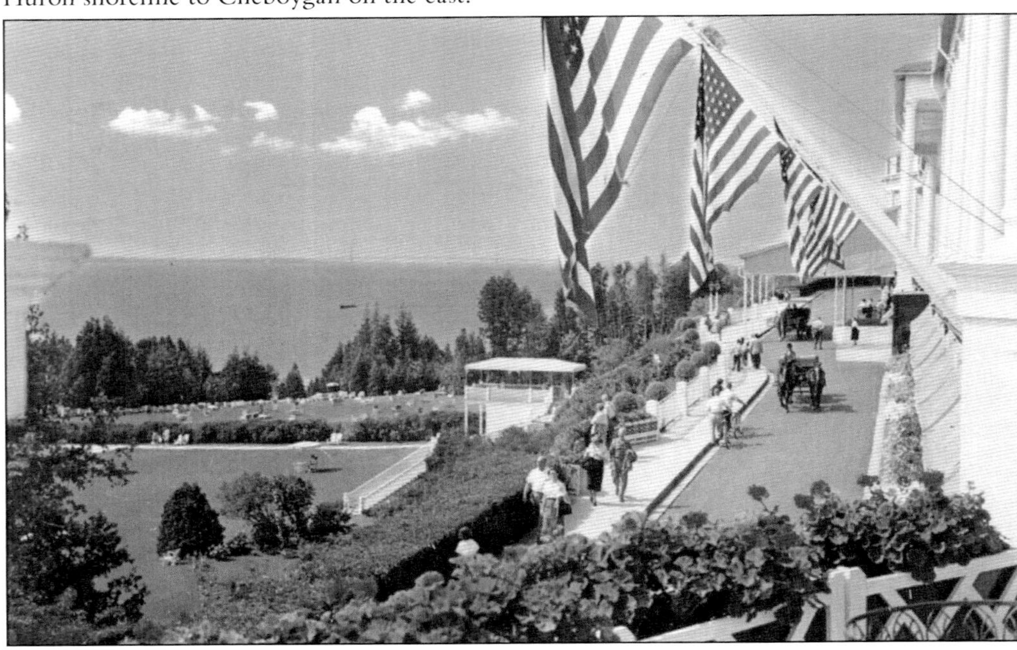

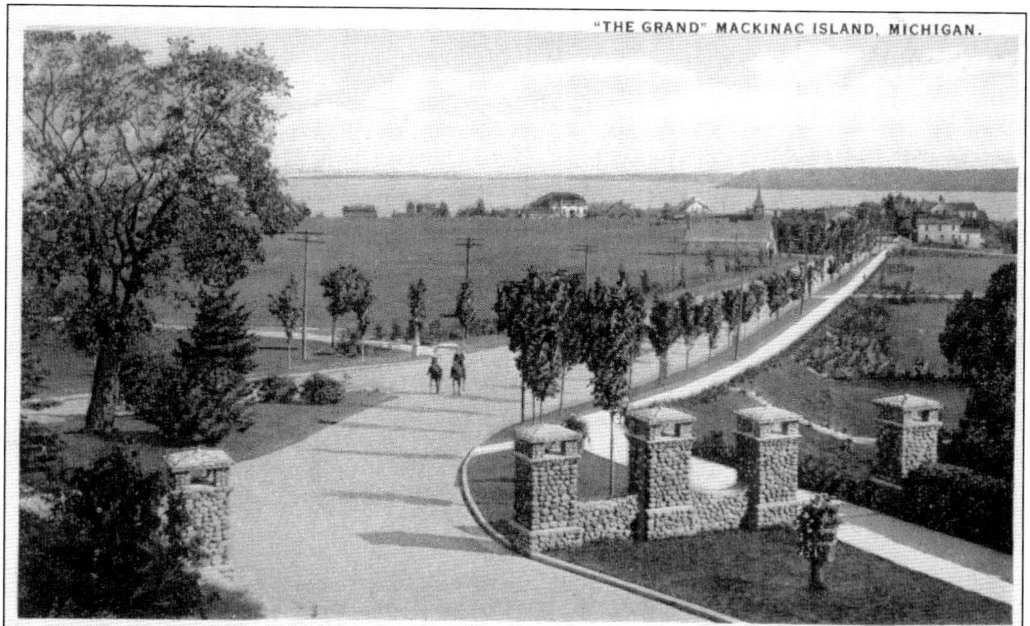

VIEW OF GOLF COURSE AND ENTRANCE TO GRAND HOTEL. 96683

The above image looks towards The Straits from halfway up Cadotte Avenue at the entrance to Grand Hotel. In later years, trees and buildings would fill in the open spaces. The postcard below depicts a magnificent view from the west end "cottages" looking east, with Grand Hotel in the background. Notice the elaborately trimmed shrubs and gardens in the front yards; however, the American flag on the first home in the image below was likely added by the postcard printer. These grand homes on both the east and west bluffs were called cottages and were subject to continued repair and restoration from the ravages of inclement weather. All supplies had to be purchased on the mainland, shipped over, and carried on drays to the appropriate address.

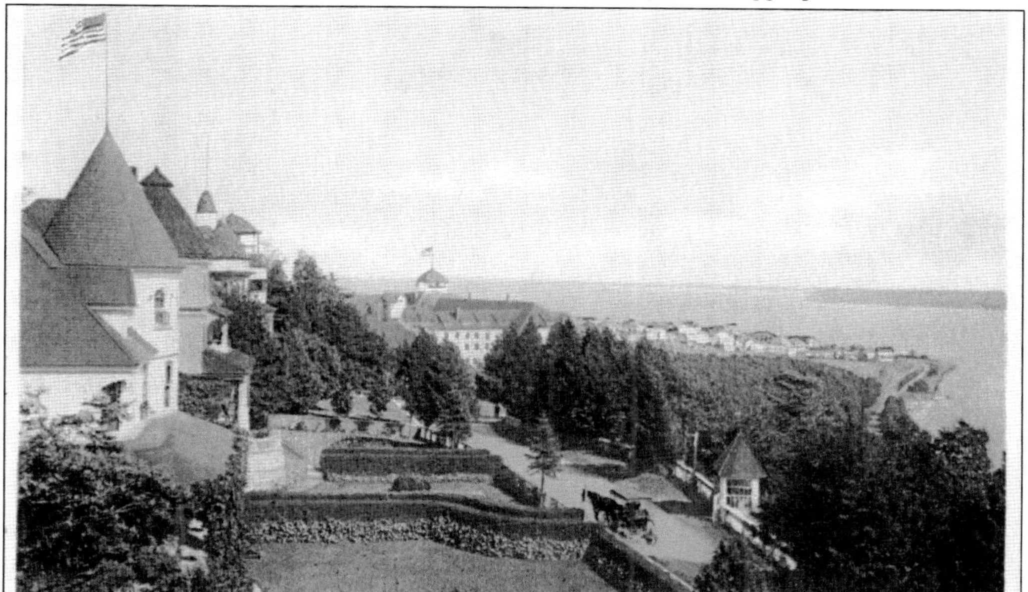

12050 WEST END COTTAGES, MACKINAC ISLAND, MICH. COPR. DETROIT PUBLISHING CO.

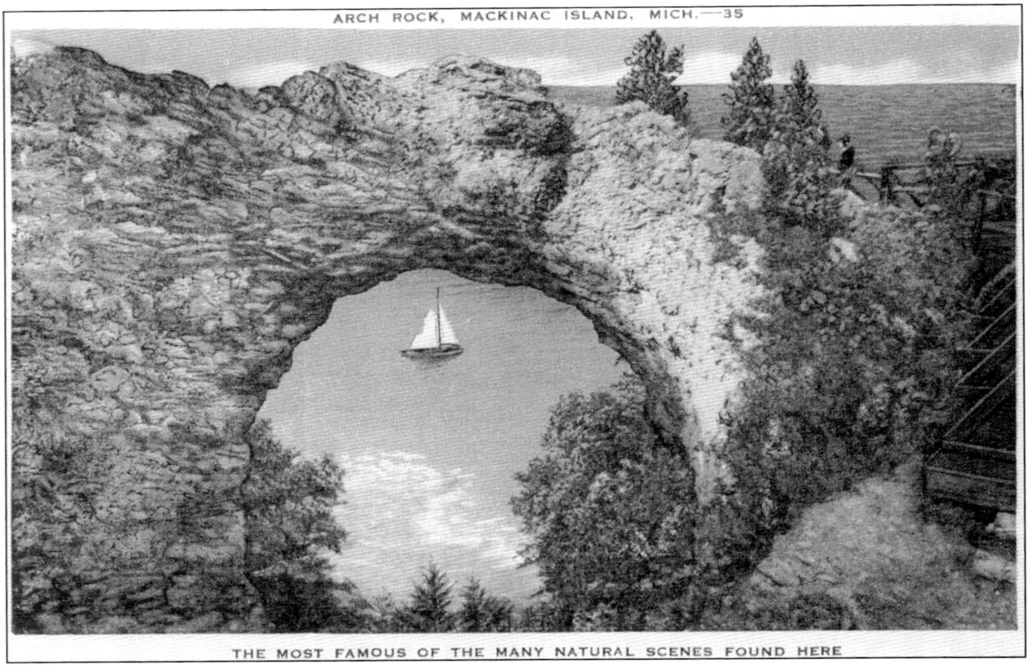

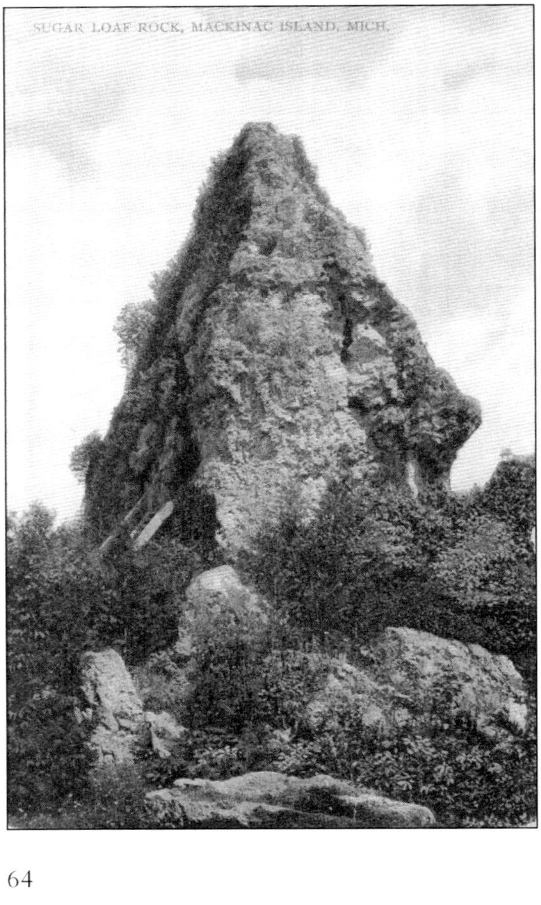

Native Americans had intriguing legends and lore regarding the wonders of nature on Mackinac Island, which has its share of sea stacks and breccia formations. Arch Rock (above) is located on the east side of Mackinac Island and is probably the most photographed of all of the area's natural curiosities. This limestone marvel was naturally formed by glaciers, erosion, wind, and water, but the native people thought the island's "fairy" spirits entered and left through its center. The sailboat in this view was added by the postcard printer. Sugar Loaf Rock (left) no longer has quite the high peak it did in this 1910 postcard, but it still attracts visitors and boasts its share of photographs. A ladder leading to a small cave is on the left. Legend says it is the home of Gitchie Manitou.

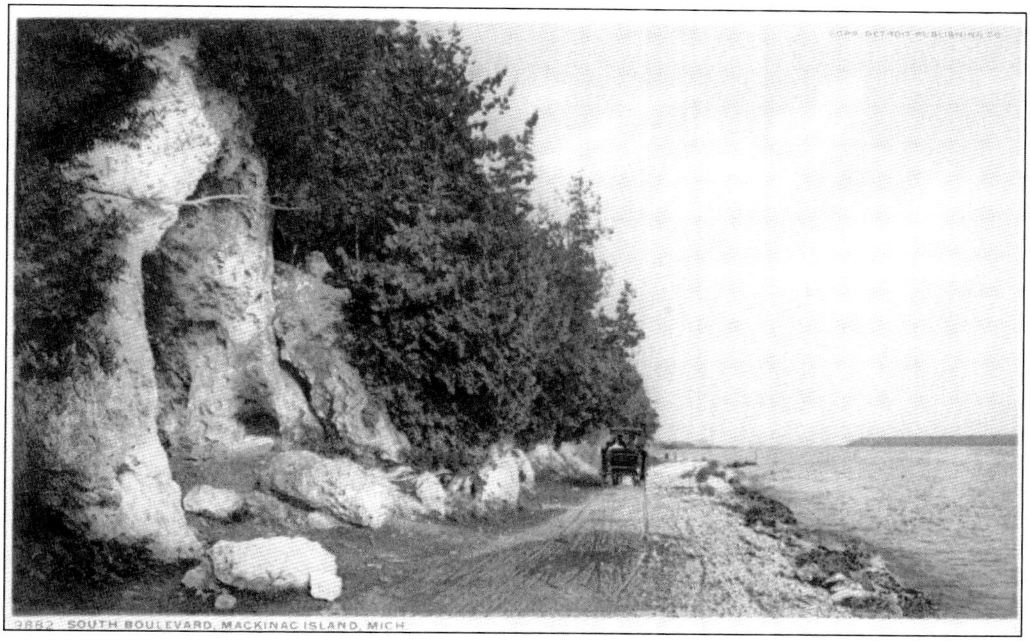

Another popular limestone cave is on South Boulevard (above), which is now a paved Michigan highway winding its way around the shoreline of Mackinac Island overlooking Lake Huron. Robinson's Folly (right), at the easternmost point of the island, rises high above the water. The legend of Robinson's Folly has many versions, including one where Capt. Daniel Robertson, an English officer at Fort Mackinac, fell in love with an Indian princess. Her father, an Ojibwa chief, was enraged and came to grapple with Robertson at the top of the peak, where Robertson had built a small house. In the ensuing struggle, Robertson (whose name was corrupted to Robinson) fell over the side to his death. The princess was so distraught that she too met her end at Robinson's Folly.

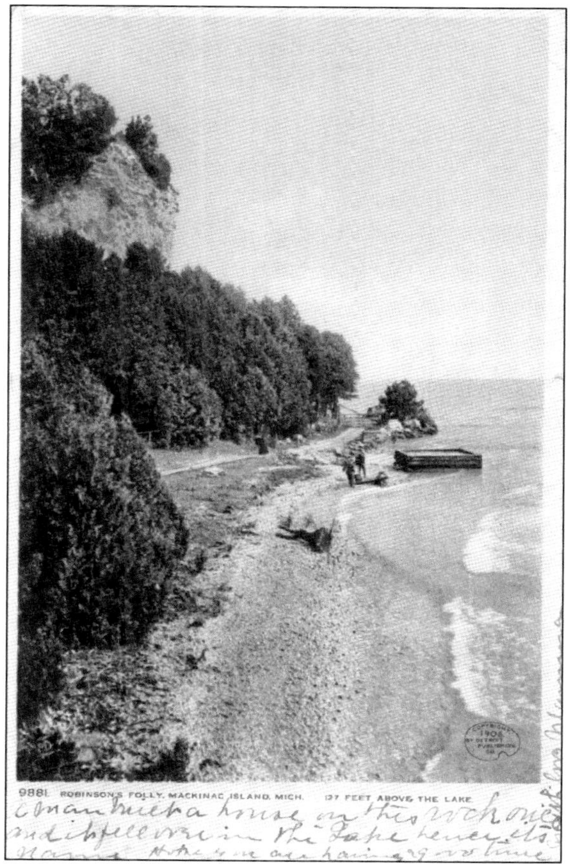

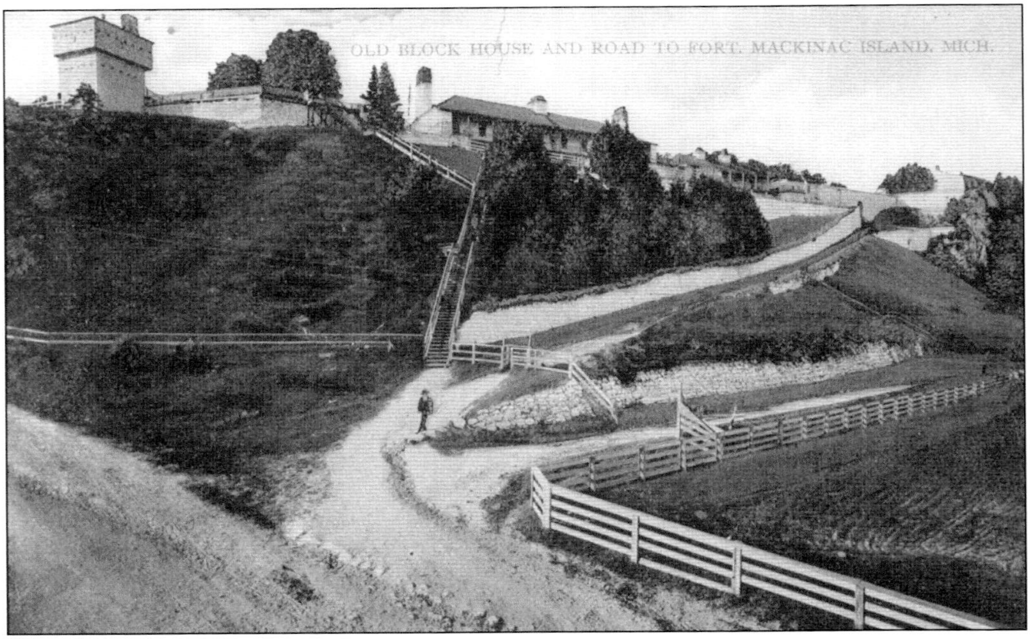

The first military fort on the Straits of Mackinac was Fort de Buade at St. Ignace, the second was Fort Michilimackinac at Mackinaw City, and the third was Fort Mackinac on Mackinac Island as seen in this 1908 postcard. Sitting high on a bluff, it was a more strategic location than its predecessor, offering the British a good vantage point to watch for enemies. (Courtesy of Larry and Janice Knapp.)

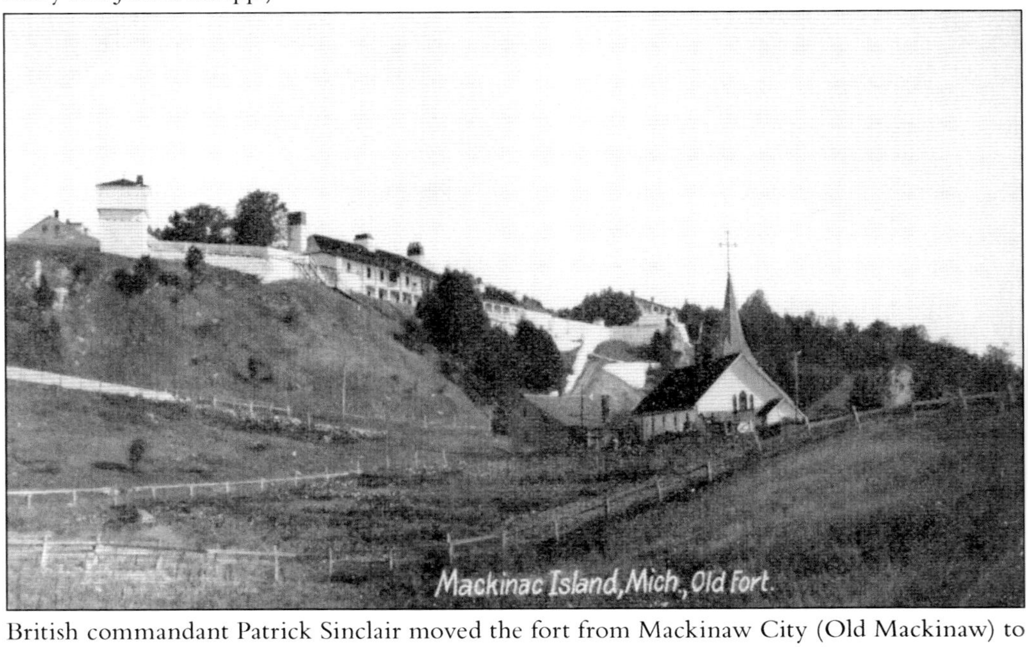

British commandant Patrick Sinclair moved the fort from Mackinaw City (Old Mackinaw) to the island around 1780 during the American Revolution. Americans took control of it in 1796, but in the War of 1812, the British took it back. Americans finally regained control of the fort for good at the end of the war. Trinity Episcopal Church, built in 1882, sits in the foreground.

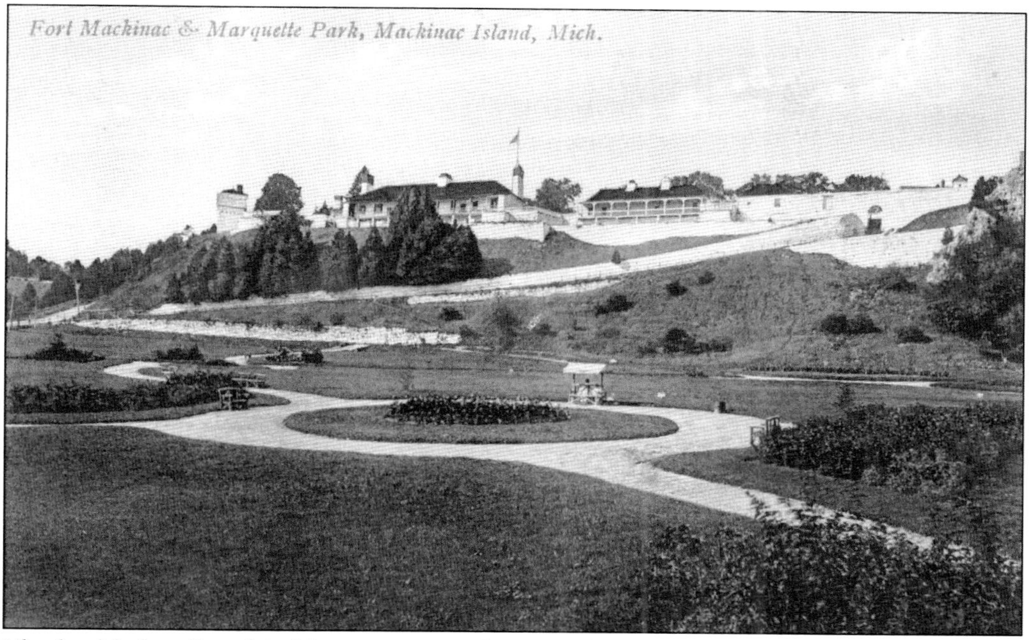

The land below Fort Mackinac was a grazing area for the fort's cattle. Transformed into a park, this postcard, postmarked 1908, shows the area before the bronze statue of Fr. Jacques Marquette was erected in 1909. The fort buildings, many of which were dismantled at Fort Michilimackinac and reassembled on the island, have been restored by Mackinac State Historic Parks. The entire fort is now a living history museum.

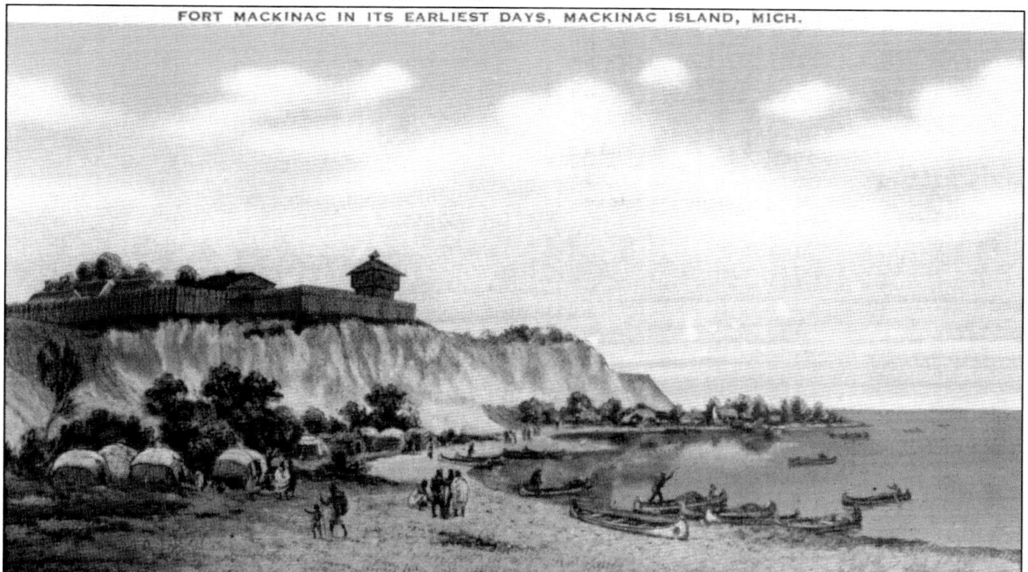

This postcard is an artist's depiction of Fort Mackinac in its earliest days. Hundreds of Native Americans from many tribes camped on the shore below. They came to fish and to try to keep claim on their sacred island. In 1895, the fort was closed as a military post. Formerly a part of the second national park, Fort Mackinac is now a proud attraction in Michigan's first state park.

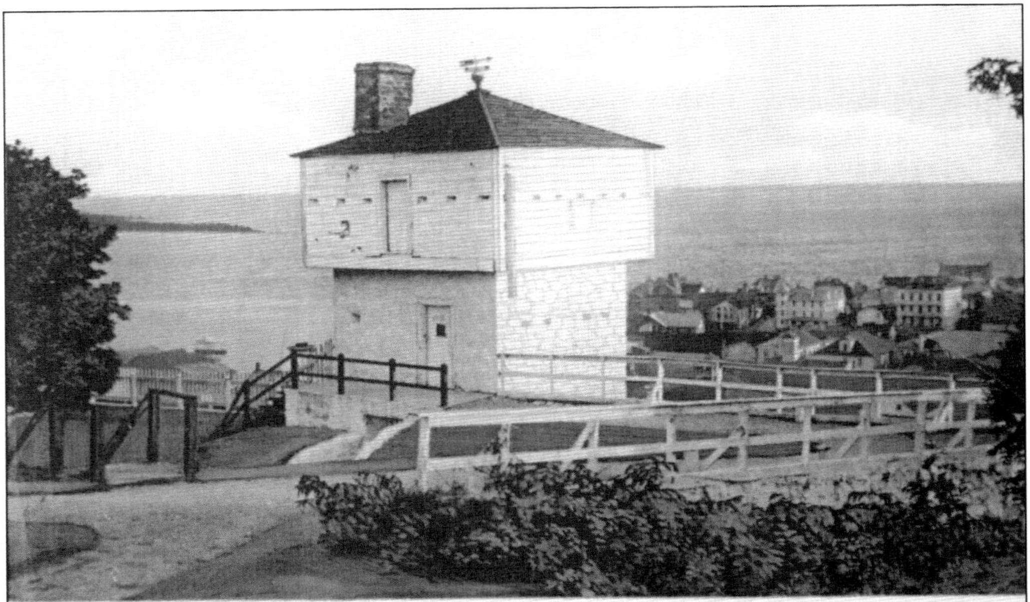

13012 THE OLD BLOCK HOUSE, MACKINAC ISLAND, MICH.

The above image is a postcard of one of Fort Mackinac's old blockhouses, and the image below shows the fort's south sally port and south wall. Archaeological excavations at Fort Mackinac, particularly the Provision Storehouse, have provided a wealth of information about early life there. Carefully recovered artifacts include shards of ceramics, household and military buttons, bottles, ironware (including hooks, nails, screws, hinges, and spikes), clay smoking pipes, pieces of musketry, coins, and even human teeth.

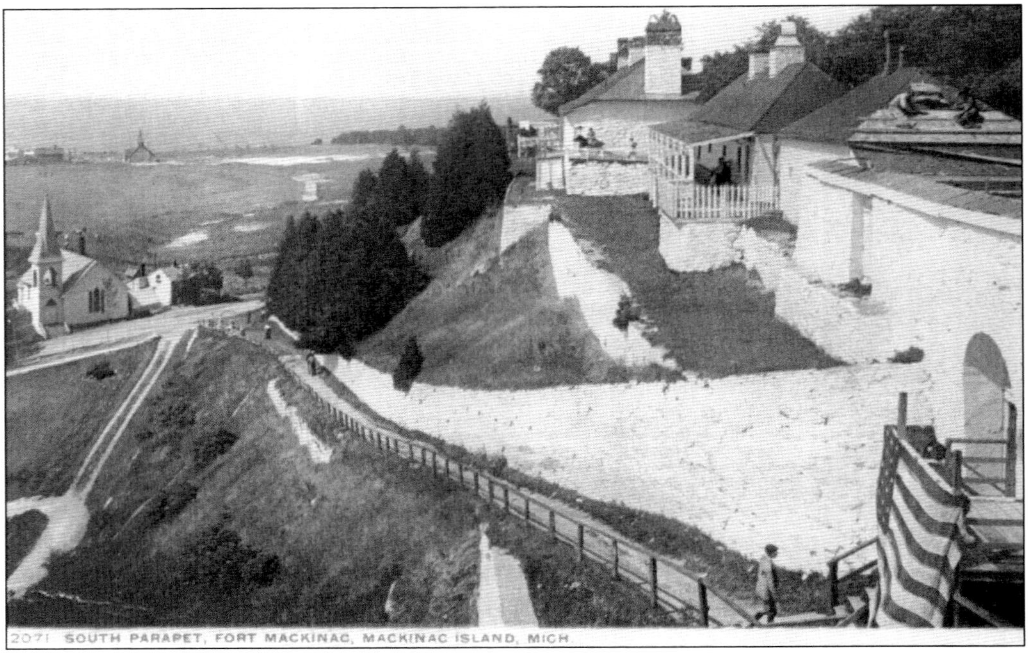

2071 SOUTH PARAPET, FORT MACKINAC, MACKINAC ISLAND, MICH.

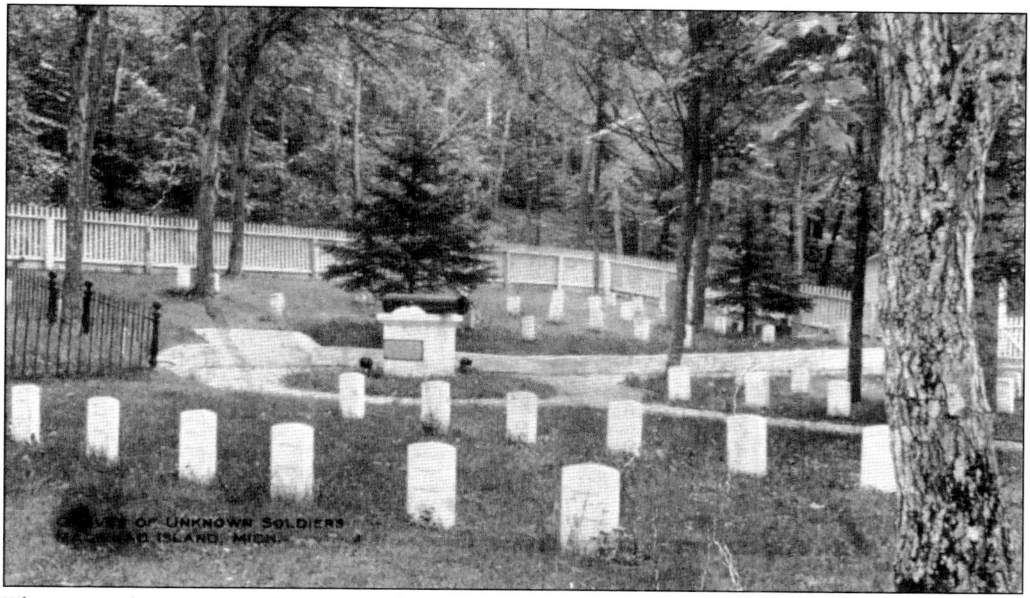

There are three cemeteries on Mackinac Island, grouped rather closely together: a Catholic cemetery, a Protestant cemetery, and the Post (or military) Cemetery. The current Catholic cemetery originated in the mid-1820s, when St. Anne's Church was moved from its original location; many graves were relocated as well. The Protestant cemetery was established around 1830 after the first Protestant mission was established on the island. The Post Cemetery, with its white-picket fence and arched entrance, contains the remains of over 100 Fort Mackinac residents, both military and civilian. Unfortunately, many of the graves have not been identified, including those of probable British soldiers. Noted causes of death included drowning, inflammation of the lungs, typhoid fever, peritonitis, gunshot accidents, suicide, and "hanged for murder."

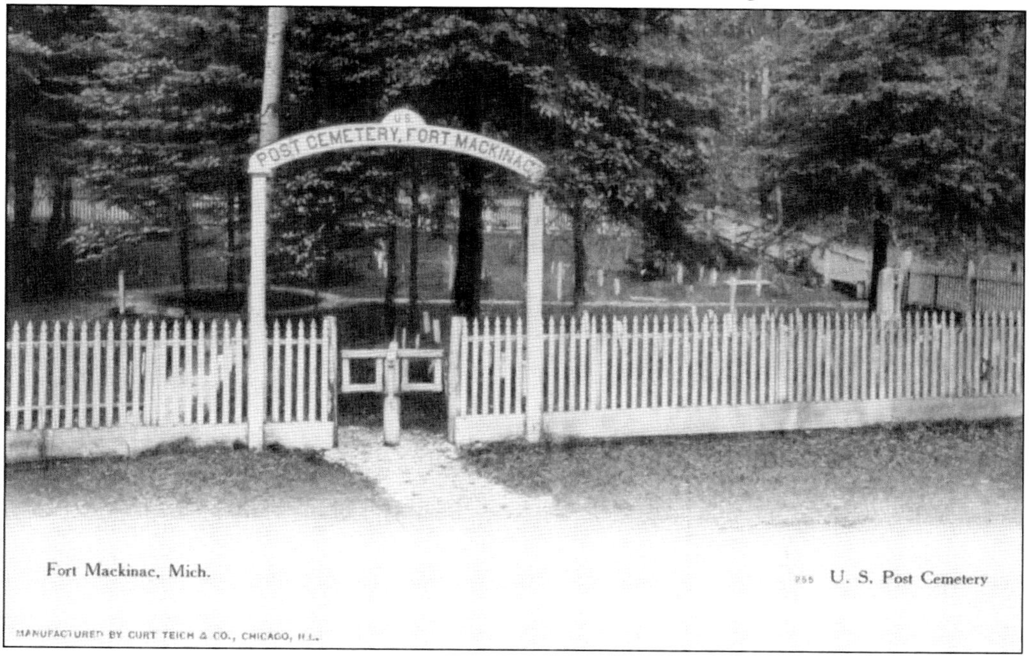

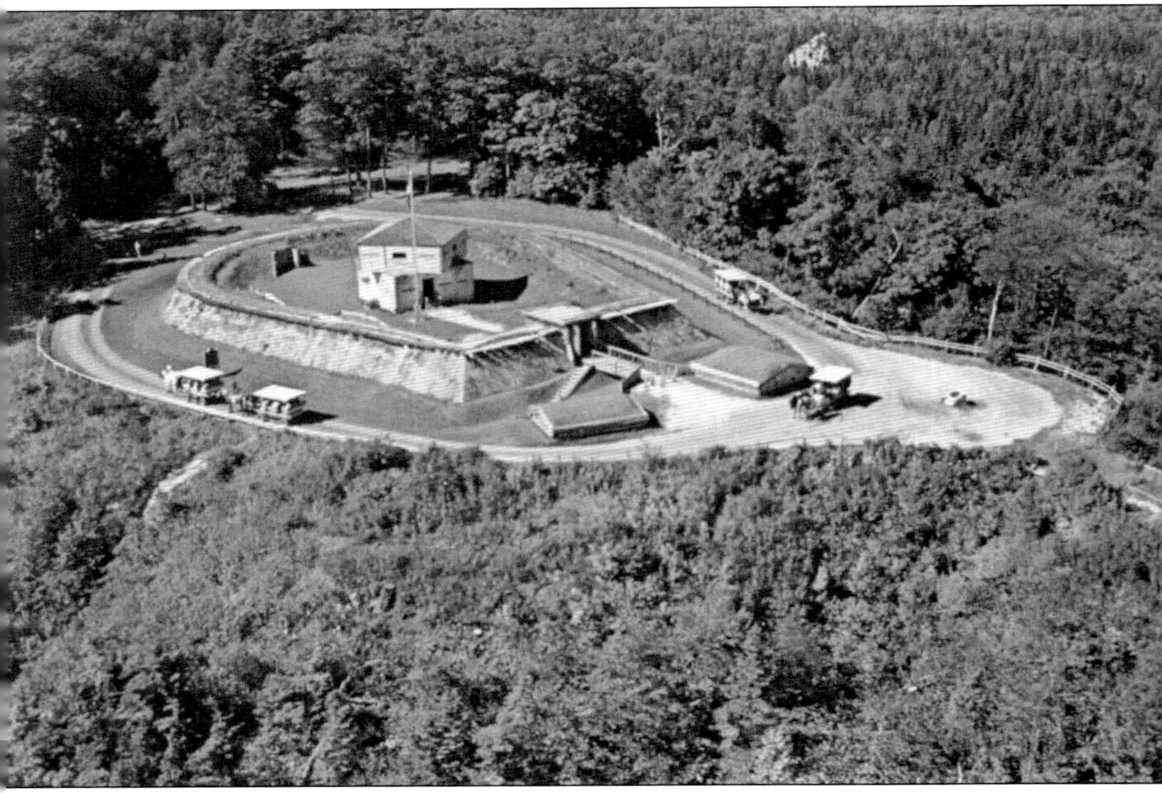

Located at the highest elevation on Mackinac Island, over 300 feet above lake level, is the fourth fort on the Straits of Mackinac, Fort Holmes. Built during the War of 1812, it was originally named Fort George by the British soon after they captured Fort Mackinac. When American major Andrew Holmes perished after an attack against the British on the island in 1814, the fort was renamed in his honor. Soldiers stationed at Fort Holmes were transient, as there was not a regular water supply, and all accounts of activity ceased there around 1817. Today, little remains of Fort Holmes except for historical markers, but the magnificent view of The Straits remains unchanged. Native Americans had a legend about this hilltop. The faithful Me-cos-te-wan-da waited day after day for the return of her beloved husband, Che-to-wait, who had gone to war. Then, one day, Me-cos-te-wan-da saw a strange canoe travelling slowly in the water. The sides of the boat were stone, and its sails were feathered wings. The words of the "Death Song" floated toward her, and she recognized her husband's voice—a fitting legend for a magical isle.

Four

Mackinaw City
Pe-quot-e-nonge

Mackinaw City may spell its name differently, but it proudly joins Mackinac Island and St. Ignace in a triangle of history. Native Americans named it Pe-quot-e-nonge and later it was called Old Mackinaw. Early inhabitants of the Straits of Mackinac explored, lived, and moved around all three points of this triangle.

Mackinaw City began as a Native American encampment joined by a busy fur-trading post around 1673 on the south shore of the scenic waterway. To protect their expanding commercial interests, the French built a palisade around the busy village in 1715 and named it Fort Michilimackinac. When the French military post was dismantled and moved to Mackinac Island, life at the former site changed dramatically, as it was mostly blown over with sand. Left dormant for decades, it was not until 1857 that Edgar Conkling, an Ohio businessman, began a redevelopment of the area. He was joined by George Washington Stimpson and Lewis Willets. Together, these men and their families created a welcomed stopping point for sailing vessels and steamboats passing through The Straits.

The first "enterprise" in Mackinaw City was Conkling's cordwood business, then Stimpson's hotel, followed by Willets' dry goods store. Unfortunately, two major fires, one in 1900 and another in 1916, devastated most of the early structures. Today, Mackinaw City is a village of about 900 residents situated in both Cheboygan and Emmet Counties. It sits at the tip of Michigan's Lower Peninsula at the southern end of the Mackinac Bridge, just a short water distance southwest of Mackinac Island, and is home to many historical sites.

Fort Michilimackinac (now called Colonial Michilimackinac), Old Mackinac Point Light, McGulpin Point Light, Historic Mill Creek, and the decommissioned US Coast Guard Cutter/Icebreaker *Mackinaw* welcome and share history with thousands of visitors every year. A new attraction at the Headlands, a 600-acre Lake Michigan shoreline property, is the exciting International Dark Sky Park, which hosts stargazing experiences for celestial-loving crowds. Mackinaw City's motto is "Living History, Making History."

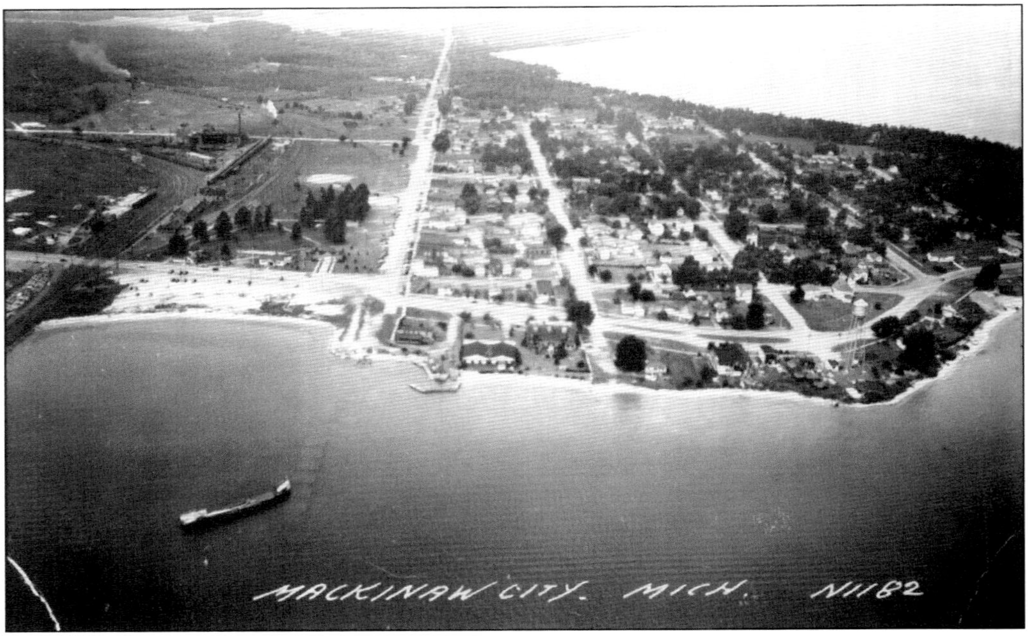

Mackinaw City lies at the very heart of the Straits of Mackinac. It is surrounded by water on three sides: Lake Michigan to the west, The Straits to the north, and Lake Huron to the east. The view in the above postcard looks west from the Lake Huron side toward Trails End Bay in Lake Michigan. The wide street running vertically is Mackinac City's present-day main street, Central Avenue. A Great Lakes freighter is in the foreground. The 1960s postcard below looks north, showing Mackinaw City at the southern end of the Mackinac Bridge, which connects Michigan's two peninsulas. The ferry docks and old railroad dock are on the right.

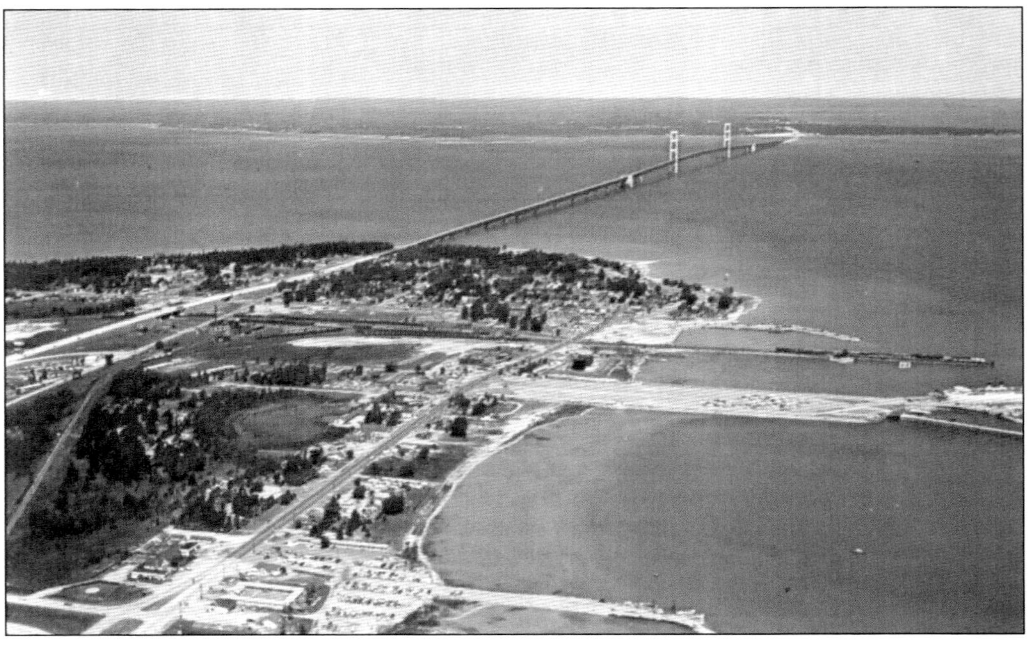

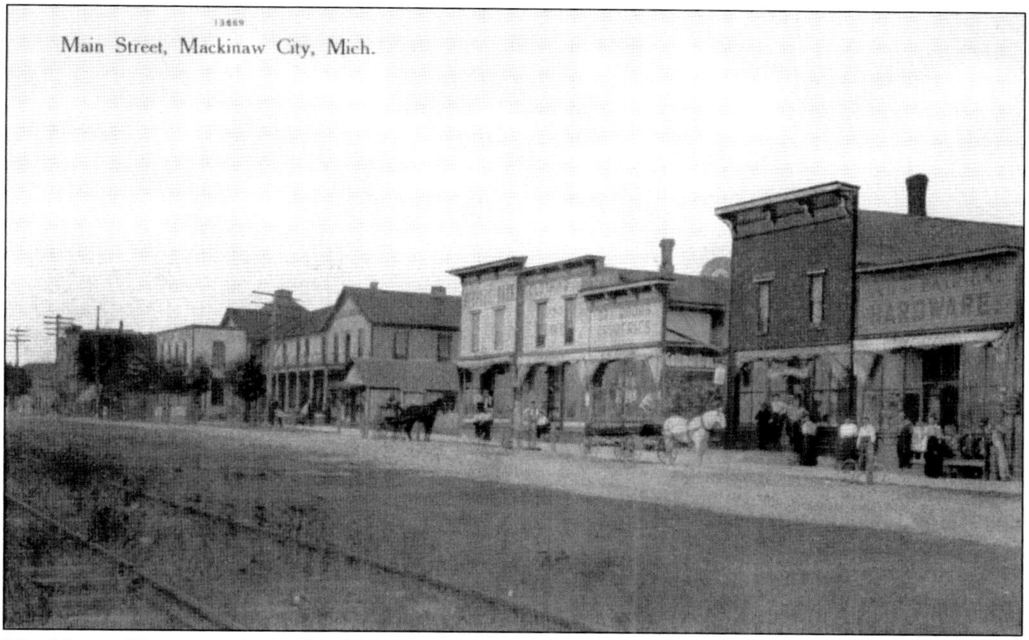

Mackinaw City was originally platted by its founding father, Edgar Conkling, in 1857. Conkling published an exposition about Mackinaw City and its surroundings, stating, "Mackinaw City evidently occupies the most commanding natural position for a city of the first class; surrounded . . . by a widely extended territory, abounding in elements of the greatest wealth, affording the utmost encouragement to the manufacturer and mechanic in the widest diversity of employment, and without the possibility of a competing city in any direction nearer than Detroit on the south." Conkling dreamed of creating a bustling metropolis on The Straits, and he advertised it as such. The above image looks west down Central Avenue, and the postcard below is an eastern view toward the water with a Michigan State Ferry boat in the distance.

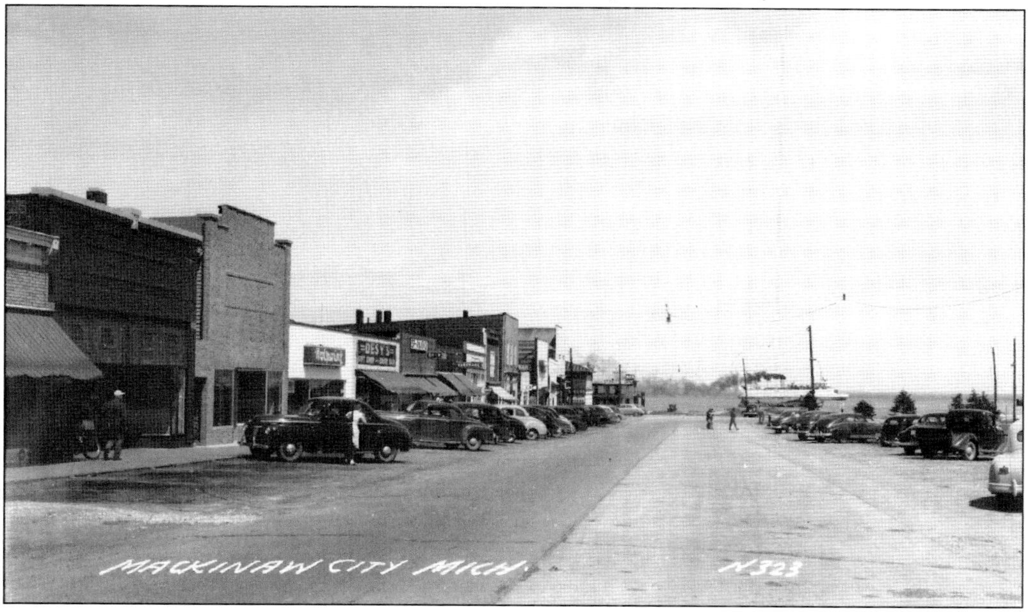

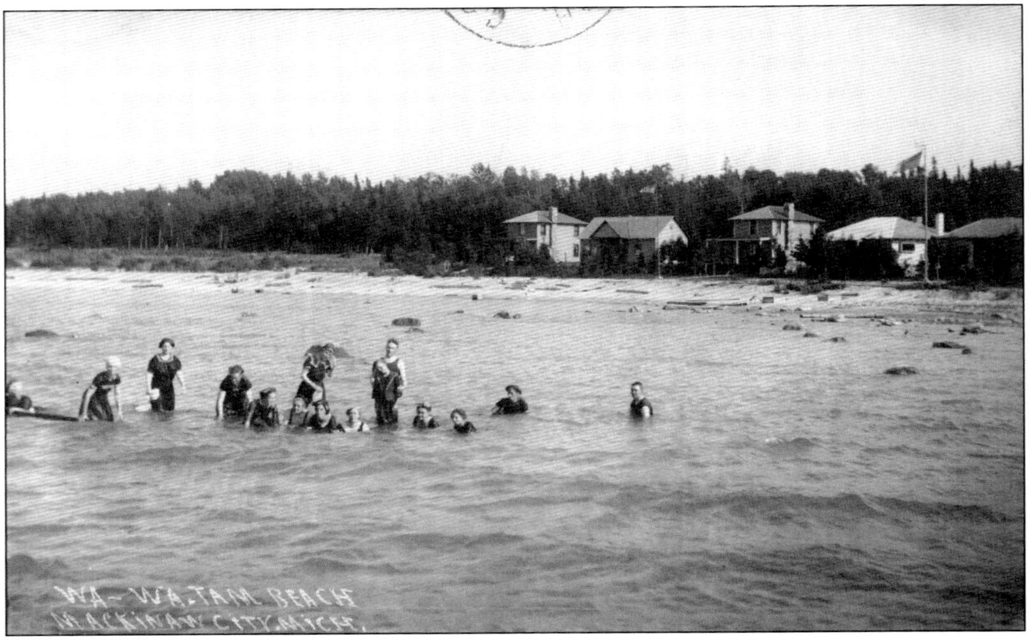

Long before any structures were built, Edgar Conkling proposed a sale of his platted lots for "the low price of five dollars per front foot, and water lots at double that, payable either in labor, improvements, or on a satisfactory credit." Another Mackinaw City entrepreneur, Vine Harding, developed the west side of Mackinaw City in the 1880s along the shoreline area known as WaWaTam Beach. Harding sold waterfront lots and had splendid cottages built for families looking for resort properties. Named after an Ojibwa chief, WaWaTam Beach was primarily a summer residential area and later became a pristine residential community. A sidewalk along the water's edge stretched the entire distance of the beach area, from the State Park to McGulpin Point; remnants of the sidewalk remain today. The above postcard, postmarked 1911, shows happy vacationers in vintage bathing attire cooling off in Lake Michigan.

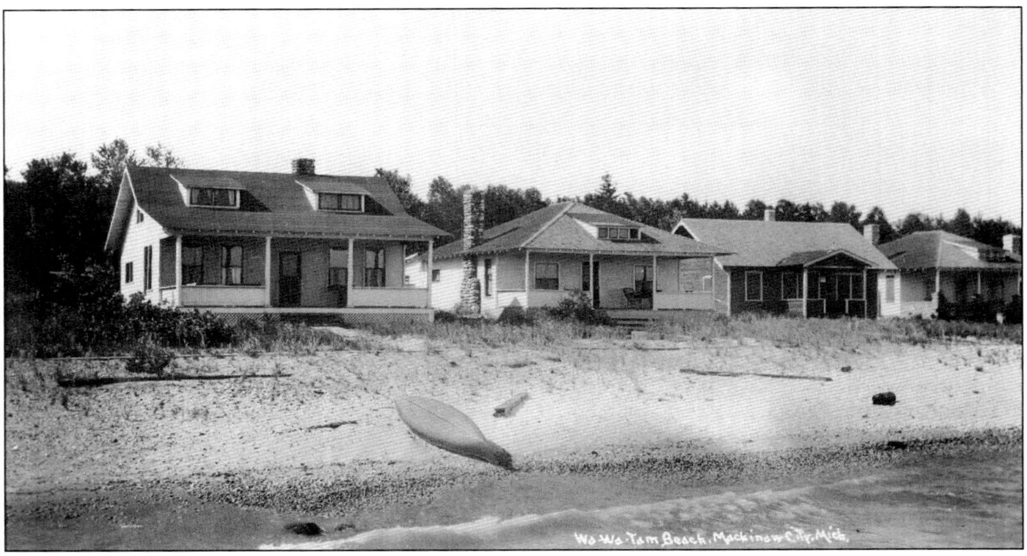

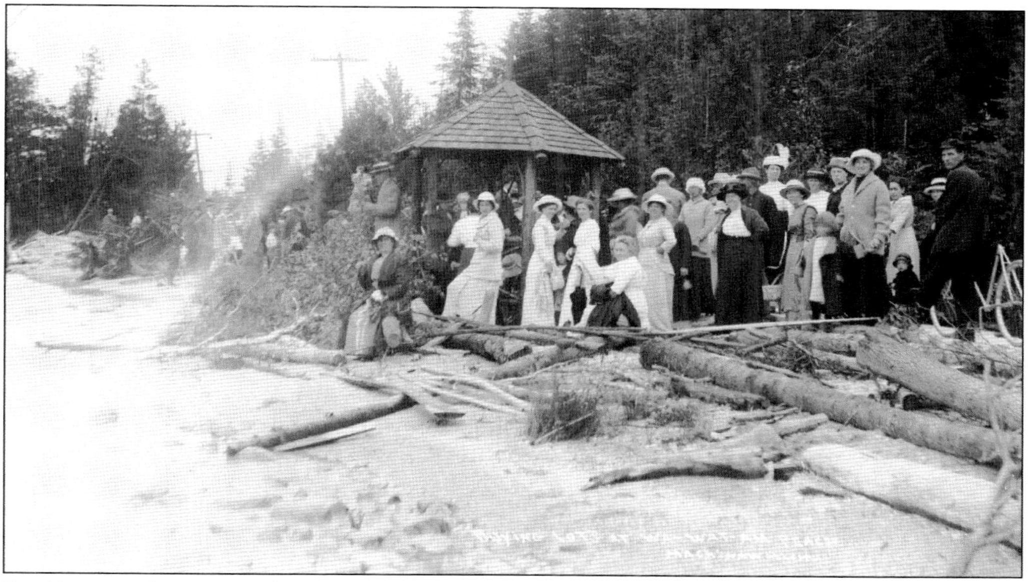

Residents and visitors of WaWaTam Beach were a lively bunch, always getting together for picnics, parades, card parties, and special events. Eager to populate the area, they formed an association with regulations and bylaws; dues were $5 per year. Today, properties on historic WaWaTam Beach have remained in families for years and are highly desirable but rarely come up for sale. Many streets in Mackinaw City were changed from numbered streets by an early Mackinaw City resident and author of children's books, Frances Margaret Fox. After a request from the village council, she renamed the streets after French and British soldiers and traders who were prominent in the early days of Michilimackinac. Names such as Sinclair, Langlade, Etherington, Ducharme, Depeyster, and DuJaunay appear on street signs as well as in history books. Both of these images are from the early 1900s. (Courtesy of John Marsh.)

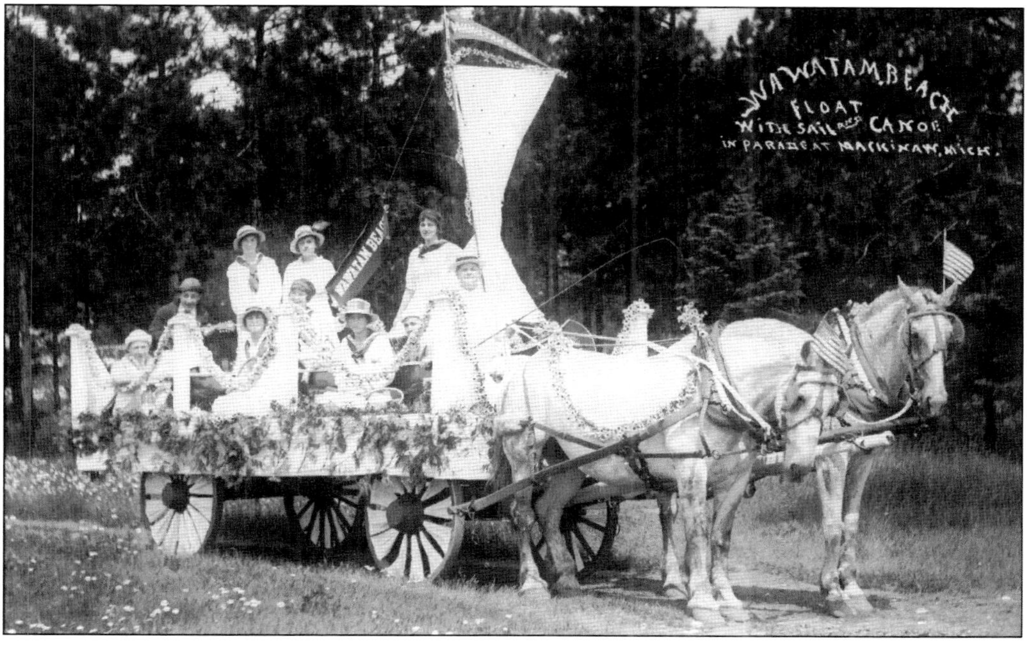

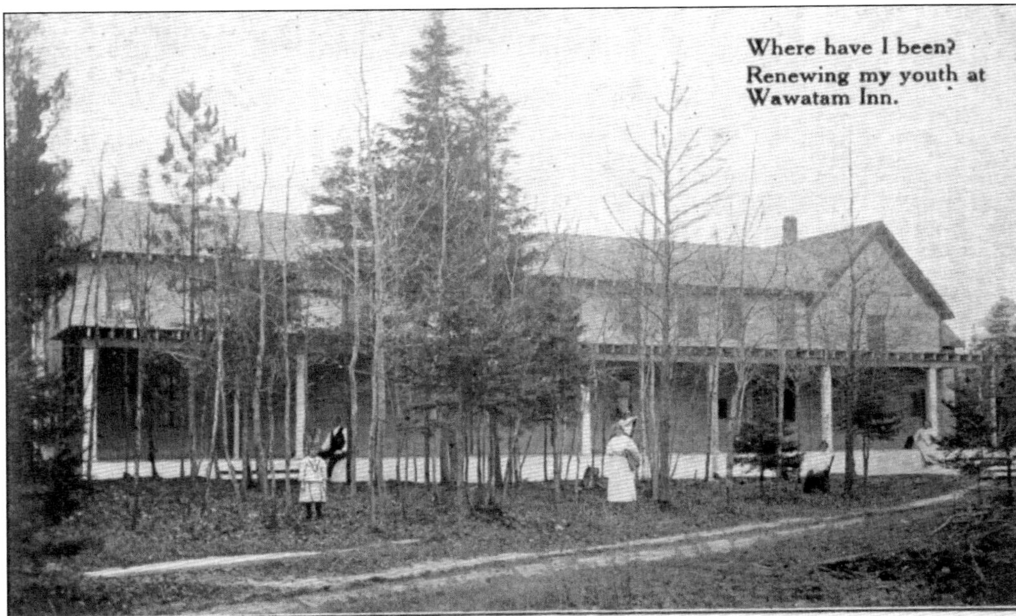

WAWATAM INN, MACKINAW CITY, MICHIGAN

Advertisements for the Wawatam area welcomed newcomers by boasting, "Attractive furnished cottages on the Straits of Mackinaw, Mackinaw City, Mich. reached by three railroads and numerous boat lines." Rates were $100 to $200 per season or $40 to $75 per month. The Wawatam Inn, a fancy new hotel, advertised running water and electric lights in every room and a "large, airy dining room, a screened-in porch, and a table furnished with fresh farm products." Recreation activities included lawn tennis, croquet, bathing, fishing, and boats to let. Rates were $2 and $2.50 per day or $8 per week. Vine Harding and Silas Sousie were the salesmen and proprietors. The ice-cold bubbling springs that popped up intermittently near the beach were another plus for residents, along with a magnificent view of the water and passing steamboats.

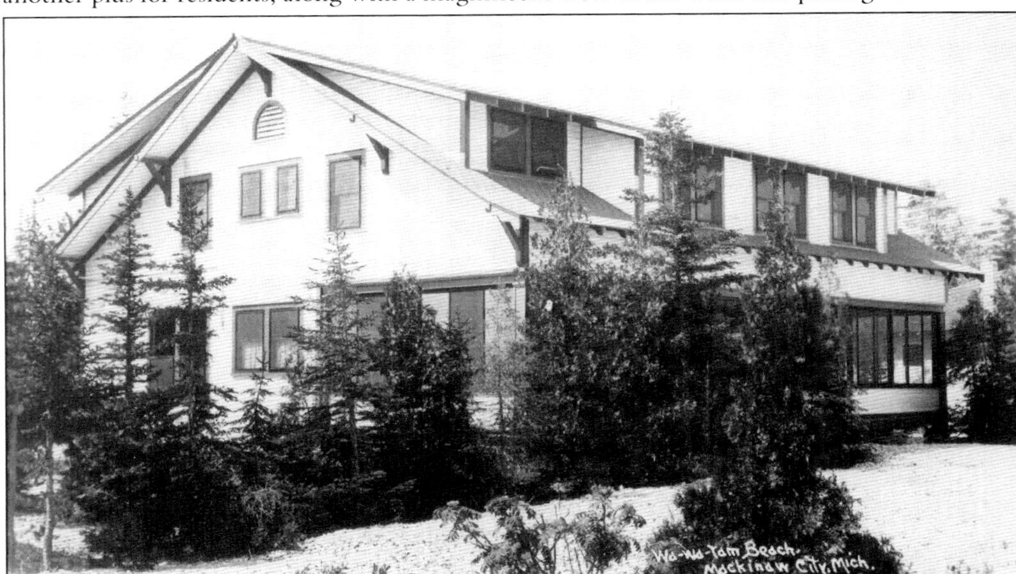

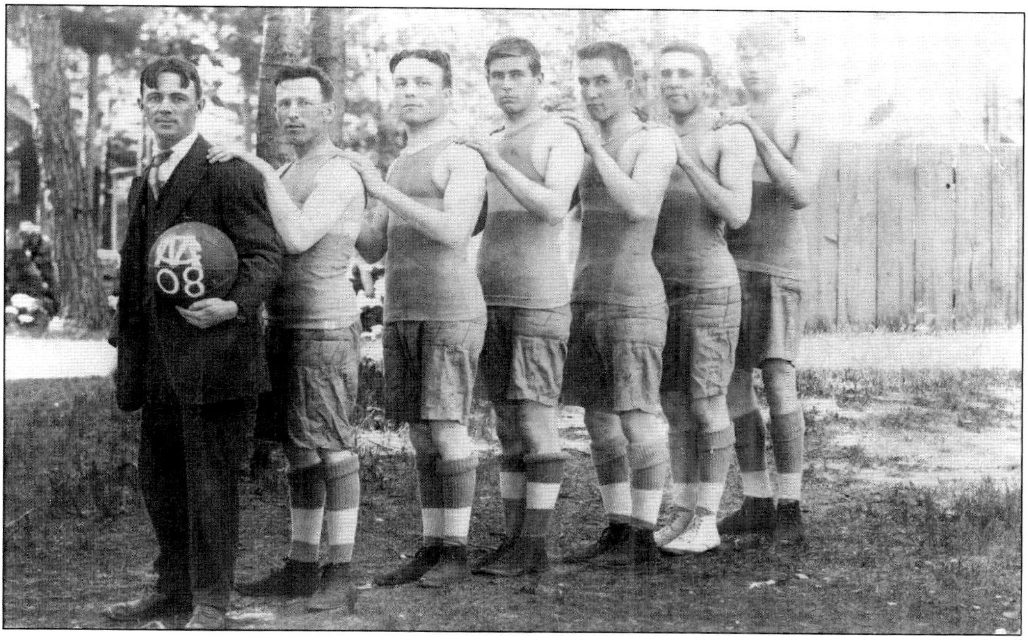

Early Mackinaw City was a progressive community, which included men's and women's basketball teams. Above is the 1908 men's team, identified on the back of the postcard as Buhler, Desy, McAlaster, Misac, McVay, Myers, and Smith. In the postcard below, postmarked 1915, the women are not identified, but the coach appears to be Mr. Desy from the men's team. Note the women's interesting uniforms of middy blouses, leggings, and bloomers with saucy hair bows to complete their ensembles.

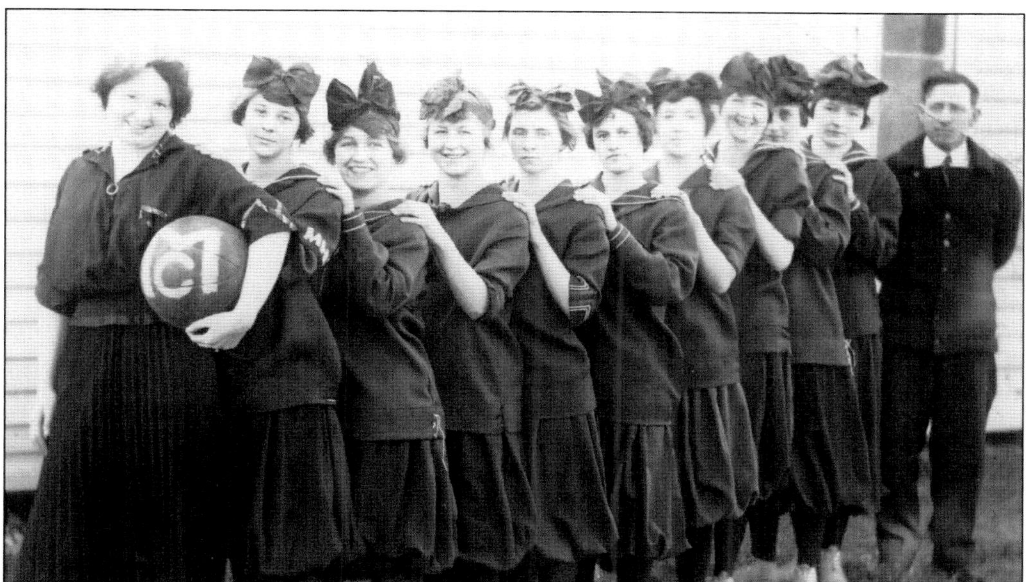

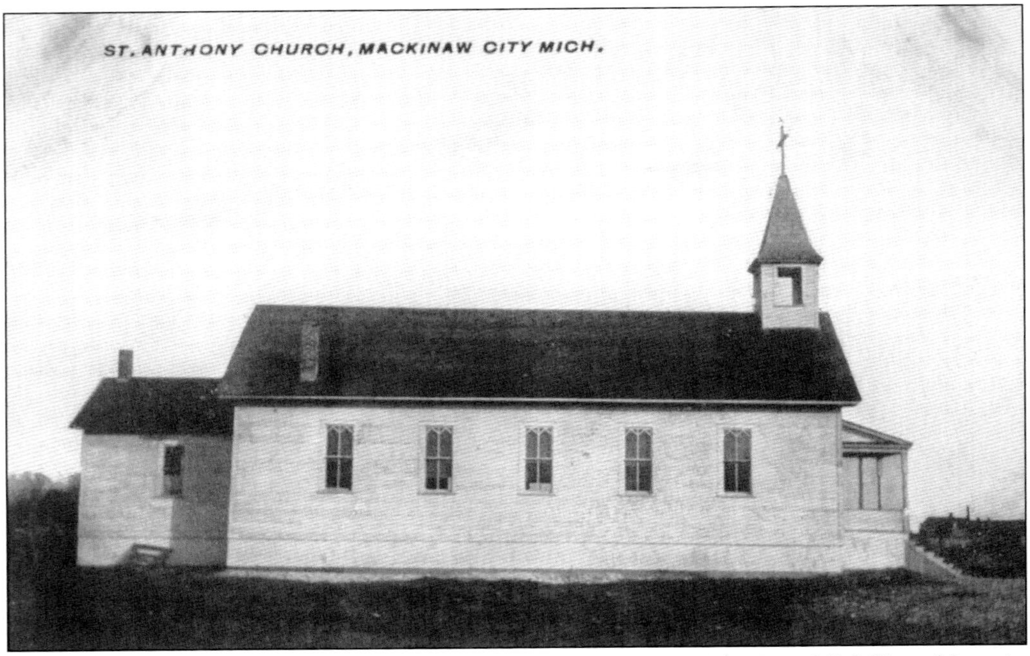

The first Catholic mission in the Mackinaw City area was inside Fort Michilimackinac in 1715. Many years later, when Mackinaw City incorporated as a village, services were held in homes and hotels. The devout parishioners held many fundraisers for their dream of a church to become a reality in 1907. This image shows St. Anthony Church as it looked in 1912.

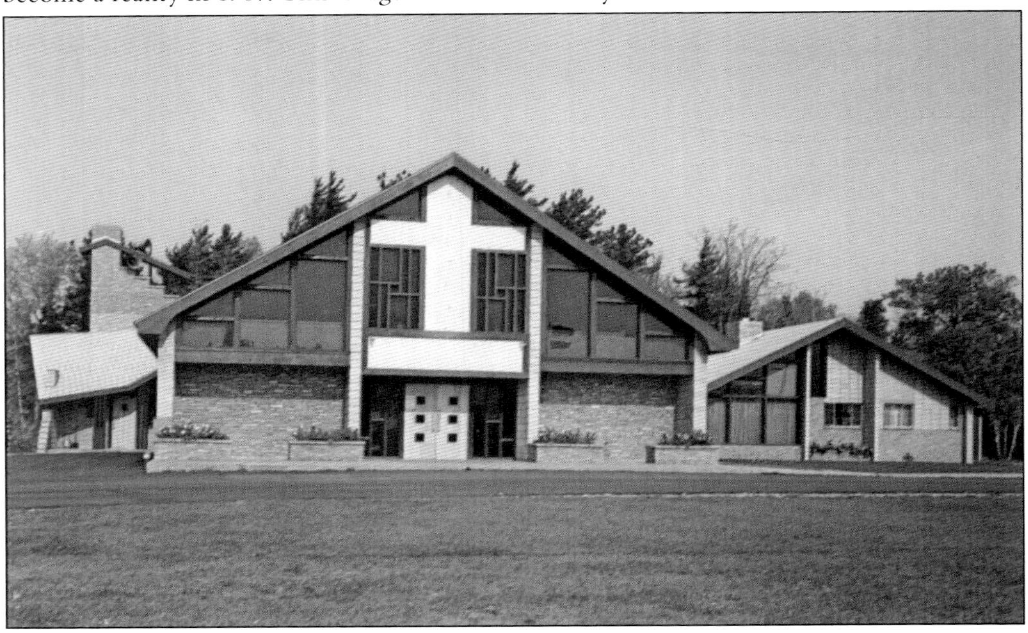

The old church served the community well but eventually fell victim to age. It also needed expansion; in the summer months, six masses were held every Sunday. In the late 1950s, a new church building was erected on West Central Avenue. It was named St. Anthony's of Padua Shrine, and its first Mass was said on July 3, 1959.

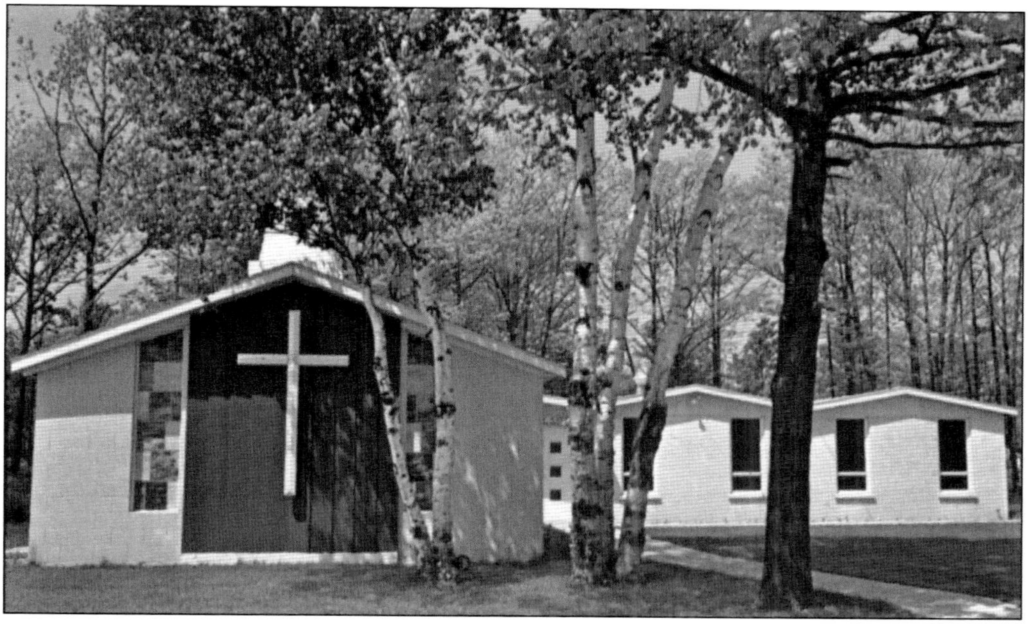

The Mackinaw City Bible Church was built in 1968 and is located on West Central Street. It was founded by Rev. Lyle Hoover, who established the church in 1960 with services originally held at the Wawatam Town Hall. The church continues today with morning and evening services. Its motto is "A Bible-Believing, Bible-Teaching Church."

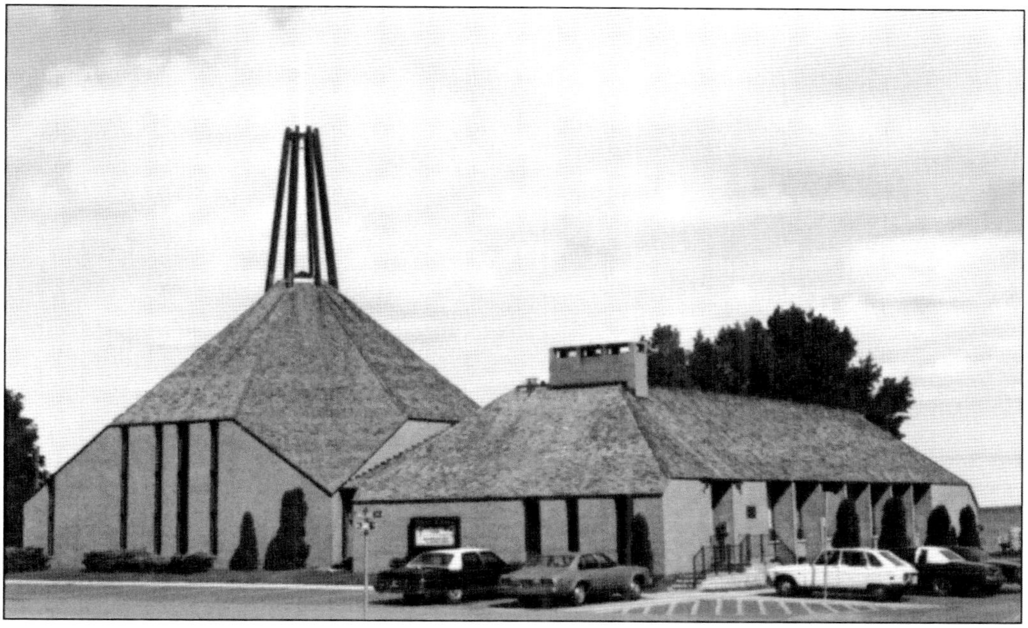

The first protestant church service held in Mackinaw City was a Methodist service in George Stimpson's home in 1870. The Presbyterians have roots back to 1881, holding services in Stimpson's hotel. The Church of the Straits originated from combining these two congregations in 1962. Older churches were torn down to make way for this new building. Located within view of the Mackinac Bridge, it was completed in 1966.

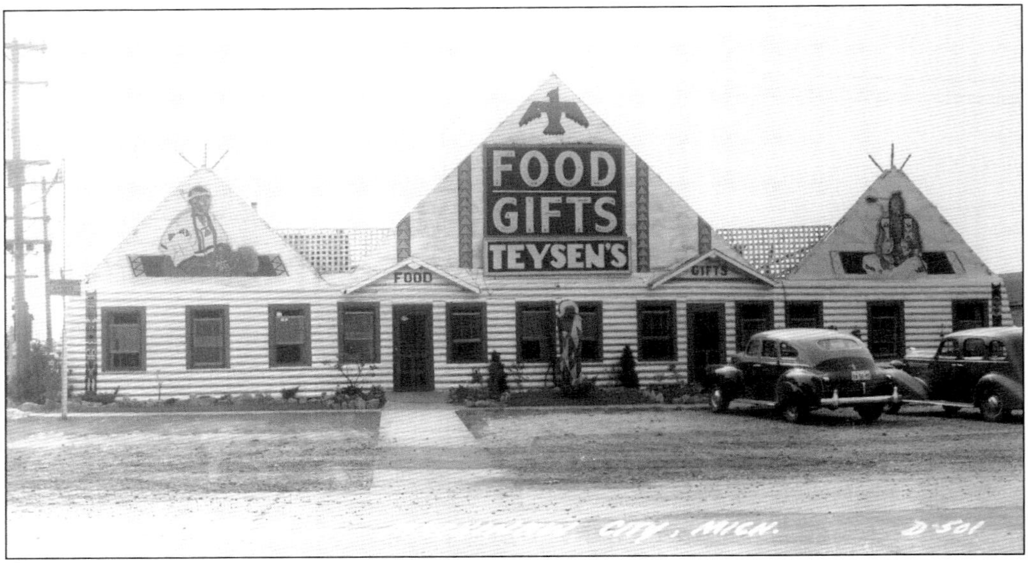

Gift shops and restaurants began to spring up in Mackinaw City, including the popular Teysen's. Mackinaw City resident and historian Kenneth Teysen collected Native American artifacts with his father, Harry Teysen, for many years. In the 1940s, the family opened Talking Bear Museum on the second floor of its restaurant, located across from the bustling ferry docks. (Courtesy of John Marsh.)

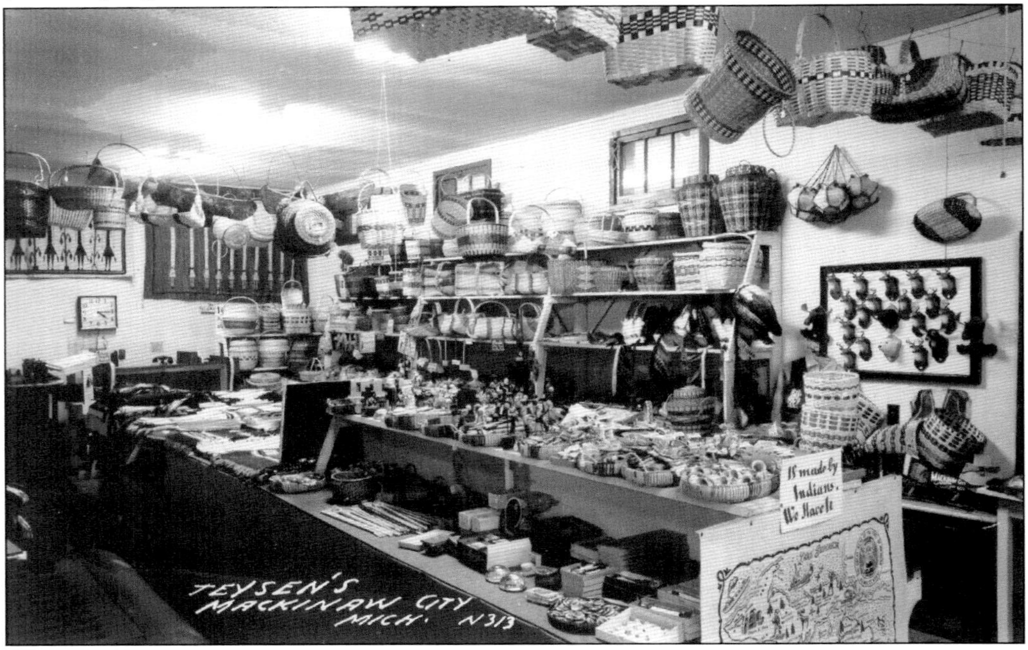

After the restaurant became increasingly busy, a gift shop was added, featuring crafts and handiwork by Native Americans from the Mackinaw and L'Arbre Croche area. This interior view shows handmade baskets on display and a sign in the foreground reading, "If made by Indians, we have it." Over the years, the shop was expanded and remodeled. Today, the Teysen family continues its retail hospitality in a new location in the Mackinaw Crossings mall.

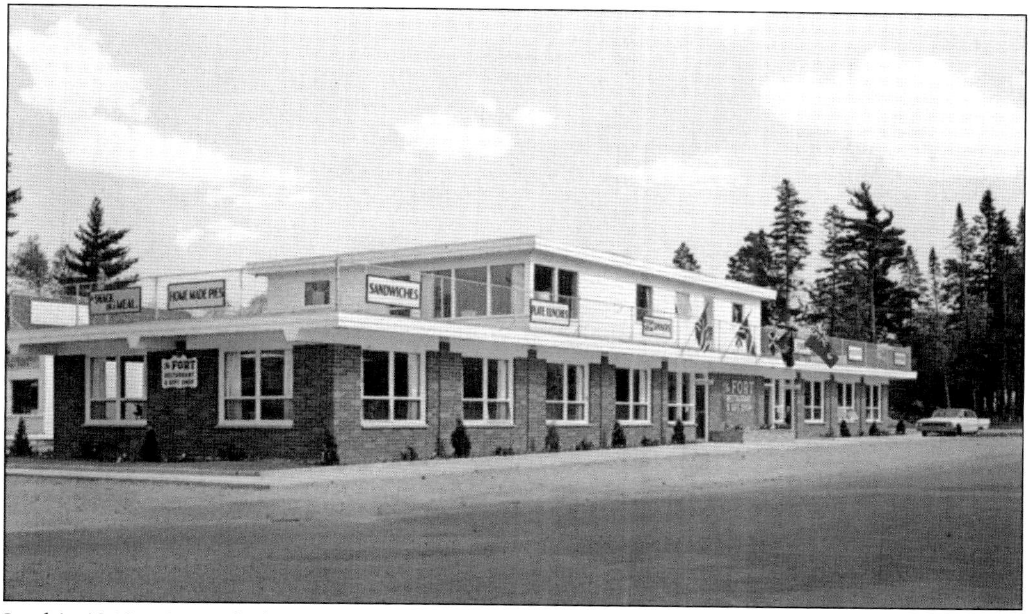

In this 1960s view of The Fort Restaurant and Gift Shop, located across the street from Fort Michilimackinac, signs advertise sandwiches, plate lunches, and homemade pies. An advertising promotion on the back of the postcard states that it is the "newest and finest restaurant and gift shop in Mackinaw City, specializing in wild huckleberry pancakes."

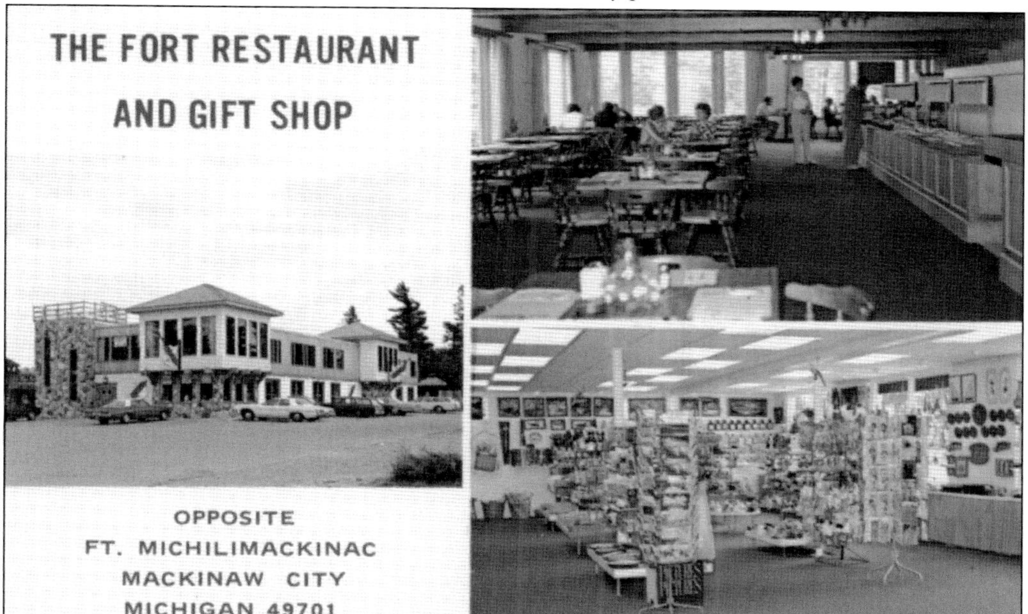

In this view, the Fort Restaurant and Gift Shop shows its remodeled exterior. Today, the building no longer houses a restaurant but two shops, The Fort Gift Shop and The Fort, Inc. Each shop has a unique souvenir and gift section, and both have added a candy kitchen offering fudge and other sweet treats. The Fort, Inc. also advertises a Mackinaw Mining Company and Hockey Room.

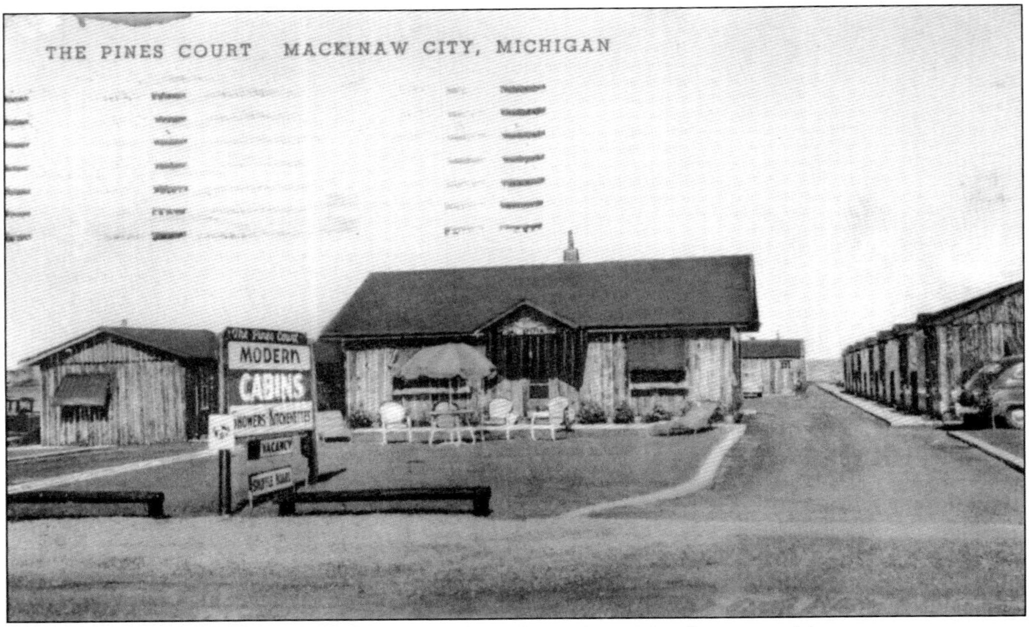

Visitors needed accommodations, so motels and tourist cabins began making appearances one after another. This 1951 postcard shows one example of an early rustic spot: The Pines Court Modern Cabins, which advertised showers, kitchenettes, and shuffleboard. These dockside cabins looked towards Mackinac Island, and the Food Basket Café was right next door.

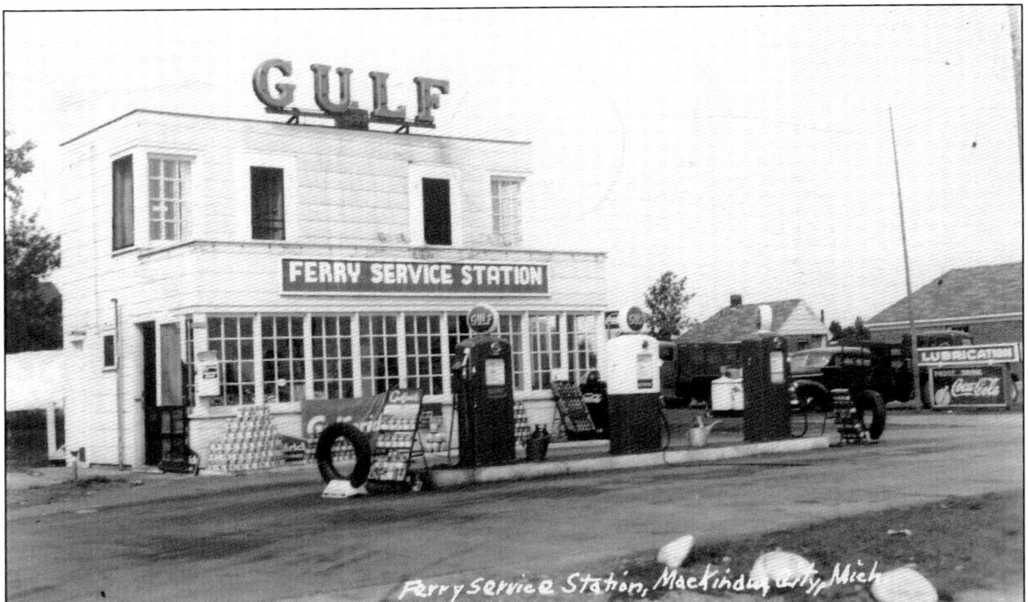

This postcard, postmarked 1949, is captioned "Ferry Service Station, MacKinaw City, Mich." Also located dockside on Huron Avenue, the station sold Gulf gasoline, tires, and Coca-Cola to village residents and tourists waiting to cross The Straits to Mackinac Island or to the Upper Peninsula. (Courtesy of John Marsh.)

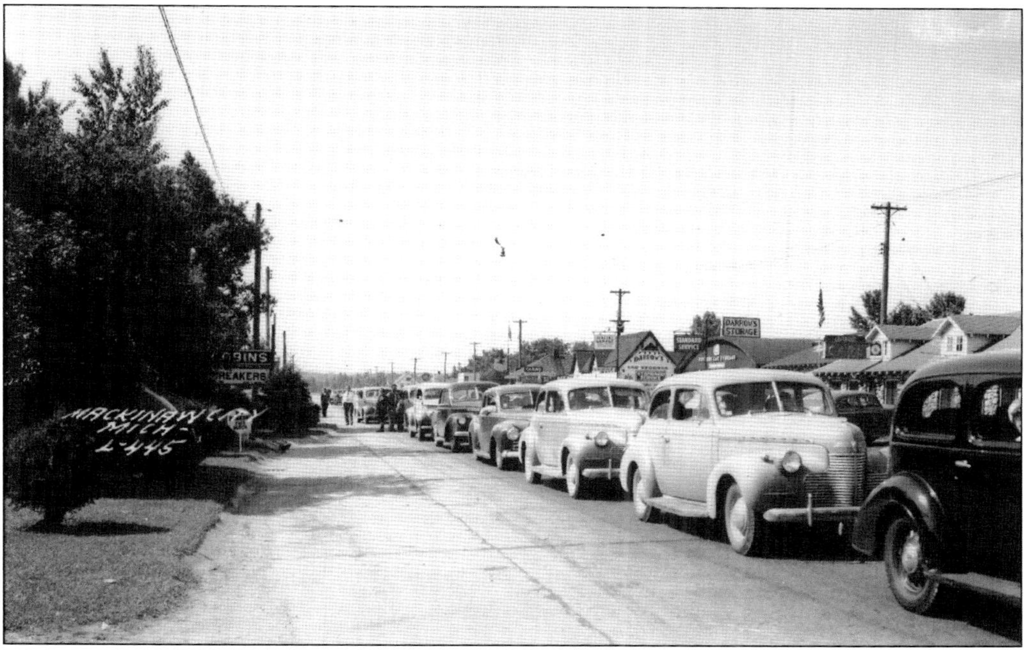

Cars wait their turn to load on a ferry to cross to Michigan's Upper Peninsula. Vehicles lined up for miles, and during hunting season, a line could reach down Highway 23 all the way to Cheboygan. Young entrepreneurs would walk up and down selling sandwiches to hungry tourists.

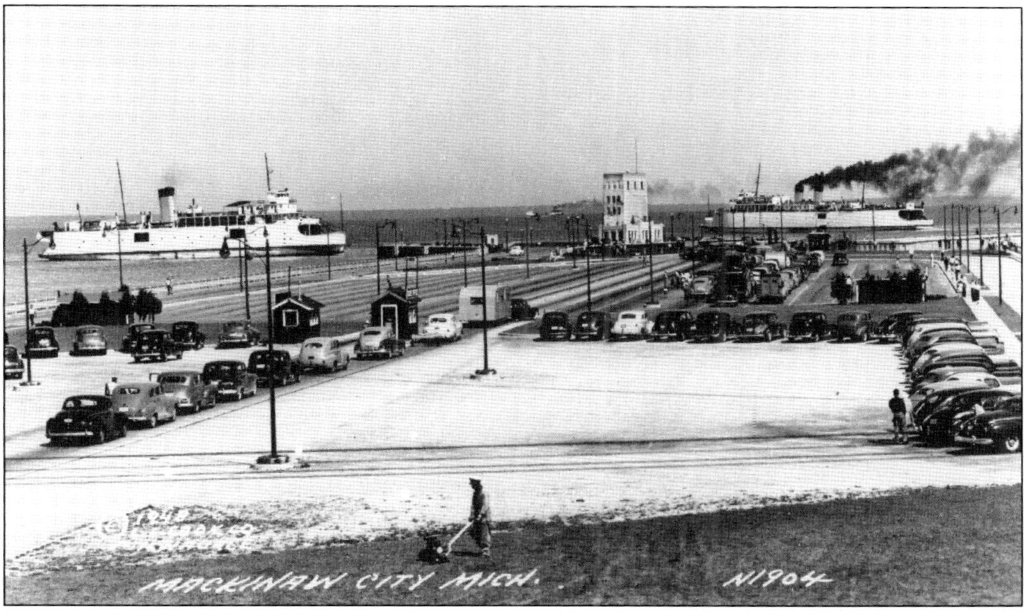

This is what the front of the line looked like. Two large, coal-burning car ferries are entering and leaving Mackinaw City's State Ferry Dock as tourists wait for a breezy trip across The Straits. Mackinaw housewives would not hang their laundry outside when the ferries were "in port." All of this activity came to an end with the opening of the Mackinac Bridge.

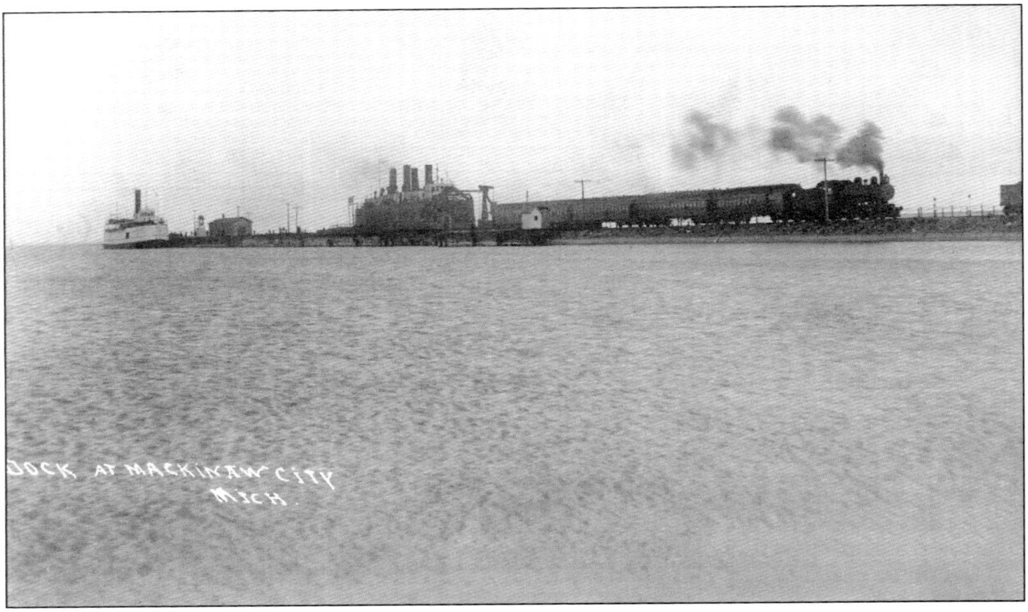

Down the road from the State Ferry Dock was Mackinaw City's railroad dock, where huge railroad cars were loaded on even bigger railcar ferries to cross The Straits. The rail dock was a busy place with all kinds of transportation: railcar ferries, train cars with locomotives belching out smoke, and passenger car ferries. If passenger cars were transported on the railcar ferries, these automobiles had to be drained of all of their gasoline before departure. It was a long and tedious process to take a passenger car on a railcar ferry. US mail and other goods were also carried across The Straits on the railcar ferries.

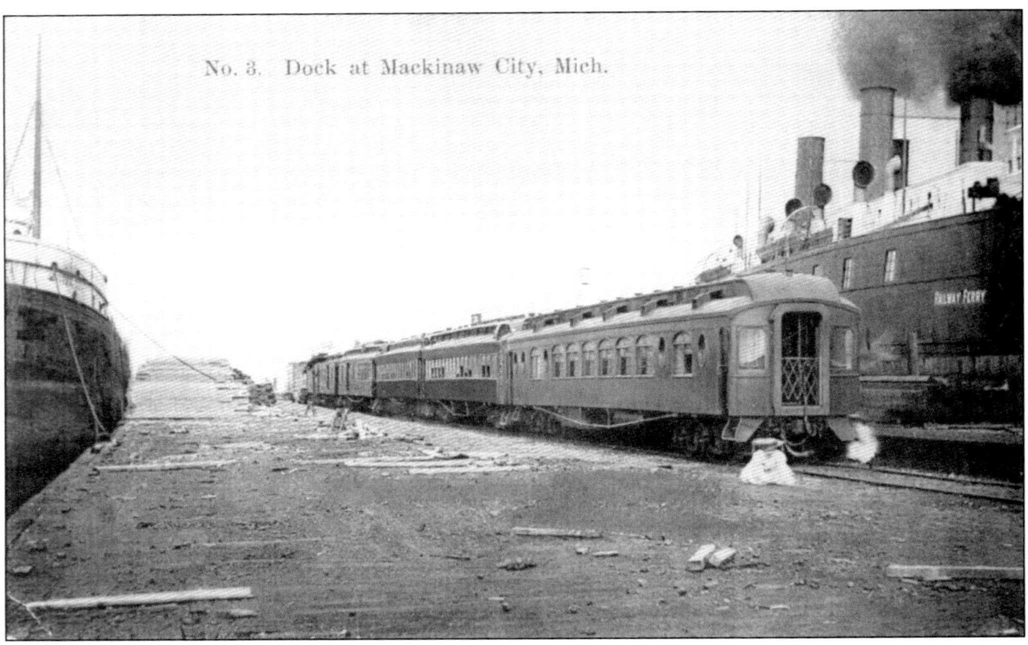

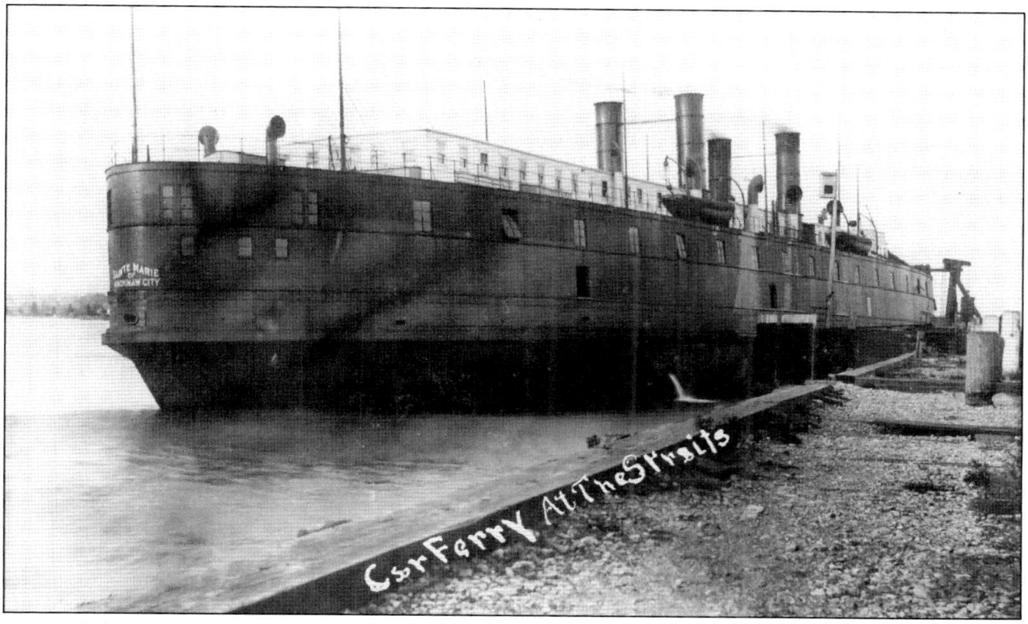

Two of the most well-known railcar ferries were the *Sainte Marie* (above) and the SS *Chief Wawatam* (below), named after an Ojibwa chief. There were actually two *Sainte Maries*, both named in honor of Sault Ste. Marie in Michigan's Upper Peninsula. The *Chief Wawatam* was the largest railcar ferry on the Great Lakes, carrying 20 railroad cars, and operated continuously for over 50 years. Besides making countless trips across The Straits, these two railcar ferries were also icebreakers. In wintertime, even a railcar ferry could get stuck in the pileup of ice in The Straits, so it was not unusual to see the *Chief Wawatam* rescuing the *Sainte Marie* or vice versa. (Above, courtesy of John Marsh.)

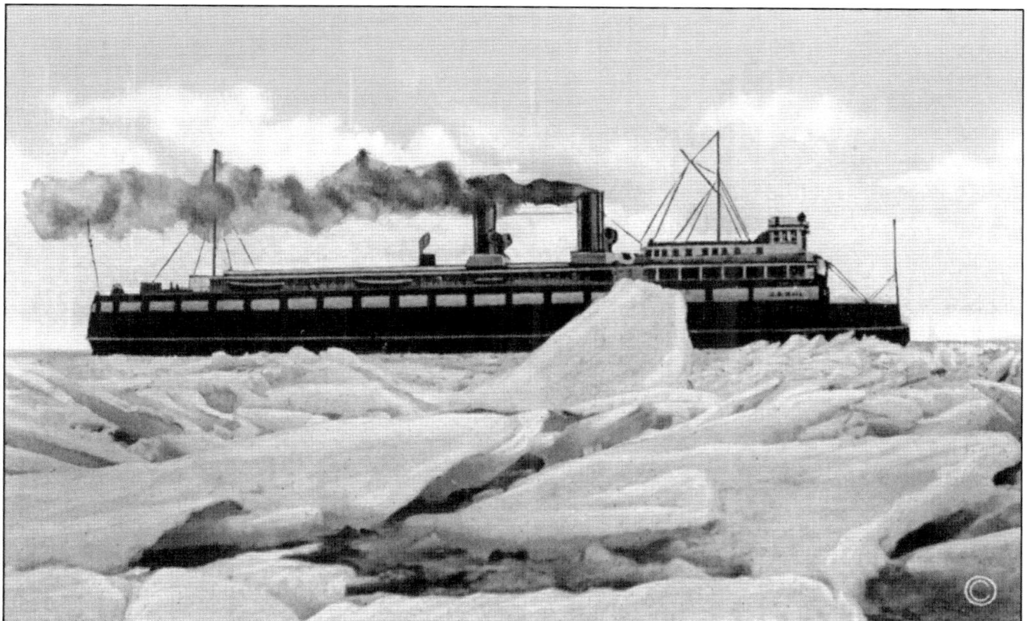

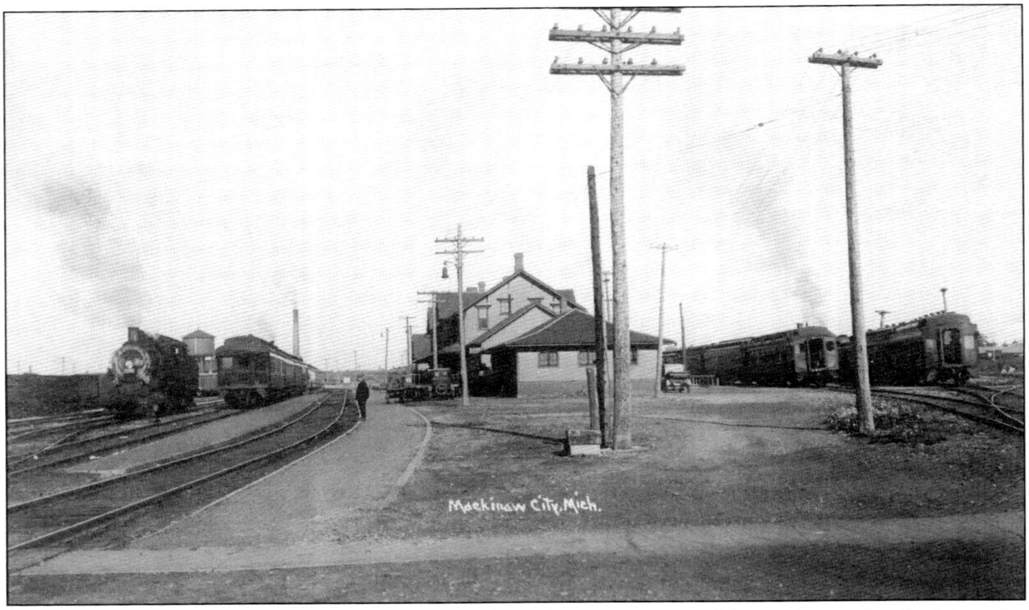

The Mackinaw City train depot was near the village center. With tracks on both sides, the depot was a busy place. In this view, the photographer stands with his back to the water looking west. Behind the photographer at the rail dock, huge railcar ferries like the *Chief Wawatam* would be loading and unloading their freight-containing railcars. (Courtesy of John Marsh.)

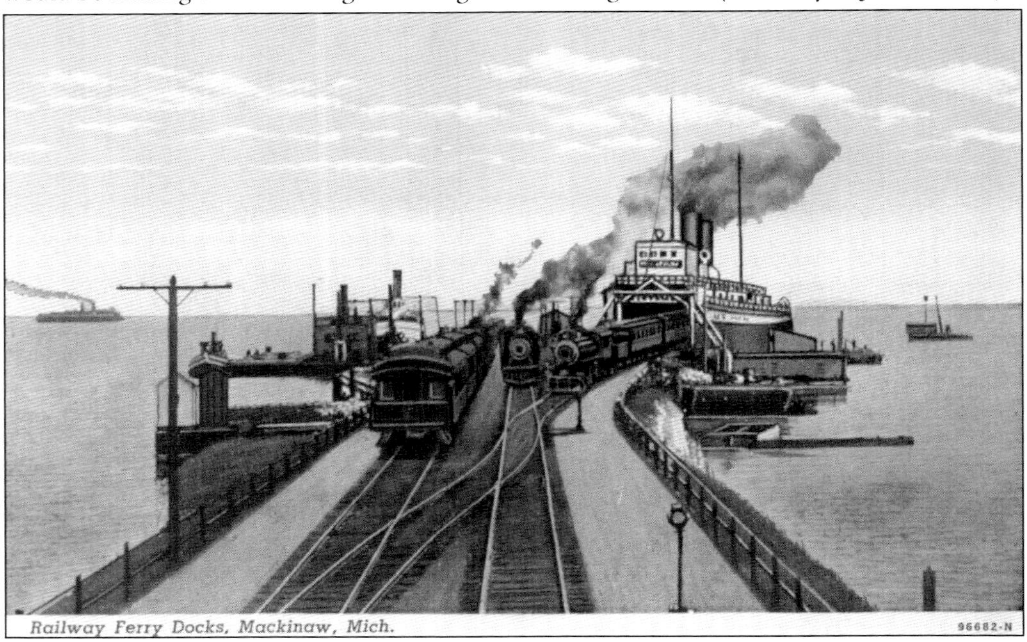

Three locomotives are on the Mackinaw City rail dock with one shown backing its cars into the *Chief Wawatam*. At one time, The *Chief* operated 24 hours a day, continually crossing and re-crossing The Straits. A former worker at the depot reported seeing 3,000 railcars loaded with lumber waiting for transport. In this image, it appears that the *Sainte Marie*, in the left background, is coming to help.

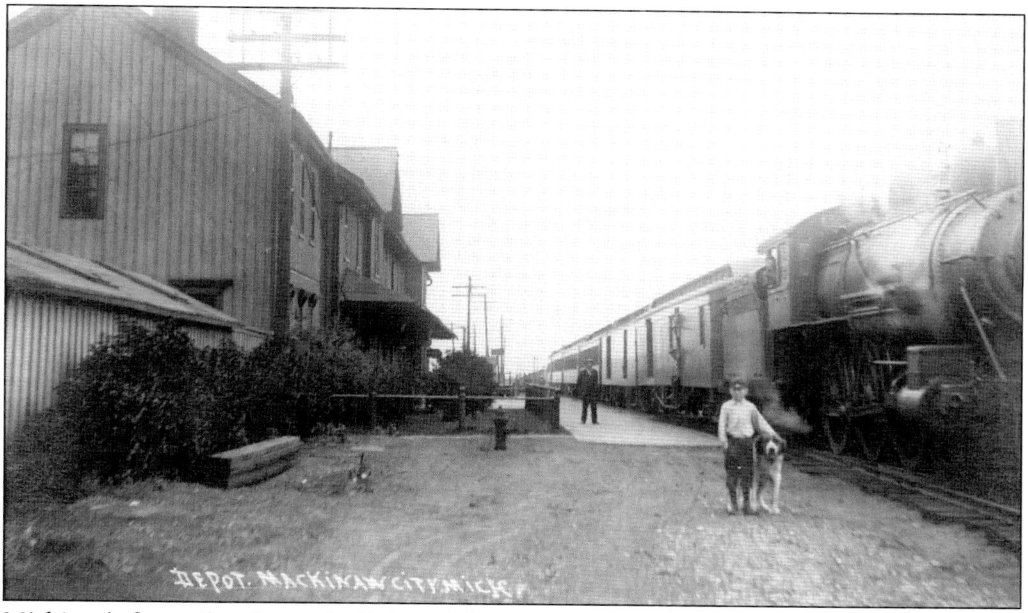

Michigan's first railroad was the Erie & Kalamazoo in 1836 and was horse-drawn. Mackinaw City saw its first railroad in 1881 when the Michigan Central Railroad ended its line there. Shortly thereafter, the Grand Rapids and Indiana Railroad reached the village. Although downsized from its original structure, the Mackinaw City depot has been restored and now houses a restaurant. (Courtesy of John Marsh.)

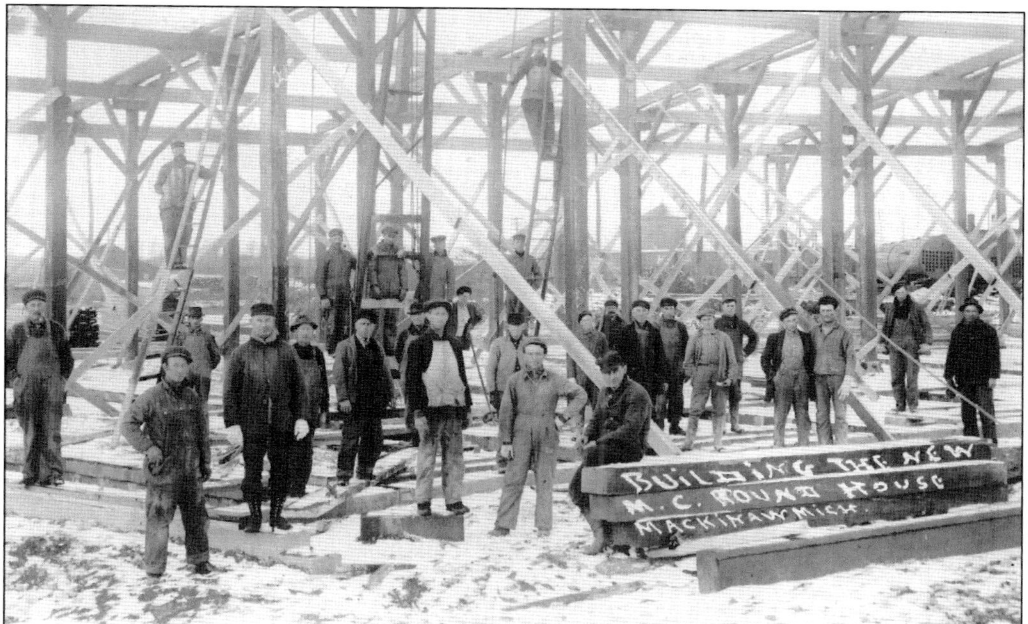

Workers pose during the construction of the new Round House in Mackinaw City. Two boilers provided the steam heat for all of the depot buildings. It took 50 tons of coal each day to "feed" the boilers, allowing for three extra jobs on the property. Today, a grocery store is located where the Round House used to stand. (Courtesy of John Marsh.)

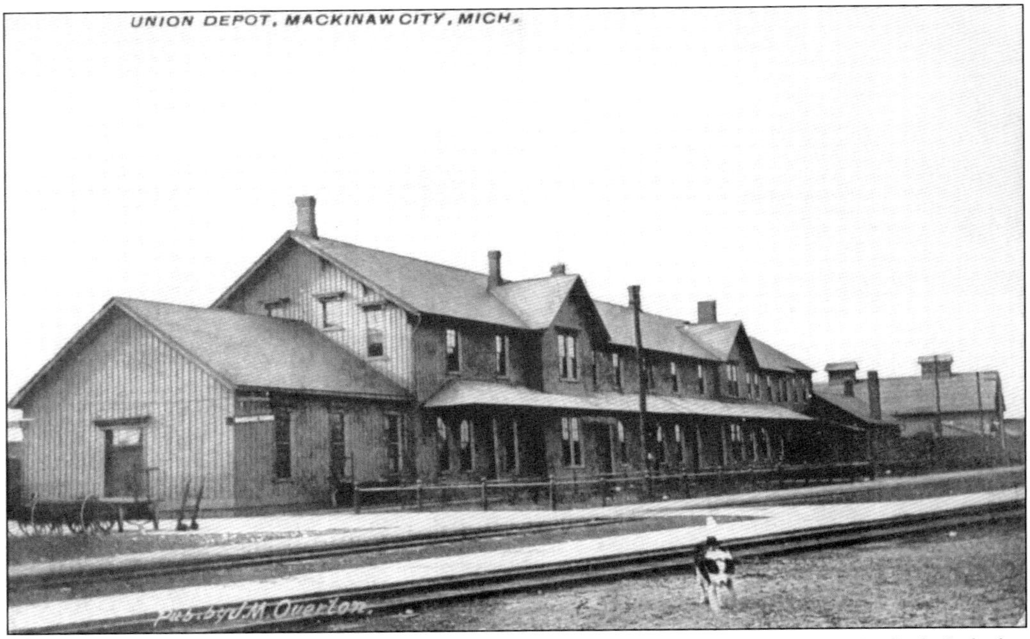

In addition to a restaurant and the Michigan Central agent, the depot operation included clerks, a stenographer, car checkers, transport men, and a janitor. Men were also needed to sell tickets, operate the telegraph, and handle baggage. Well-known Mackinaw City names at the depot included Sunday Desy, Charlie McVey, Chet Rouche, Ludwig Millhausen, Vern Niles, Frank Duffina, and Ralph Preston.

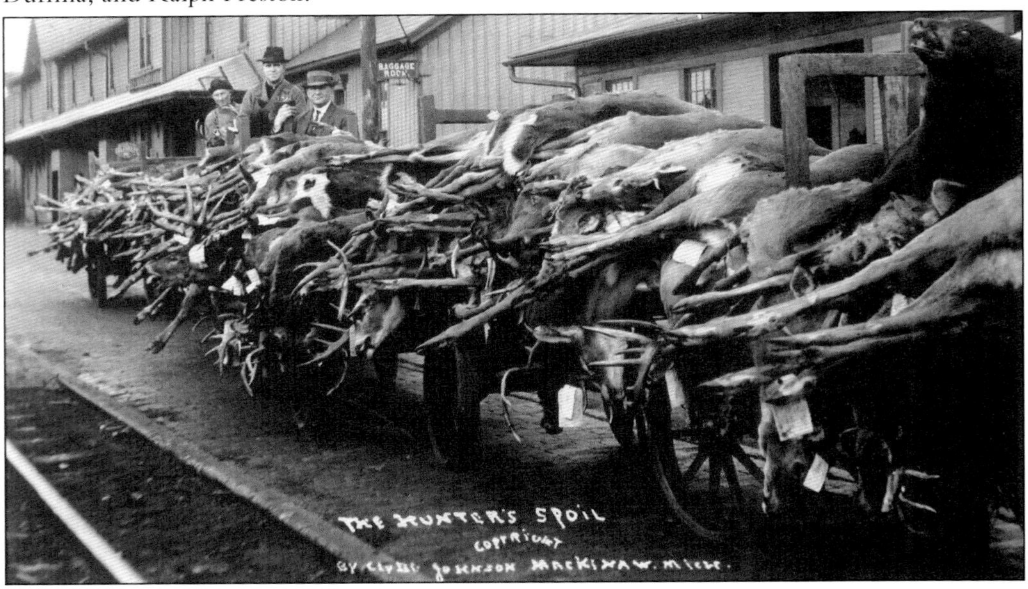

This postcard is entitled "The Hunter's Spoil." Hunting season was a busy time at the Mackinaw City depot. Here, several freight wagons are piled high with whitetail deer, or *waw-mawsh-kay-she-wog*, as hunters waited for their prize to be shipped back home. Even a black bear, or *maw-kwa*, awaits transport. In early years, hunting season was equated to a northern Michigan gold rush. (Courtesy of John Marsh.)

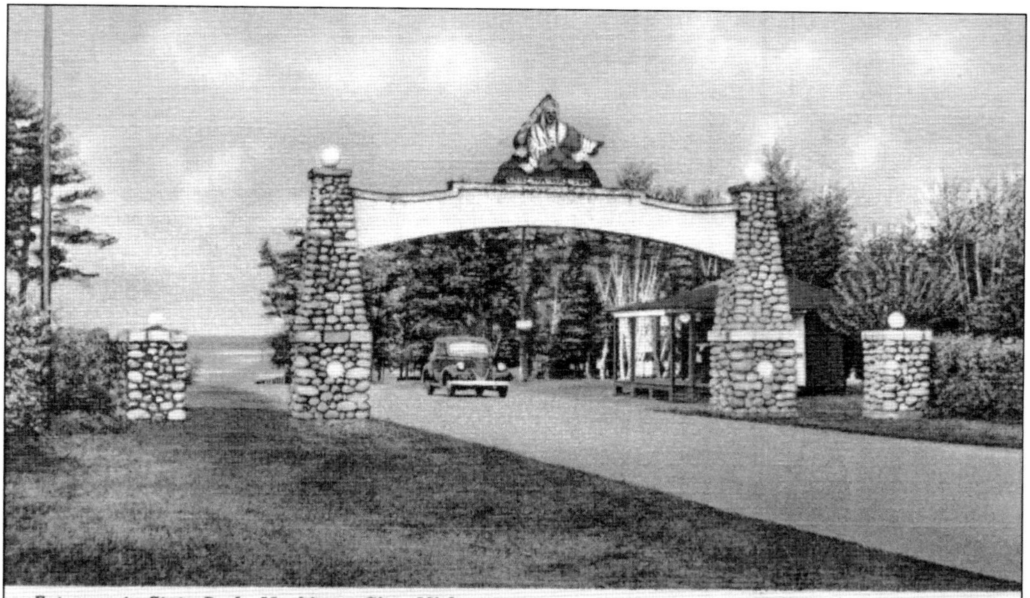

Entrance to State Park, Mackinaw City, Mich. 7A-H3601

Perched on top of the stone arch at the entrance to Michilimackinac State Park was a Native American chief painted by Mackinaw City resident Lloyd Desy. In 1904, the park was referred to as the State Park and Automobile Camp. The park's first caretaker was John Stimpson. The water in the background is the Straits of Mackinac.

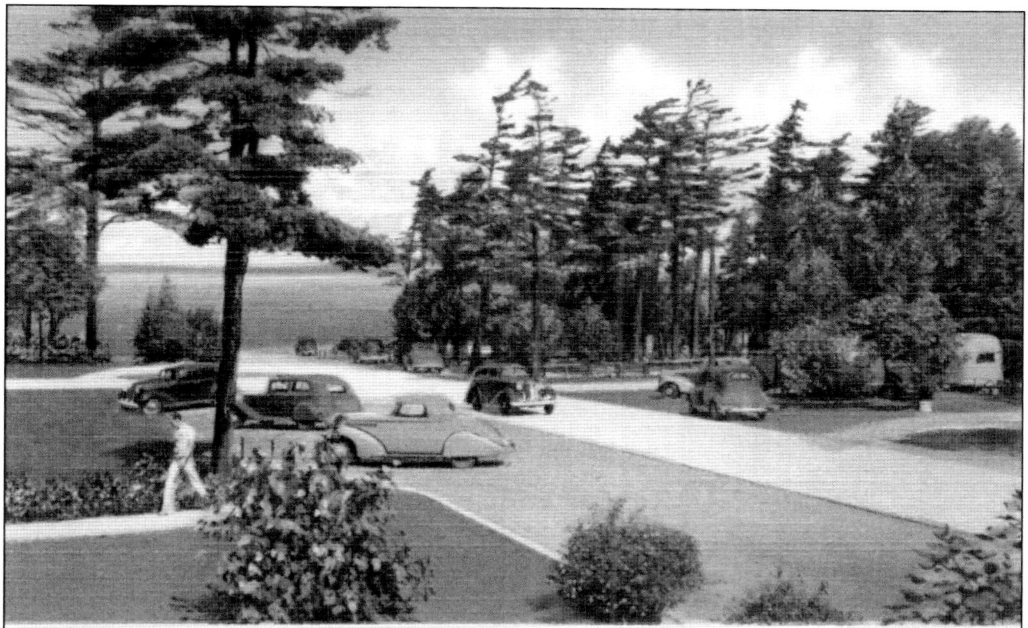

State Tourist Park, Mackinaw City, Mich. 8A-H3050

In 1857, this property was set aside by Edgar Conkling to become a village park. It was adjacent to the old Fort Michilimackinac. Camping near the water was the main attraction. No one was turned away. Rates for a camper or tent were 25¢ per night or 50¢ per week. The park offered a bathhouse, swimming dock, and kitchen amenities.

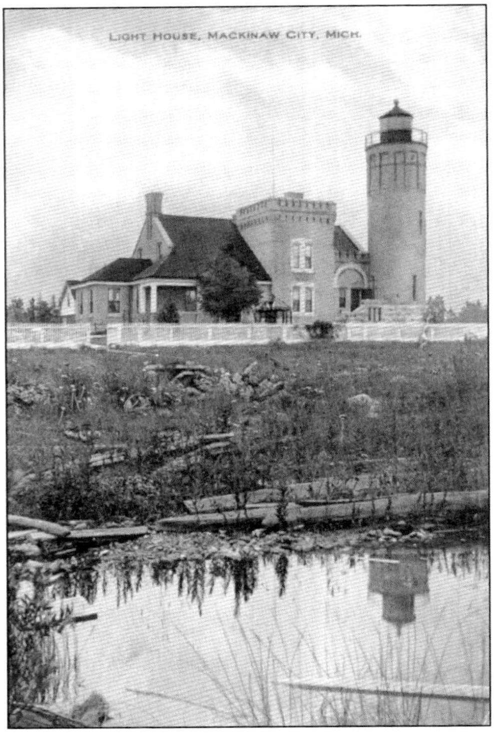

In 1857, land had also been designated as a "lighthouse reservation," but Old Mackinac Point Light Station was not constructed until 1892. It was not until the McGulpin Point Light, built in 1868–1869, was deemed nonstrategic that Edgar Conkling's vision became a reality. Old Mackinac Point Light was built with a Tudor Revival design and bore the nickname "Castle of the Straits." A lighthouse keeper and an assistant lived inside the main structure, manning the light station with constant care. Among many other duties, old-time keepers needed to wind the weights in the tower, fuel the kerosene lamp, haul oil, and polish the Fresnel lens (pronounced "fruh-nell") on a daily basis. They were also tour guides to visitors wandering over from the State Park and Automobile Camp. Old Mackinac Point Light is now a public museum owned by Mackinac State Historic Parks.

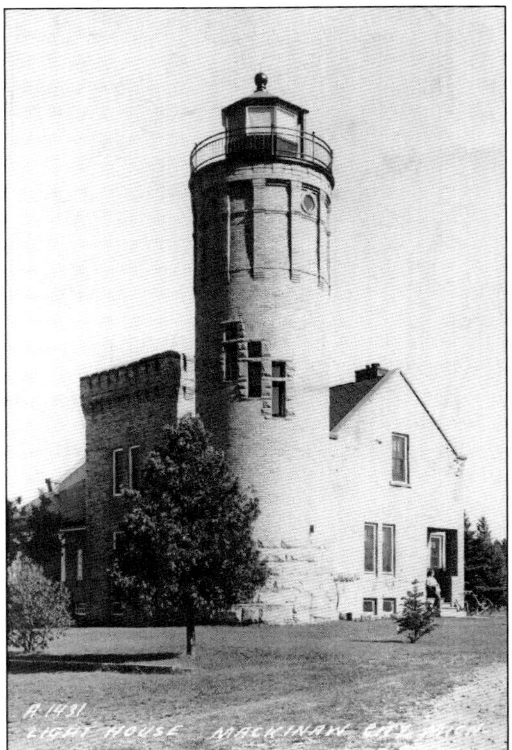

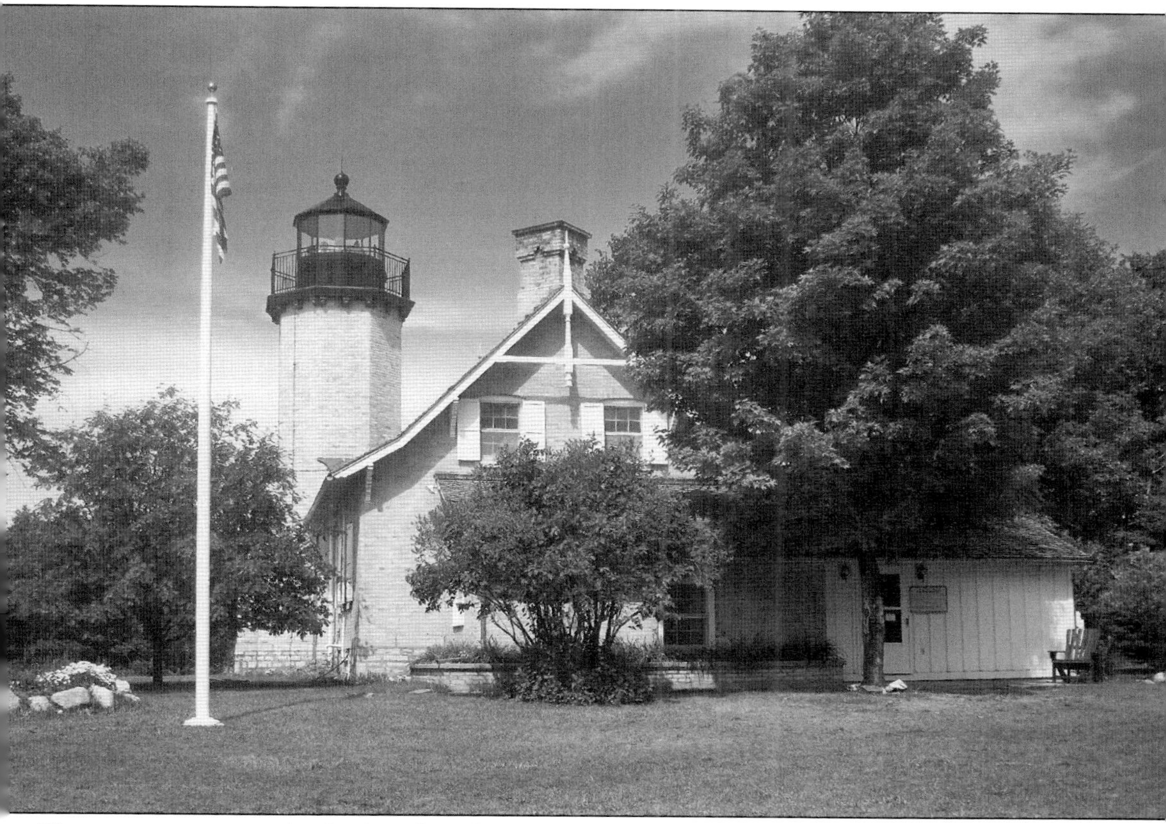

The west entrance to the Straits of Mackinac at Waugoshance Point in Lake Michigan was a treacherous place for navigation. The Waugoshance Light marked the entrance, but there was no light nearer to Mackinaw City. Patrick McGulpin once owned the land adjacent to the shore near Waugoshance, as far back as 1811. Previously it was an Odawa settlement. In 1854, funds were made available by Congress to build a light station at McGulpin's Point, but work did not begin until 1868. When completed, the living quarters included a parlor, kitchen, and two bedrooms on the first floor, two more bedrooms on the second floor, and an oil-storage room in the basement. Cast-iron spiral stairs wound their way up the tower. In 1906, the light was determined no longer strategic for use and was deactivated. From 1913 until 2008, it was a private residence, changing ownership several times. Now open to the public, the McGulpin Point Light is under the care of Emmet County and the Great Lakes Lighthouse Keepers Association and enjoyed a relighting ceremony in 2009 with the Odawa people as participants.

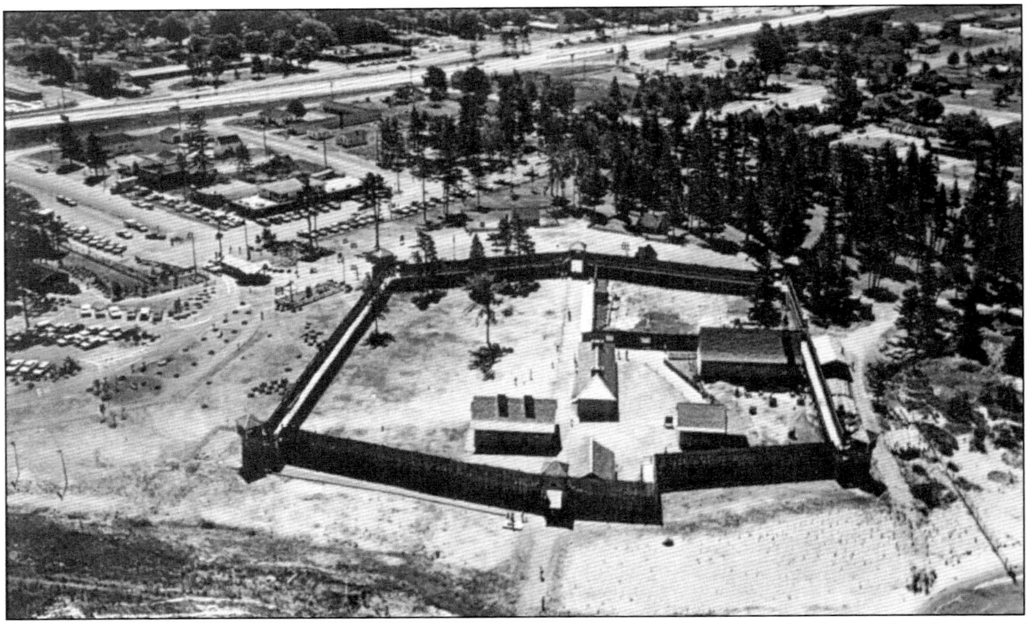

This is the spot in Mackinaw City where the second French fort was built on the Straits of Mackinac, the first having been Fort de Buade at St. Ignace. The new post was named Fort Michilimackinac. The 1960s aerial view above was taken from over the water looking toward the southern approach to the Mackinac Bridge. Before the fort was built, this shoreline was a busy place. The community consisted of a Native American encampment, a French Canadian fur-trading post, and a small mission chapel. The military post at St. Ignace had been abandoned in 1701 when Commandant Antoine de la Mothe Cadillac left to establish a fort at Detroit. In 1715, the French decided to re-establish a military presence in The Straits, but this time on the south shore. The Native people called the area Pe-quot-e-nonge.

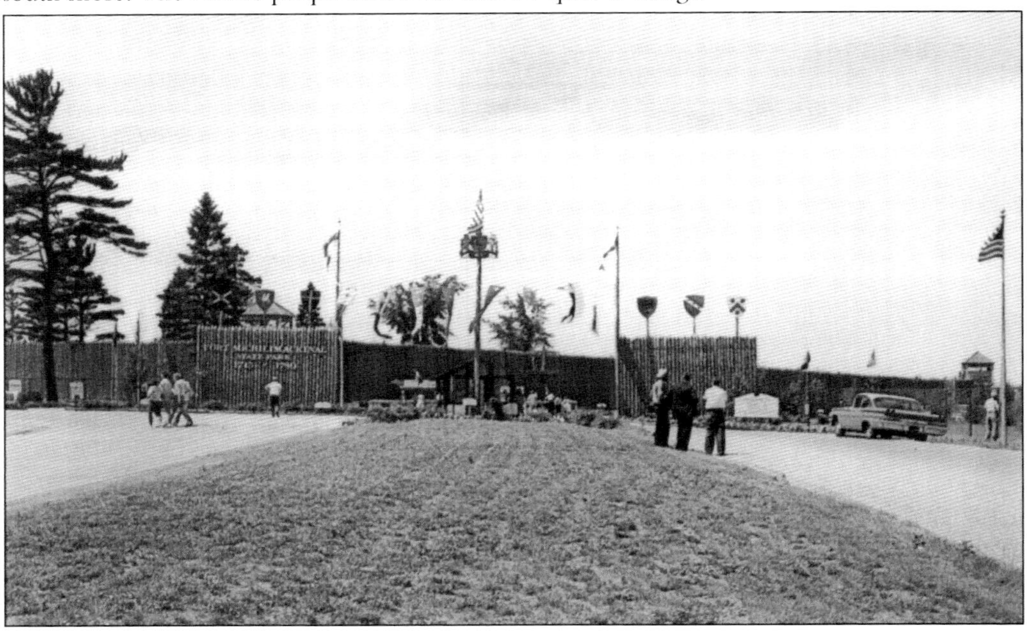

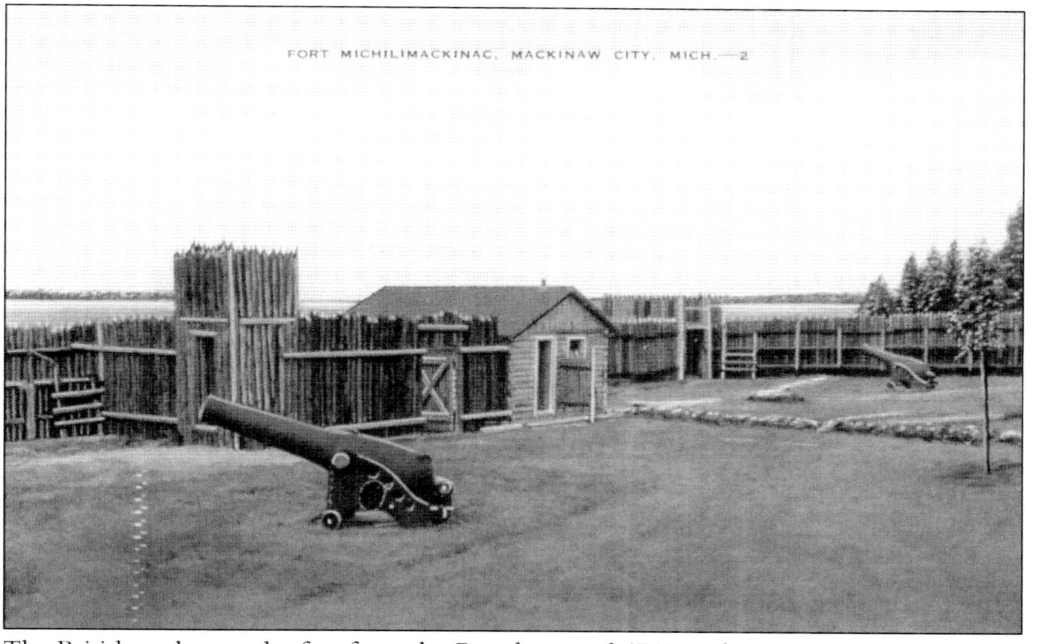

The British took over the fort from the French around 1761, and in 1780–1781 the resident commandant, Lt. Gov. Patrick Sinclair, decided to move the post to a more strategic location on the island of Michilimackinac. Buildings at Fort Michilimackinac were dismantled and moved; the rest was burned and succumbed to shifting sand. Fortunately, this military post has had two reconstructions, the first in the early 1930s (above) and the second in the early 1960s (below). During restoration, hundreds of artifacts were found from the British era and deeper in the ground from the French era. Archeological digs continue inside the fort, which has been renamed Colonial Michilimackinac, and it is under the care of Mackinac State Historic Parks. It is open to the public.

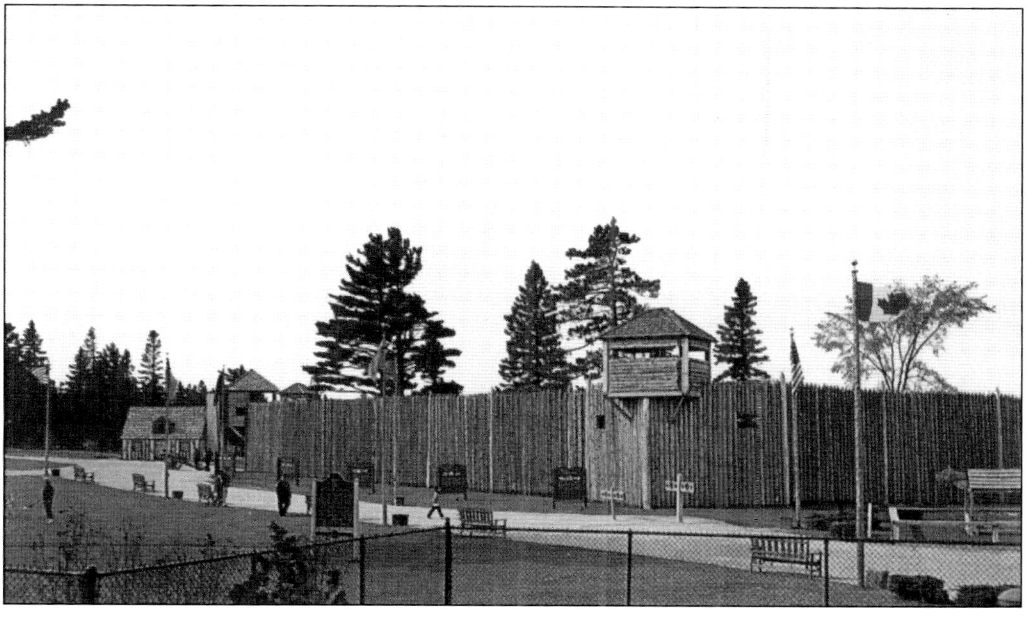

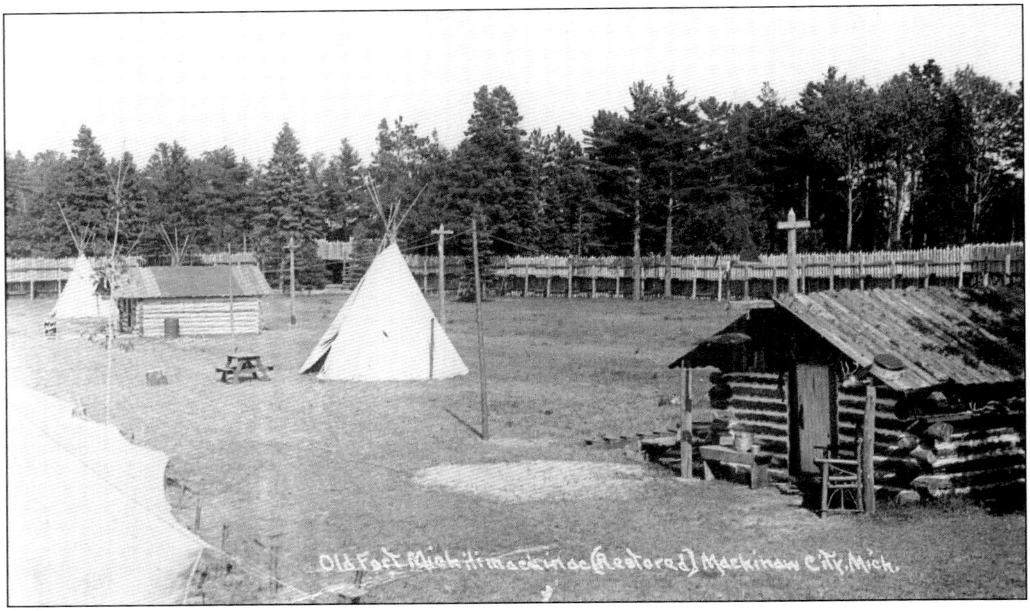

After the stockade was first reconstructed, interior structures consisted of several log cabins, including one with a museum and gift shop and one resembling a log chapel. The museum was operated by Mackinaw City resident Harry Teysen, who displayed his collection of artifacts. Real teepees were also found inside the fort. Native Americans and families in native dress were photographed inside the fort and interacted with tourists. In the 1960s restoration, interior structures were built to resemble—in great detail—the commandant's house, officers' quarters, soldiers' quarters, fur-trader homes, the provision storehouse, and Sainte Anne's Church with the priest's home adjacent to it, all to replicate the busy life at early Fort Michilimackinac. (Both courtesy of John Marsh.)

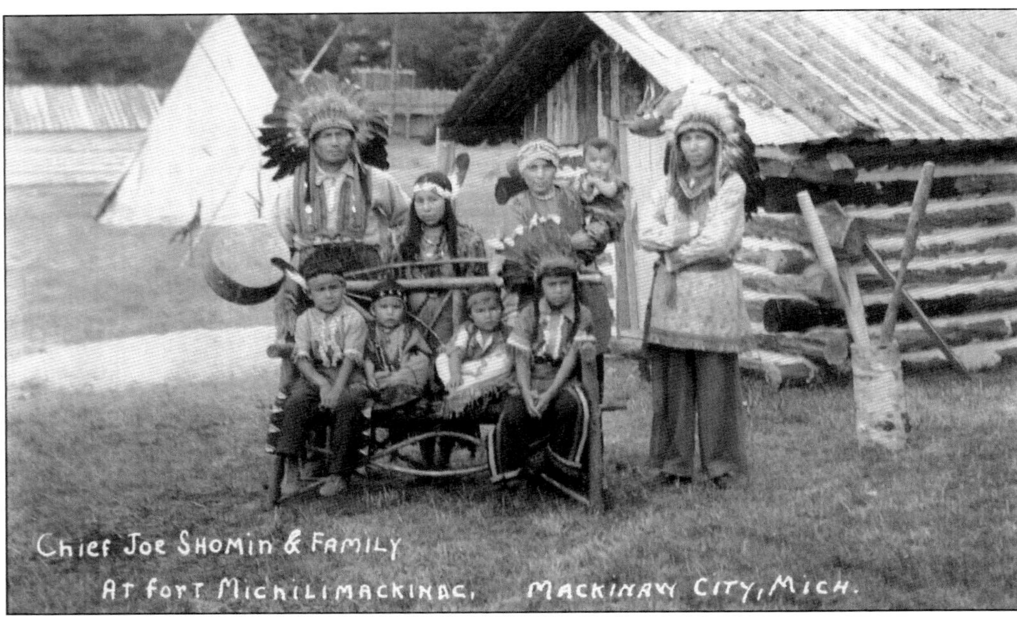

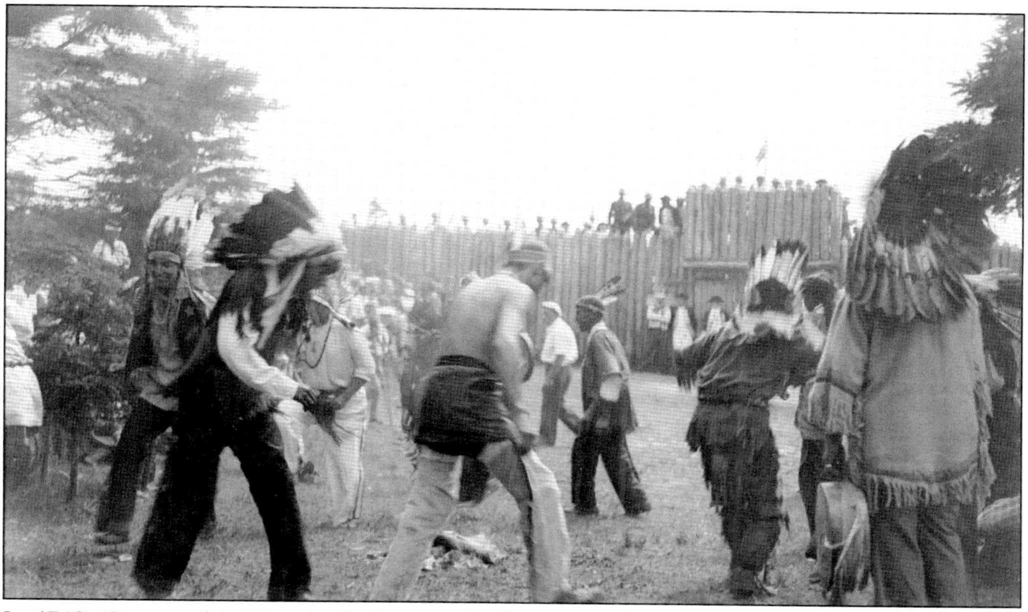

In 1763, Ottawa chief Pontiac had a grand scheme to take over Great Lakes forts, including Fort Michilimackinac. Unlike the French, the British had mistreated the native people and did not present the customary gifts. Disease and alcohol were other purposeful attempts by the British to rid the land of its native inhabitants. Chief Pontiac's mother was an Ojibway, and because the Ottawa and Potawatomi were in alliance, all three nations came together under Pontiac's great rule. His plan at Michilimackinac was a game of baggataway (lacrosse), where the rowdy participants ended up inside the fort to attack and slay the British inhabitants. The French residents were left untouched. Today, those events are replicated by reenactors in period costume each year during Memorial Day weekend at the Colonial Michilimackinac Pageant. (Both courtesy of John Marsh.)

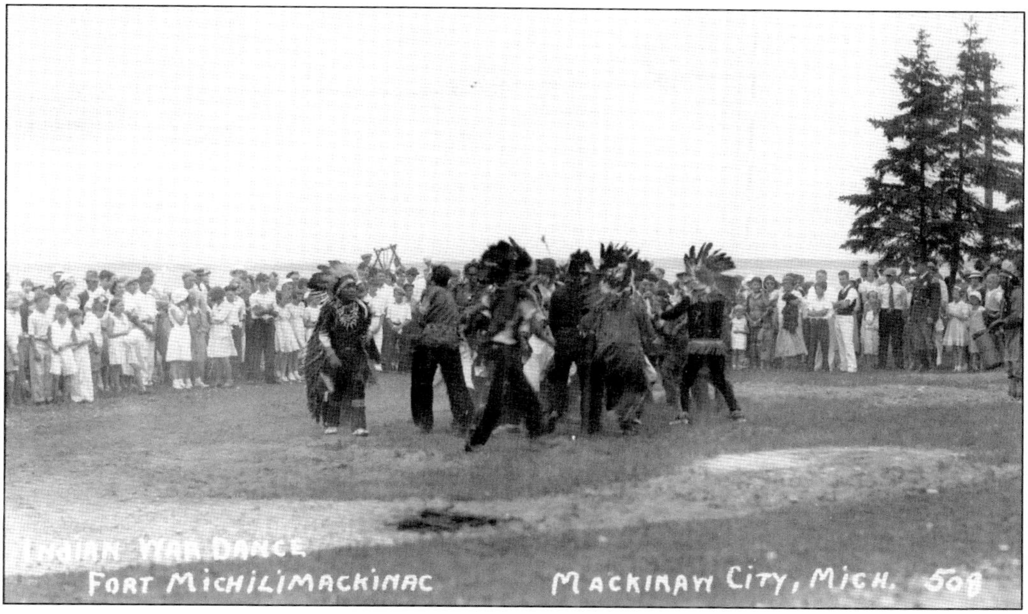

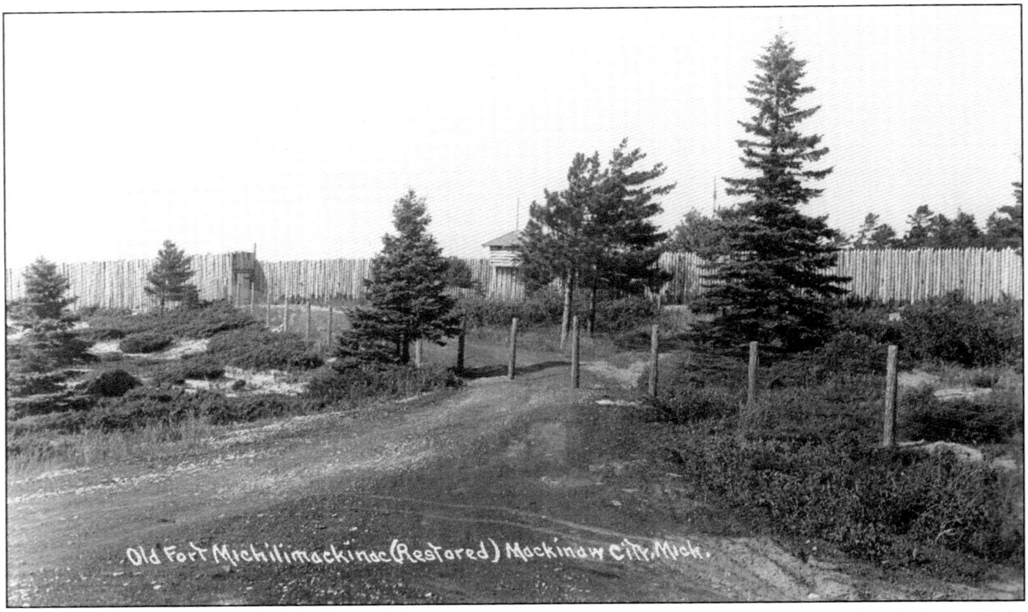

Similar to the artifacts found in excavations at Fort Mackinac on Mackinac Island, incredible pieces of history have been found in Mackinaw City. For example, from the military inhabitants, gun parts, gun ornaments, and French and English regimental buttons were found; from the religious, crucifixes, rosaries, rings, and medallions; and from the carpenters, nails, fasteners, chisels and files, locks and keys, and a compass. Other personal items included combs, pins, cuff links and chains, buckles and pencils, pipes and chess pieces, coins and beads, and needles and thimbles. From the kitchens, glasses and bottles, shards of china and pottery, knives, forks and spoons, candlesticks, and utensils were discovered. And recovered from the garbage piles were remnants of wild cherries, fish, pigs, wild ducks, passenger pigeons, deer, beavers, and seagulls—a treasure trove of early life in the Straits of Mackinac. (Above, courtesy of John Marsh.)

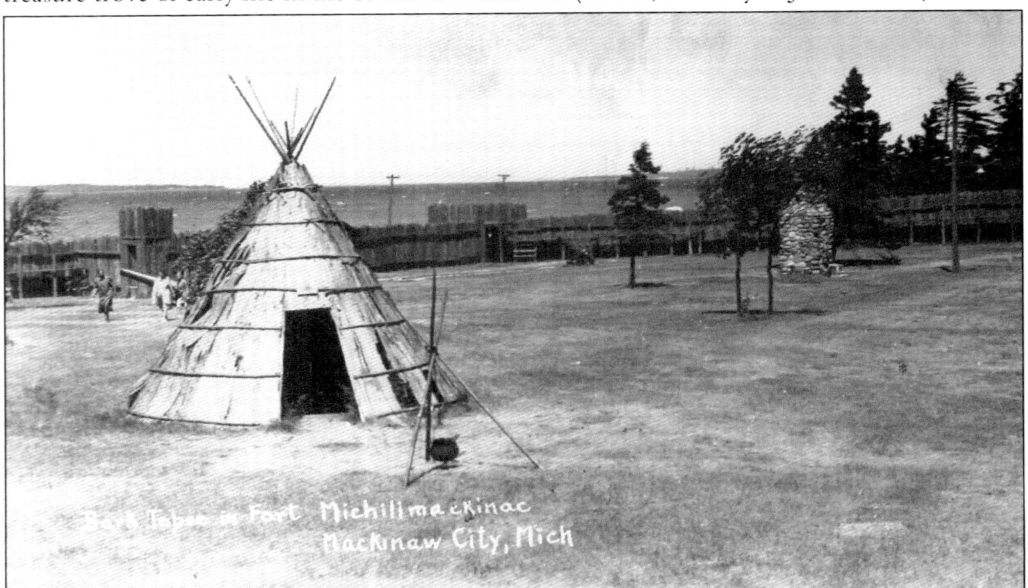

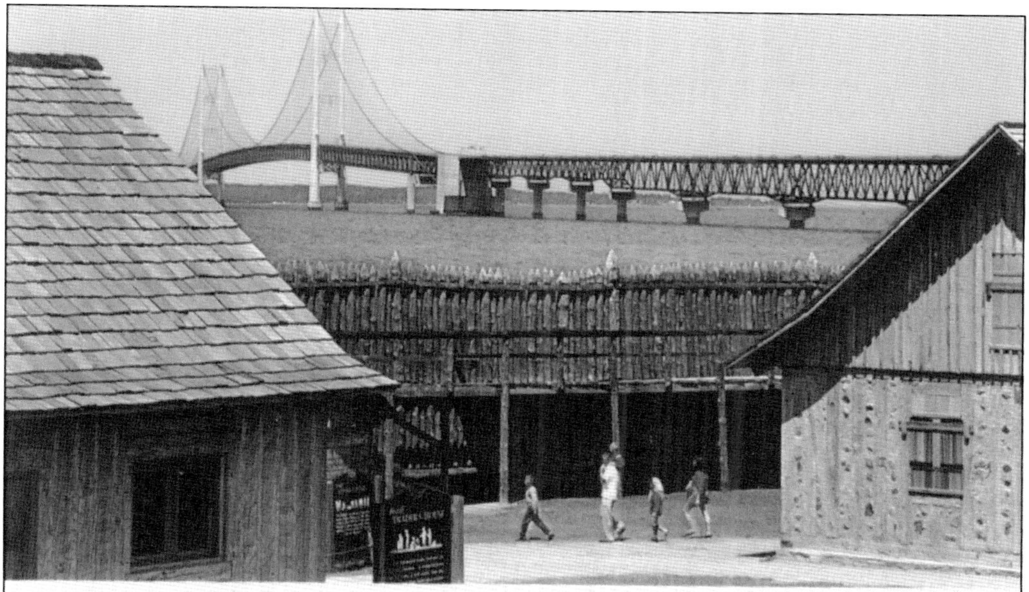

Inside Fort Michilimackinac with Mackinac Bridge in background

These two 1960s postcards combine views of the old and the new. Fort Michilimackinac sits a stone's throw from the water's edge and commands a magnificent view of the modern Mackinac Bridge. Famous explorers like Brûlé, Nicolet, Jolliet, and LaSalle travelled through here, but they called the great waters Lac des Hurons and Lac des Illinois. The main function of the fort in its early years was to control and protect the fur trade. Armadas of canoes arriving from Quebec and Montreal would stop to take on food and supplies or make necessary repairs before journeying north to Lake Superior or south to Chicago (Shikaakwa). Visitors today will find an interesting array of activities as costumed interpreters perform open-hearth cooking demonstrations, display handiwork, and fire muskets. Visitors can also attend a French Colonial wedding.

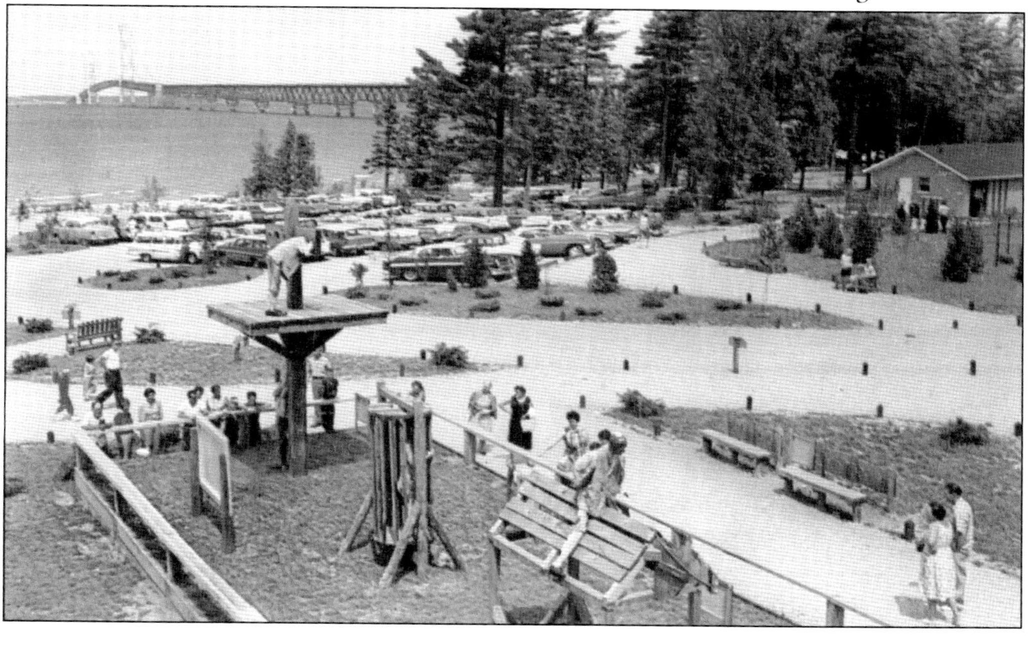

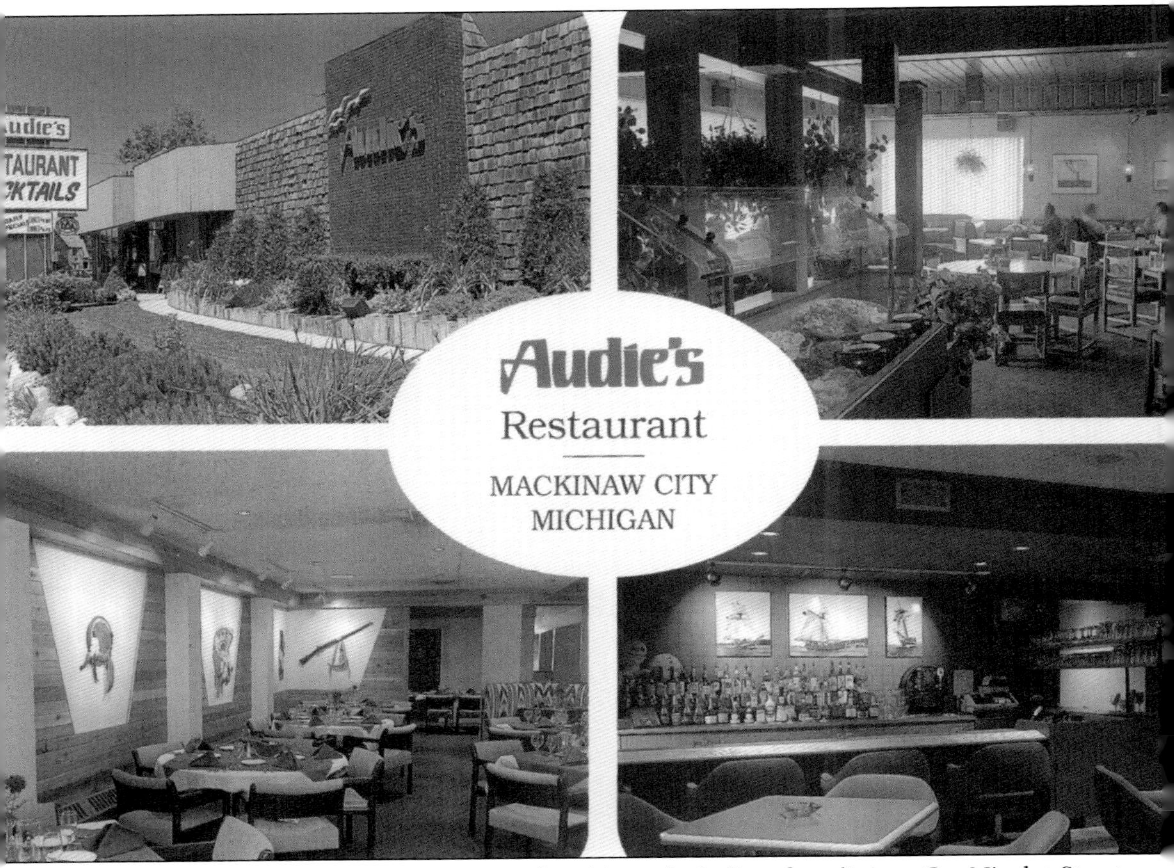

Mackinaw City has many attractions for visitors, including fine dining. On Nicolet Street, a short distance from Colonial Michilimackinac, is Audie's Restaurant. Neil and Jeanette Downing owned and operated Downing's Café on Central Avenue in the late 1950s. A few years later, they moved their café to Nicolet Street at the last Interstate 75 entrance and exit to the Mackinac Bridge. In 1974, the restaurant was purchased by Edgar and Audrey (Downing) Jaggi, and later passed it to their son Nick, a graduate of the Culinary Institute of America. Named after Audrey, Audie's has two full-service restaurants, a lounge, and private banquet rooms and offers catering services. The Chippewa Room, for casual fine dining, has Native American décor, local artifacts, and superb entrees, including wild game and mushrooms. The Welcome Lounge features fish and animal trophy mounts. The Family Room, for family dining, features artifacts and Mackinac Bridge items. Audie's motto is "Serving visitors of Mackinaw City since the Mackinac Bridge was built." (Courtesy of Nick Jaggi.)

Five

Cheboygan
Kitchi-bwa-gan

The city of Cheboygan has a colorful history on the Straits of Mackinac, just like its northern and western village neighbors. Located approximately 15 miles east-southeast of Mackinaw City on the south channel of Lake Huron, across from Bois Blanc Island, Cheboygan marks the beginning of the eastern side of The Straits. Historians debate the origin and meaning of Cheboygan's name. Variations include Cha-boia-gan, Native American for "a portage"; Shab-we-gan, for "place of entrance or "a water passage"; and Che-o-paw-gan, or Kitchi-bwa-gan, meaning "big pipe." The confusion may lie in the fact that several native tribes with differing dialects lived on each side of the mouth of the Cheboygan River, and what white men heard—and tried to spell—may be the reason for the many contemporary translations.

Cheboygan's history actually began with its sister city, Duncan. Named after a Chicago lumber baron who purchased most of the land around the scenic bay, Duncan City was located about three miles from present-day Cheboygan's city center. It was the site of the area's first post office and the spot where Jeremiah Duncan built his huge lumber mill. Later, when the mill was destroyed by fire, Duncan City began its decline, and most activity moved to Cheboygan.

Jacob Sammons was a cooper (barrel maker) at Fort Mackinac but wanted to find a place of his own. In 1844, he chose an old Native American camping ground on the mainland shore near a large river, the Cheboygan, built his cabin, and re-established his trade. Also, in 1844, Alexander McLeod arrived and built the first commercial business, a water-powered sawmill located at the river's rapids. With the fur trade dying out as animals became almost extinct, lumbering made early Cheboygan prosper. Hundreds of thousands of board feet of lumber were processed at Cheboygan, and the sawdust pile grew. Today, Duncan City is virtually gone, but Cheboygan prospers as a historical and scenic harbor town and city of hospitality on the Straits of Mackinac at Lake Huron.

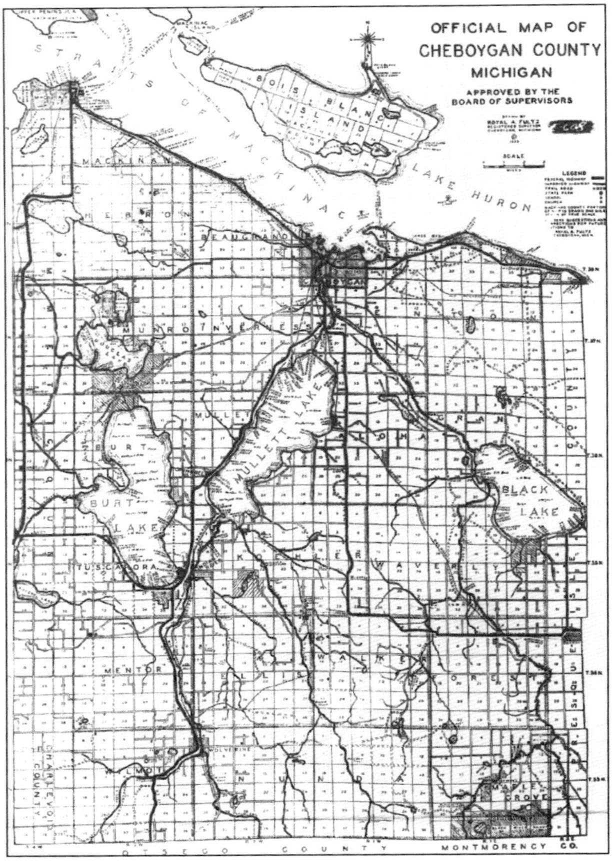

Along with the Ojibwe, Cheboygan was reportedly the home of a Huron encampment, similar to St. Ignace. The Huron were Iroquoian people and spoke a language very different from their Algonquian neighbors. The Huron wore their hair in ridges, like that of a wild boar's bristles, so the French Jesuit priests used the word *huré* to describe them. They were also called Bons Iroquois, or "good Iroquois," to differentiate them from the other warring Iroquois tribes. The huge lake Mer Douce ("freshwater sea"), around which the Huron lived, was also known as Lac des Hurons. The postcard map to the left shows the scenic town of Cheboygan at the mouth of the Cheboygan River and across the channel from Bois Blanc Island at the eastern end of the Straits of Mackinac.

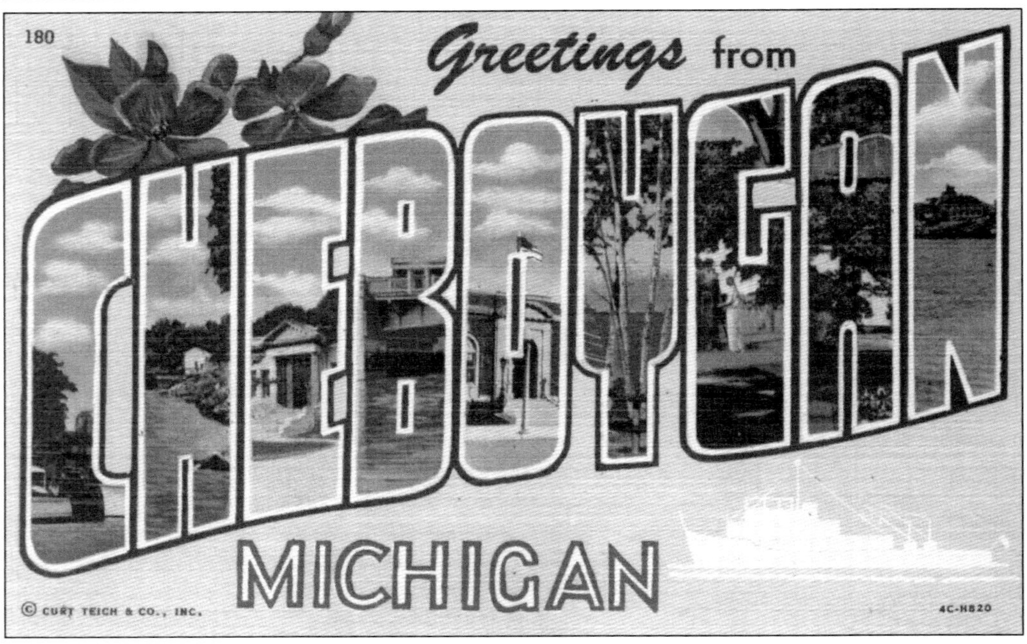

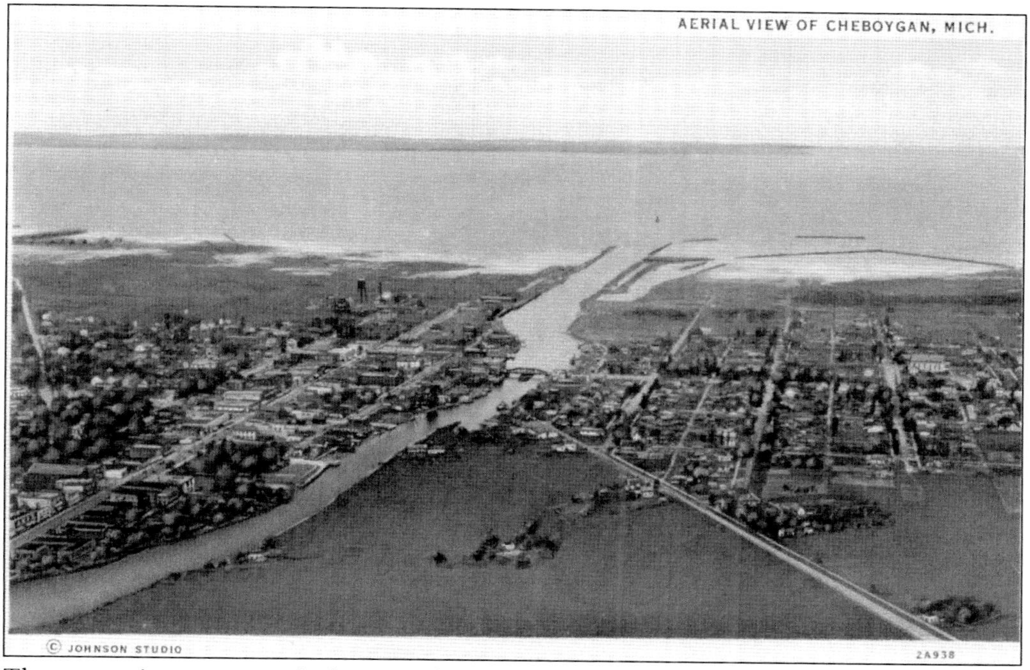

These two vintage postcards show aerial views of Cheboygan at the mouth of the Cheboygan River from both directions. The image above looks northeast into Lake Huron with Bois Blanc Island in the background, and the image below shows the mainland area to the southwest. The Cheboygan River was a natural dividing line for Native American villages and a huge natural resource for the hardy stock of pioneers who came later, braving the new frontier wilderness. While these views do not show it, early Cheboygan had immense stands of virgin pine adjacent to the river just waiting for a new timber industry to take shape. When the lumber boom came, it left its mark on Cheboygan's history.

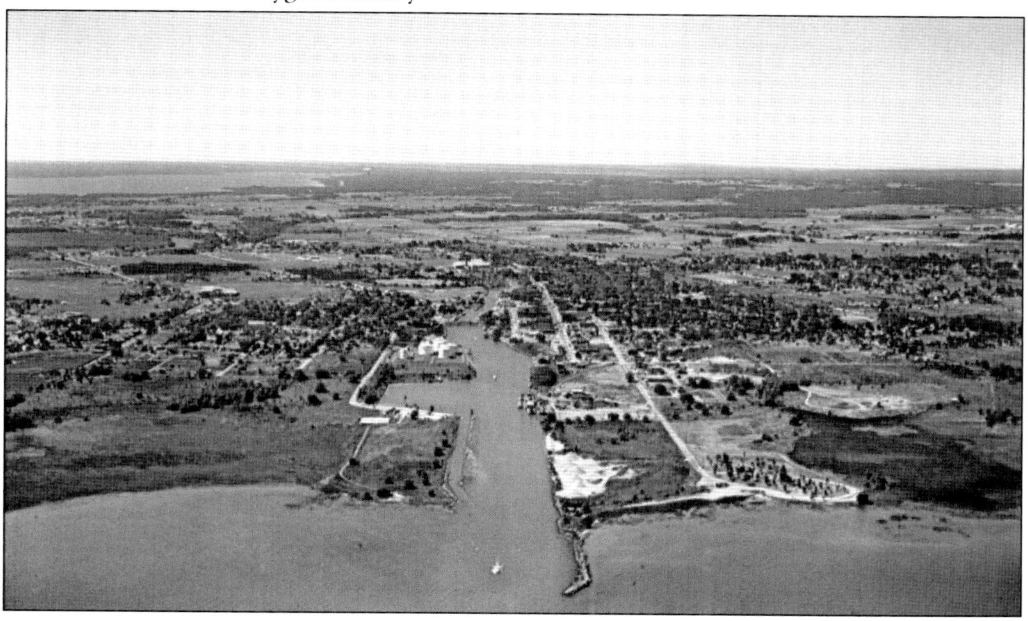

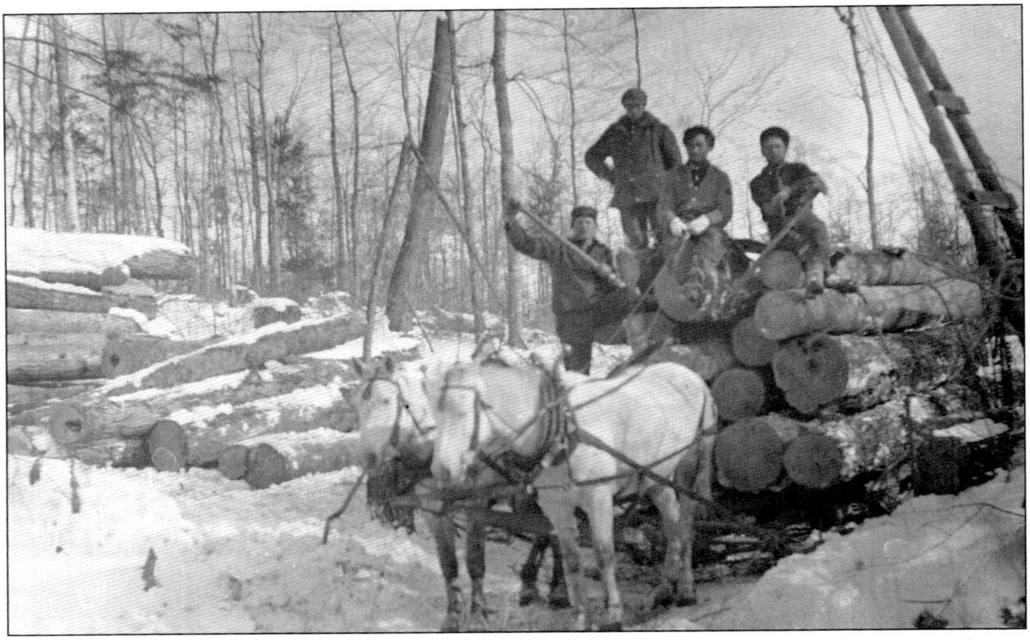

In early years, after trees were felled, the lumber was hauled from the forests on horse-drawn sleds. In most lumber camps, it was the job of a special crew, called "sprinklers," working at night to "ice down" the routes to make the hauling a bit easier, as giant sleigh loads of logs could weigh as much as 50,000 pounds. Once cut, logs were hauled to a stacking/decking area to await further transport. "Chickadees" had the task of keeping the tote roads free of horse manure. With the seemingly never-ending supply of timber, lumber camps and lumber mills sprang up in abundance, providing jobs and a means of income for the new settlers. In later years, trucks like the one shown below replaced the sleds.

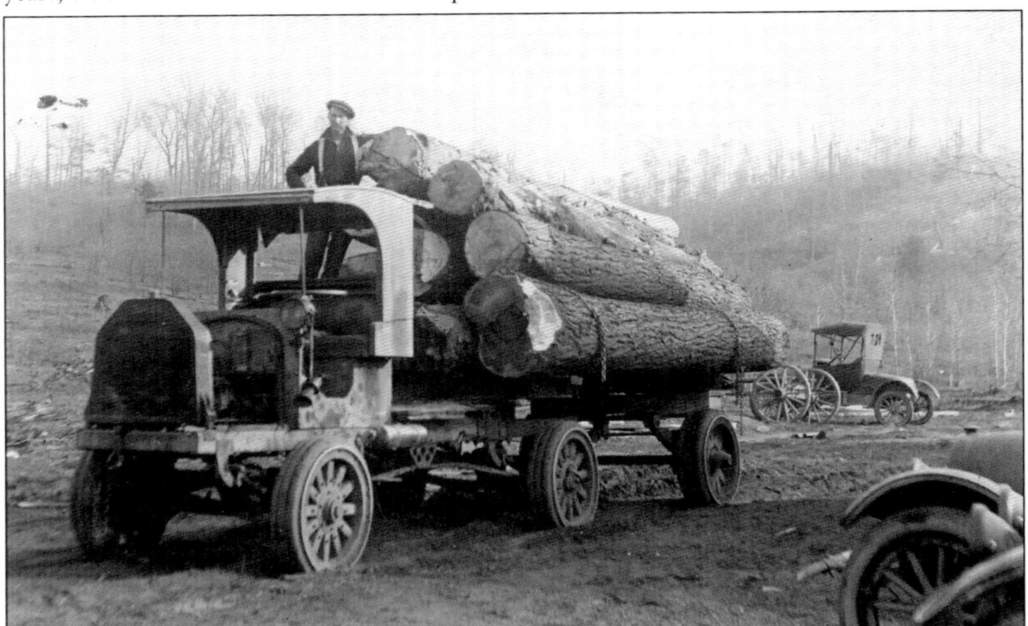

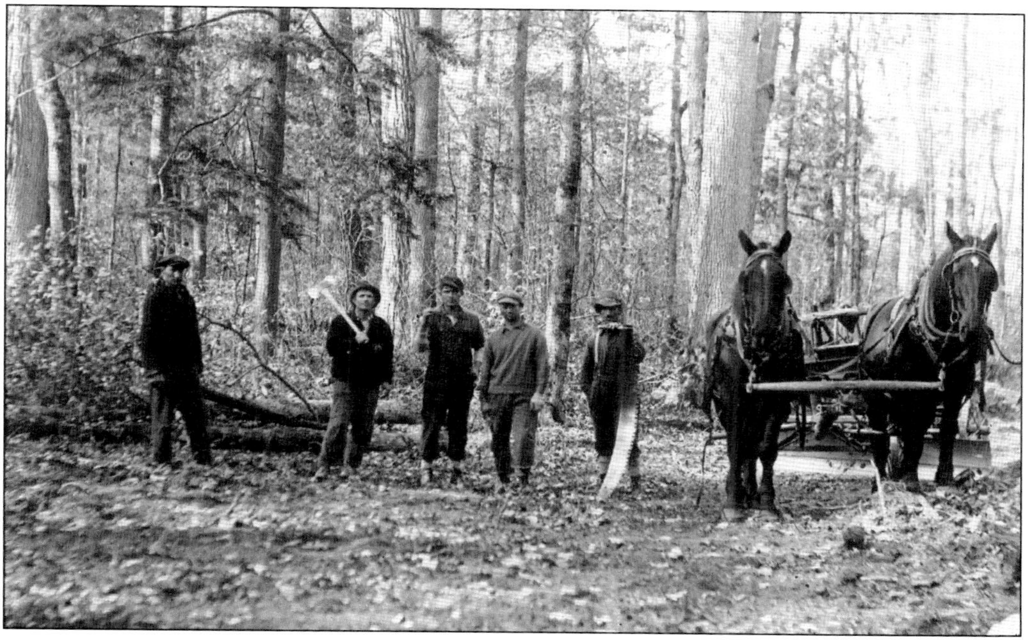

The first man on the scene was called a timber cruiser. With a compass and a primitive map, he would explore the wilderness looking for prime timber near a stream. If he found such a treasure, he would hurry to the nearest land office to register the claim. Next, a tote road would be cut to the site by "road monkeys." Then "tote teamsters" brought the equipment and supplies and created a lumber camp. When the first snow fell, a crew of "shanty boys" populated the lumber camp, eager for their task of felling the trees. The men worked hard and ate heartily.

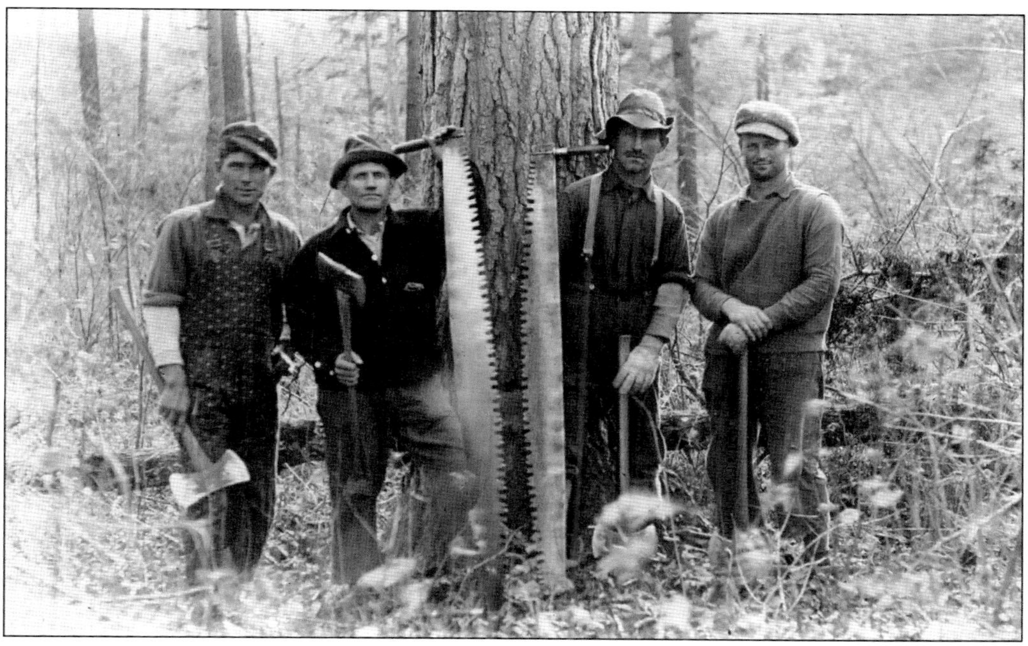

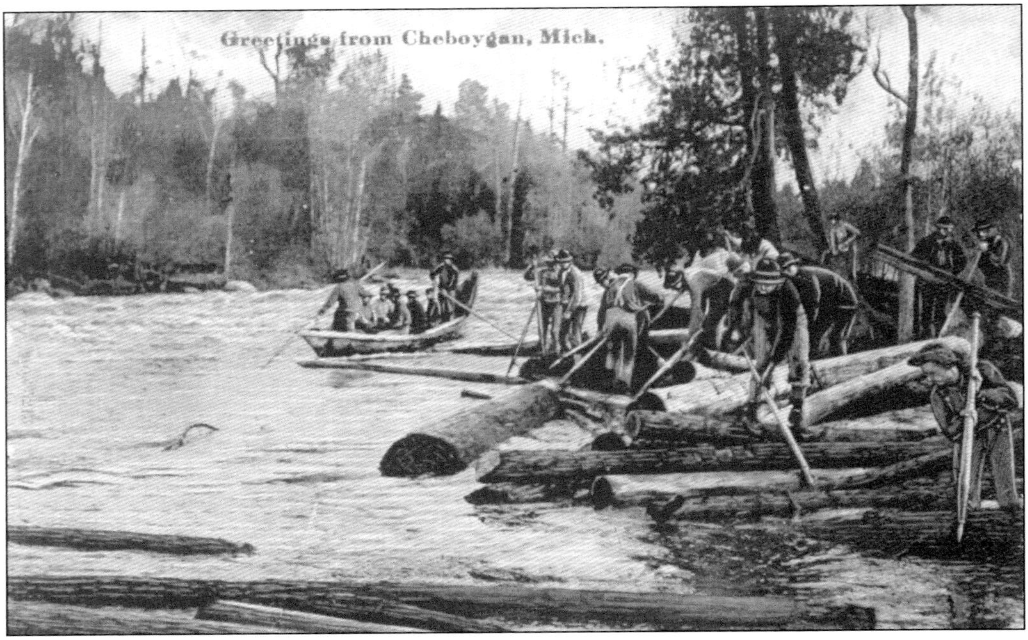

Scenes like this were common in Cheboygan's early years. From the decking area near a stream or river, logs were pushed downstream to the sawmill. It was a dangerous job for the "river hogs" to break up the huge piles of logs, which could jam up along the way. When the logs arrived at the "booming grounds," sorters were hired to identify and sort each different lumber camp's logs by a special mark hammered into the ends. These special log marks were similar to branded cattle, each one distinctive to each owner. The Embury-Martin Lumber Company, seen below in 1913, was a bustling enterprise in Cheboygan.

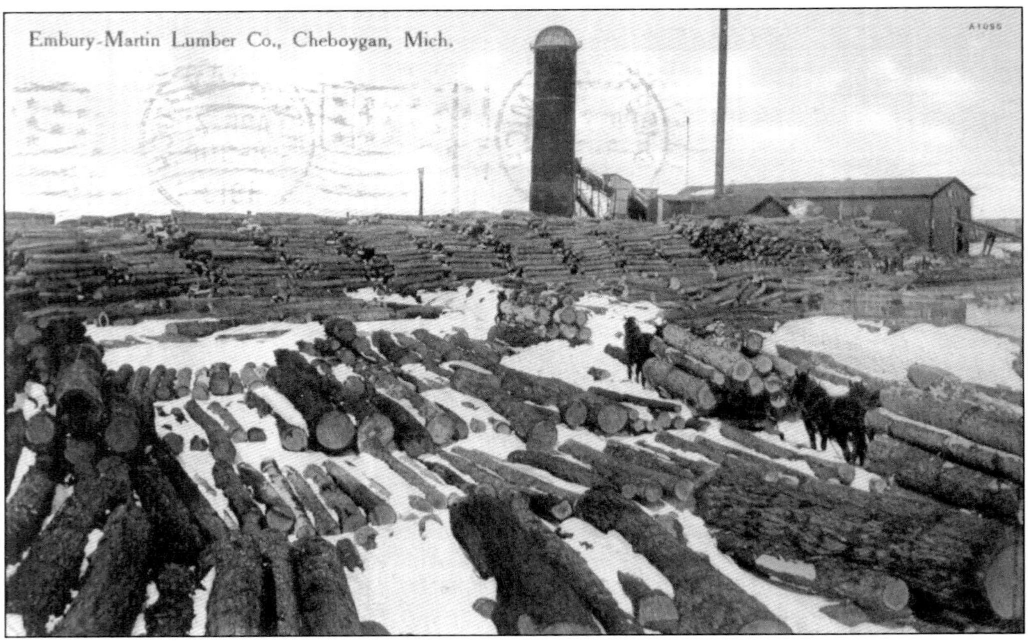

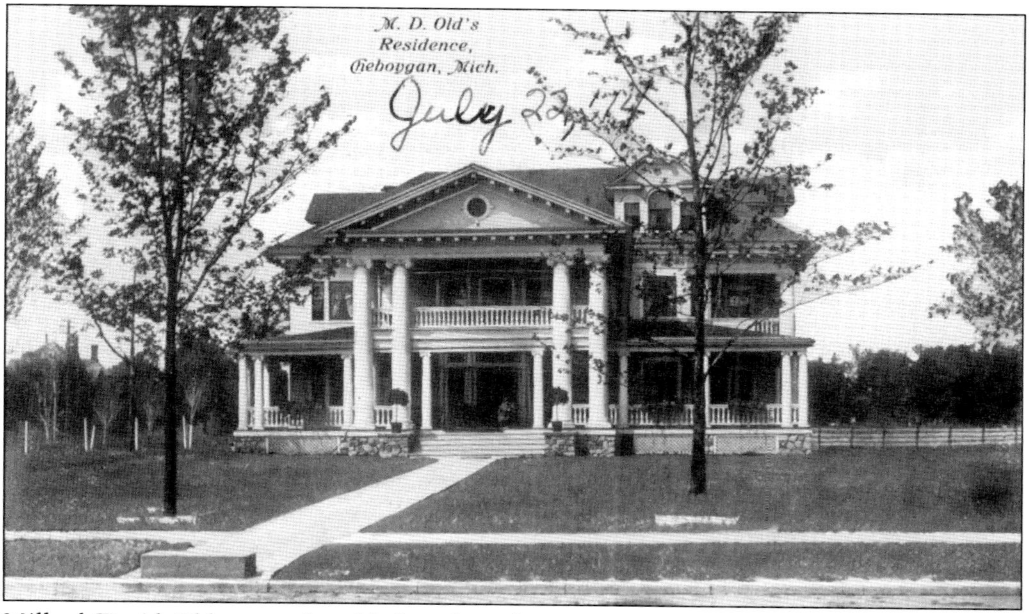

Millard David Olds was a humble but shrewd, competitive, and prosperous mill owner in Cheboygan. After moving to Cheboygan from Vanderbilt, Michigan, he built his opulent residence on South Main Street, as shown in this 1914 postcard. Olds was described as "industrious, imaginative, and an extremely capable businessman creating his own opportunities," which is fortunate for Cheboygan because he gave much back to the community. Olds even created a way for sawdust and log waste to be transported and sold to the Cheboygan Paper Company for fuel to supply their burners. The Cheboygan Paper Company, shown below, was a prominent part of early-1900s Cheboygan commerce and was the forerunner of today's Great Lakes Tissue Company.

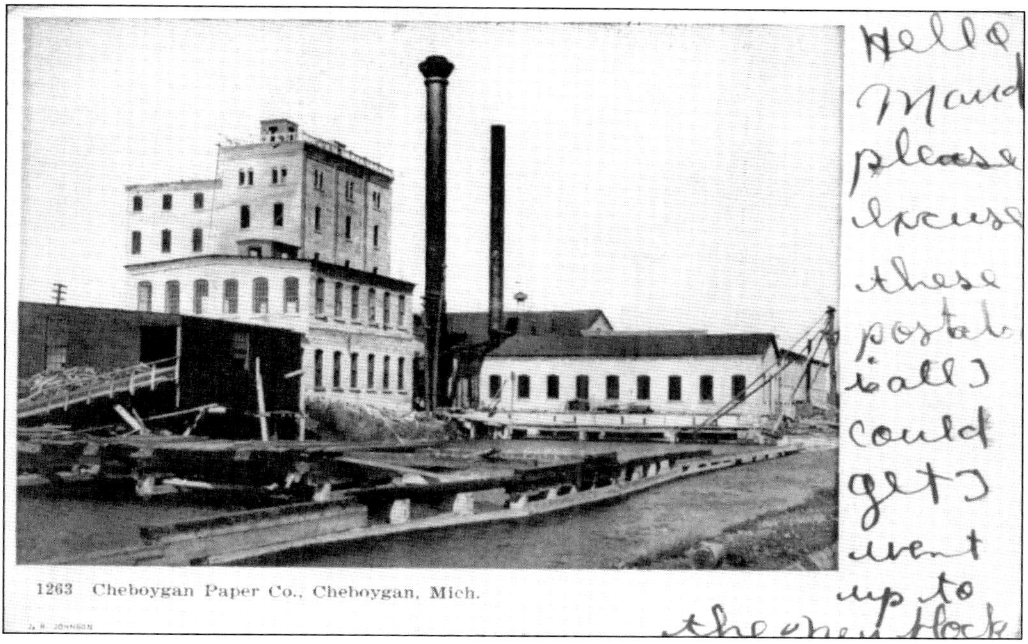

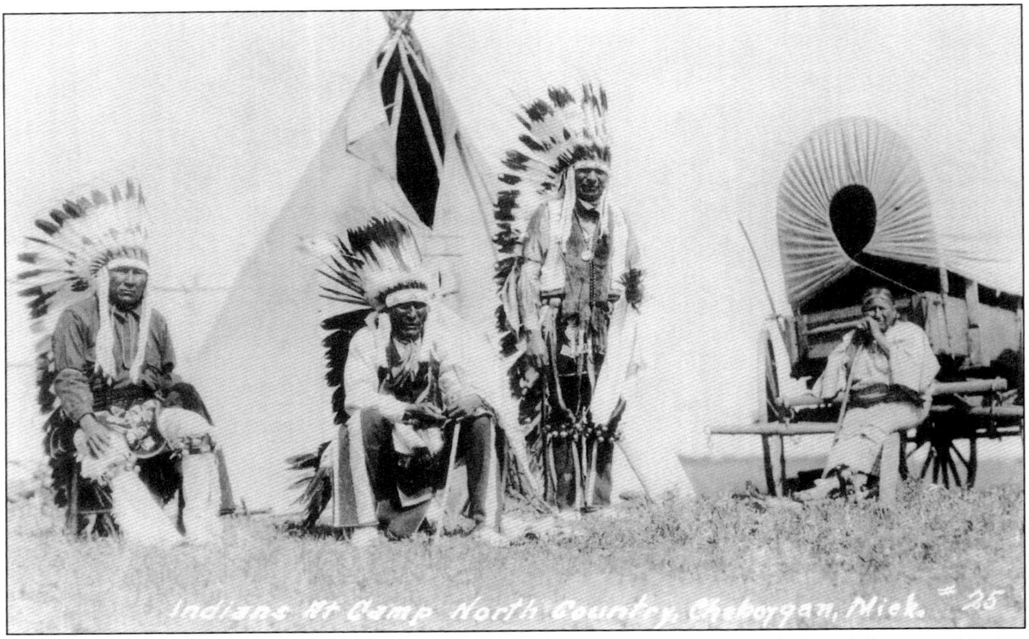

This scene is titled "Indians at Camp North Country, Cheboygan, Mich," and features Native American men wearing magnificent headdresses. Another theory of the meaning of Cheboygan claims that "the Chippewas were also called 'Cheboys,' and the term 'gan' meant water; so Cheboygan may mean 'Chippewa Water' for the adjacent river."

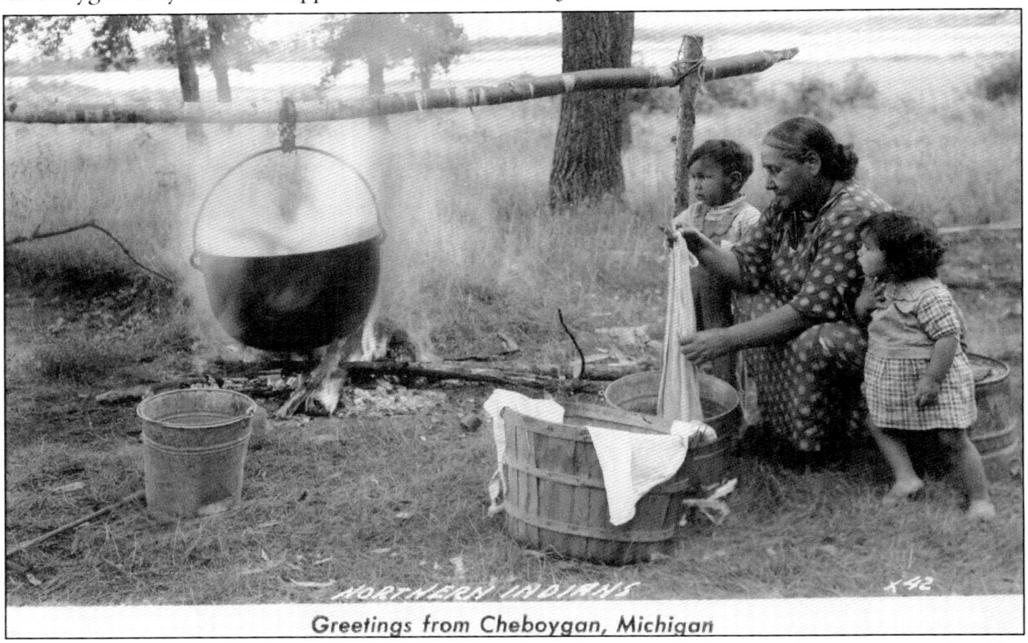

This Native American woman in contemporary dress washes clothes at her campsite. Similar fires were also built for the making of maple syrup, when fires and kettles required tending day and night. The sap had to be boiled for several days until evaporation reduced the liquid to syrup. Children were taught at an early age to respect the fires.

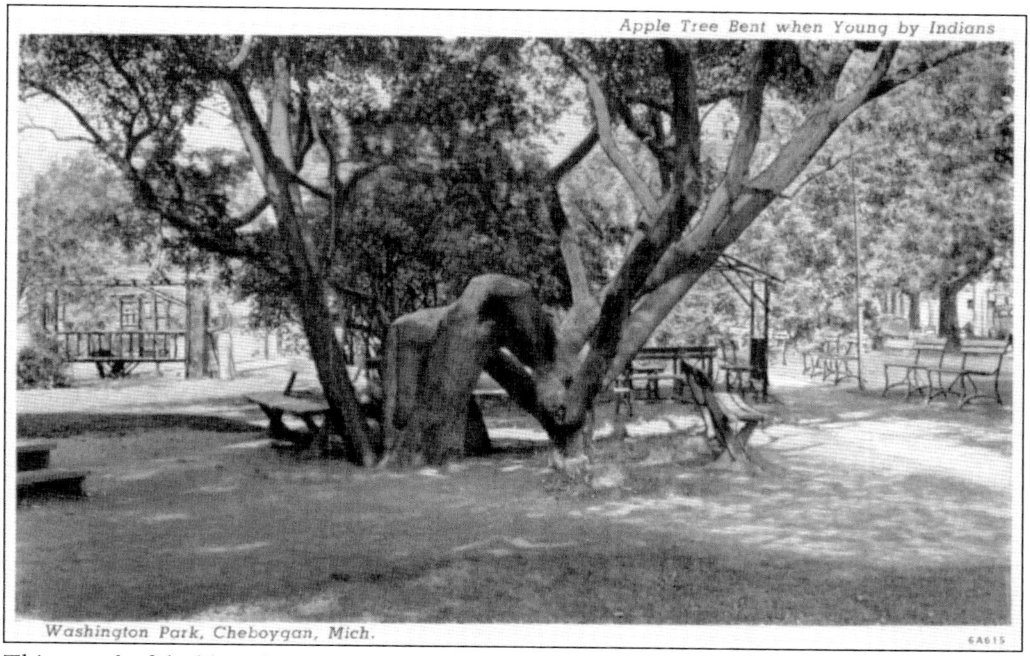

This wonderful old apple tree in Washington Park near the center of downtown Cheboygan was rumored to be a Native American landmark. The postcard title is "Apple Tree Bent when Young by Indians." Another legend states that this was a "spirit tree" for local native people. *Me-she-min* means apples and *me-she-me-naw-gaw-wosh* means apple tree(s).

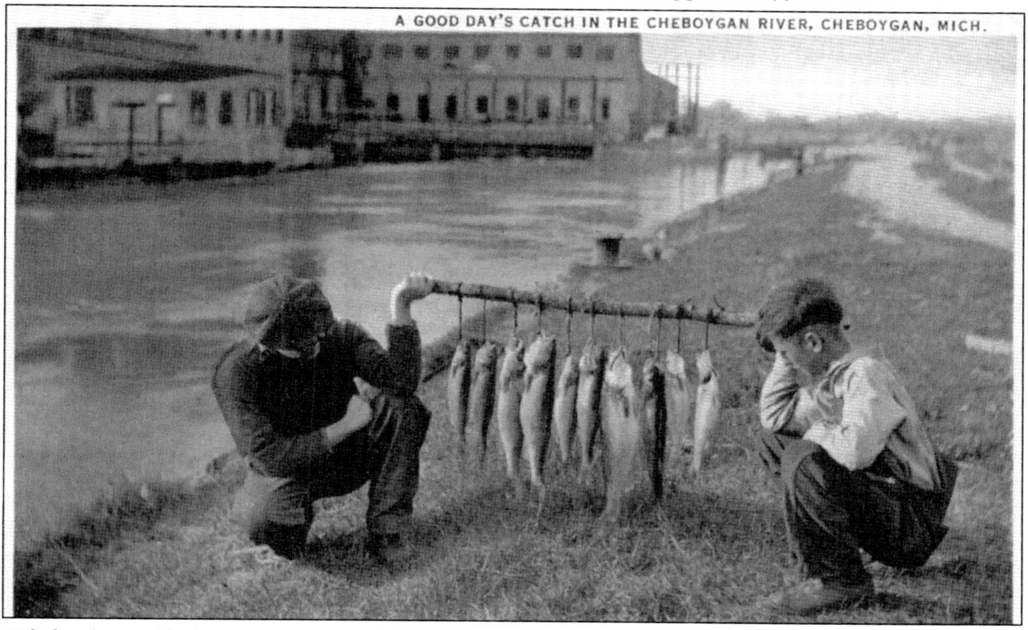

While these Cheboygan-area boys were happy with their day's catch from the Cheboygan River, Native American youth spent time fishing as well. Other leisure-time activities for the Chippewa and Ottawa included cup and pin, hoop and dart, dice and bowl, the game of straws, cat's cradle, snow snake, archery contests, and lacrosse (baggataway).

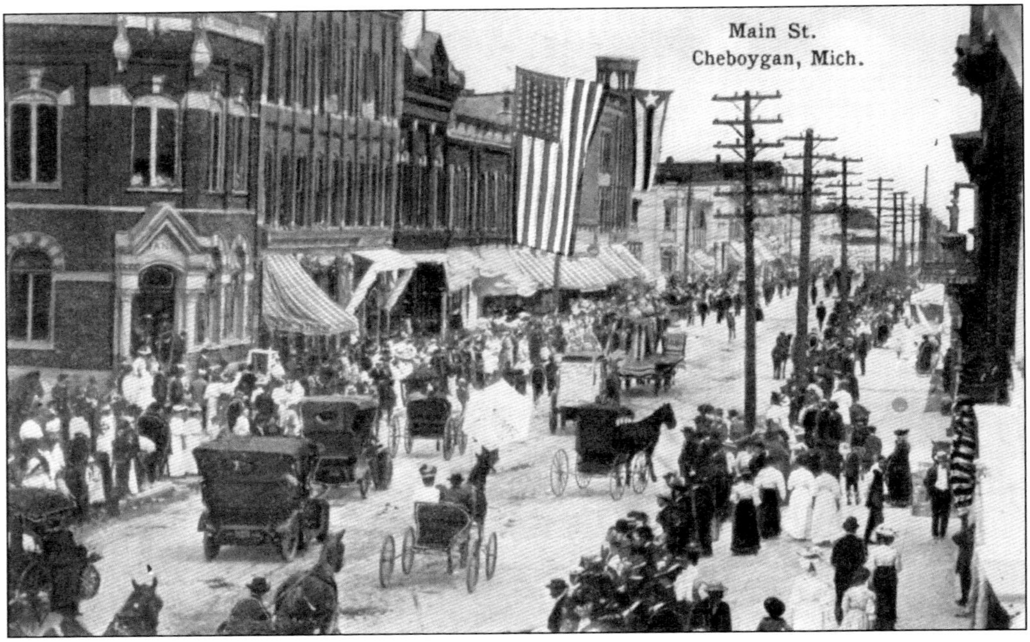

These 1910 postcards show downtown Cheboygan to be a busy place that looks quite prosperous 66 years after it began in 1844. Above, motor vehicles and horse-drawn carriages share the main street while residents line both sides. The American flag was added by the postcard printer. Unfortunately, very few of the original downtown buildings survived a 1922 fire. The image below shows Cheboygan's swing bridge crossing the Cheboygan River near its mouth. Originally built around 1877, this old bridge was operated by a hand crank.

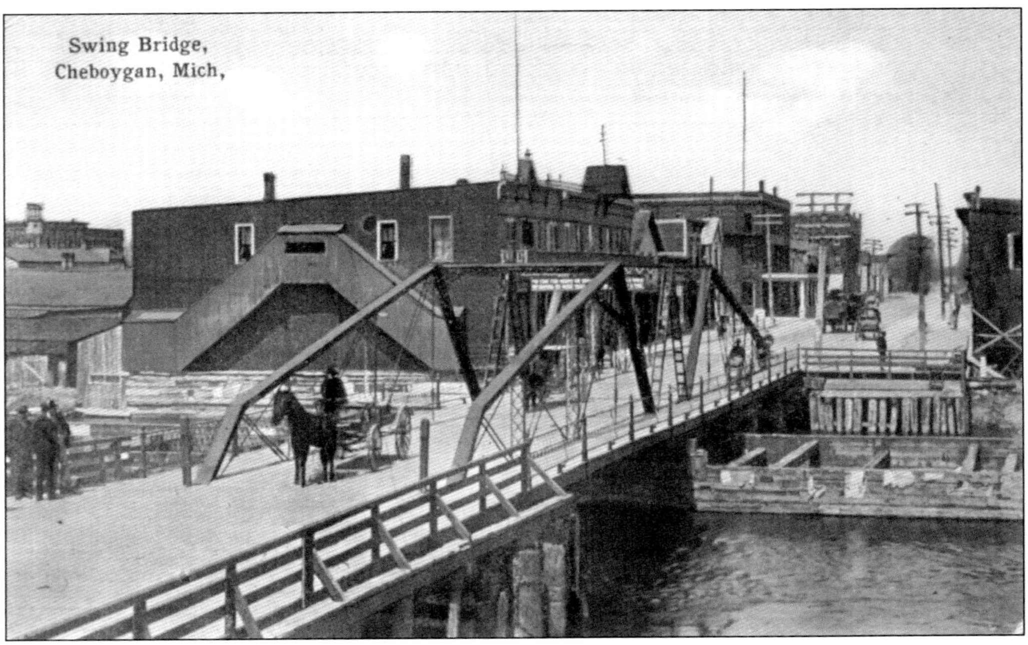

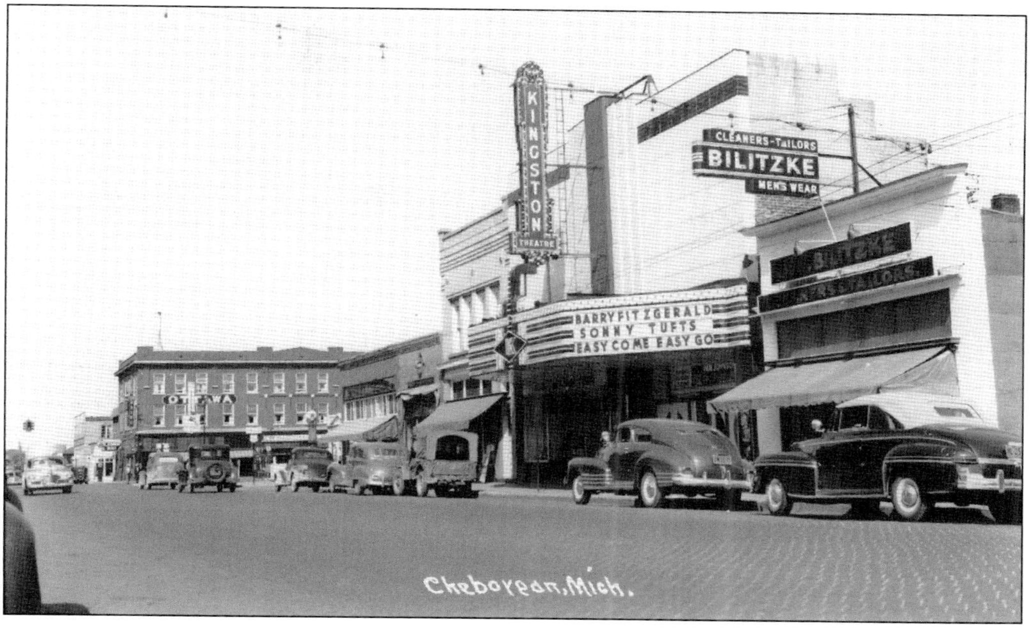

Automobiles have replaced horse-drawn carriages in these two 1940s views of Main Street. Above, the marquee on the Kingston movie theatre, which is still in operation, reads, "Barry Fitzgerald, Sonny Tufts, Easy Come Easy Go." The F.W. Woolworth store shown in the postcard below had a variety of interesting items on display in its front windows, hoping to catch the attention of potential customers passing by. The soda fountain inside was a popular gathering place to catch up on community news. An old advertisement from the 1940s for Rocky Mountain Tea sold in the store reads, "Makes the fires of life burn with a steady glow and renews the happy days of youth."

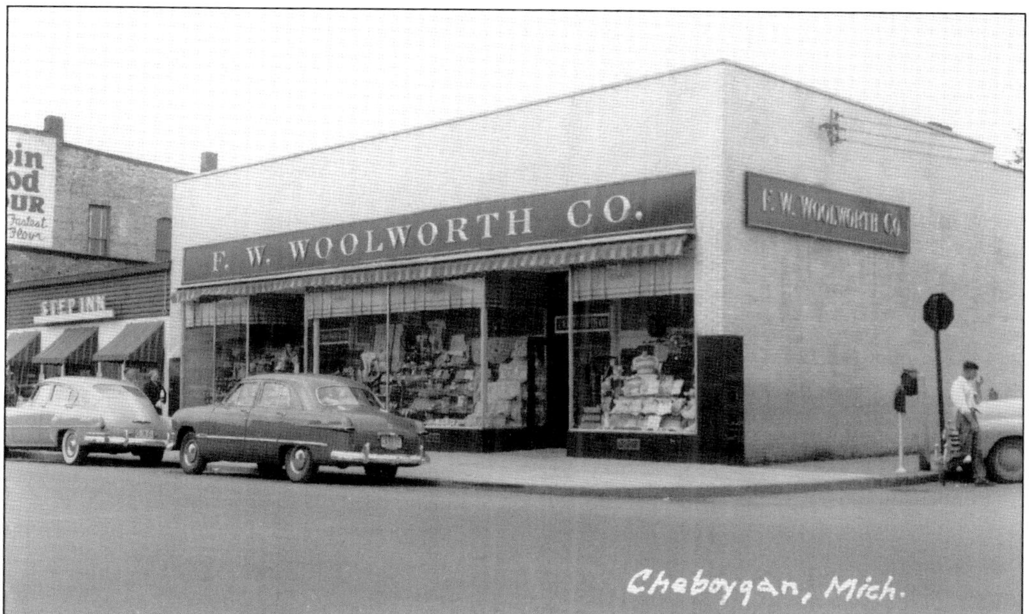

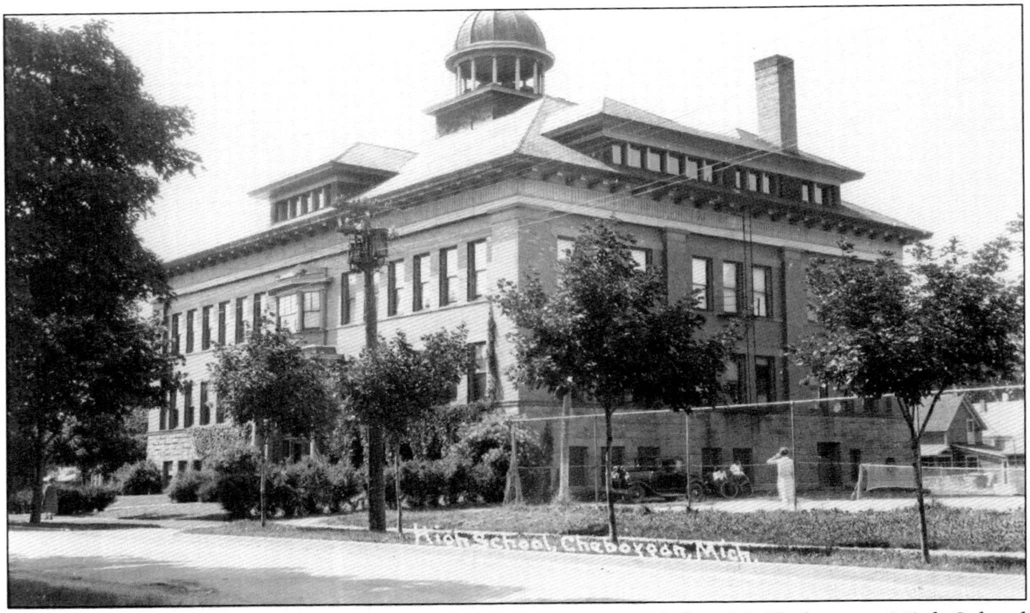

The Cheboygan School District was established in 1848, and the old Cheboygan High School was a prominent structure in the community; the cupola could be seen for miles. Built in 1909 to replace Central School, it housed students until it was razed in 1967. Note the vintage automobile parked next to the side of the school and the tennis court in the foreground. Today, the high school is located on West Lincoln Avenue, and its motto is "Home of the Chiefs."

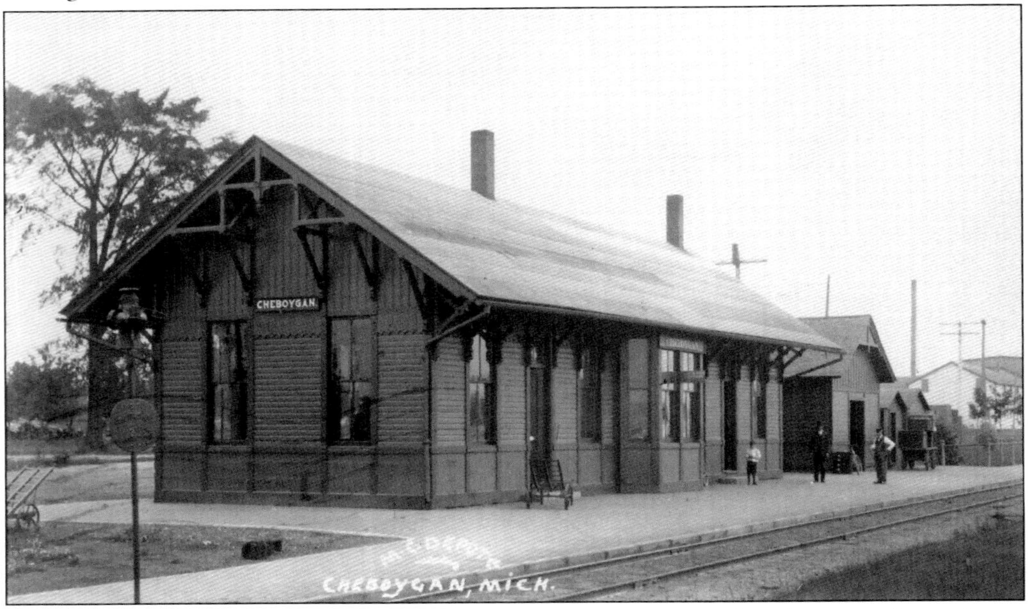

The Michigan Central Railroad arrived in Cheboygan in 1881, and its depot was located near the river. The Detroit & Mackinaw Railroad (D&M) line was extended to Cheboygan in 1904, with its depot adjacent to the business district on Court Street. The D&M line eventually reached Mackinaw City, creating rail-stop villages along the way. "Freedom" was one of those stops and was reportedly used to help escaping slaves from the South make their way to Canada.

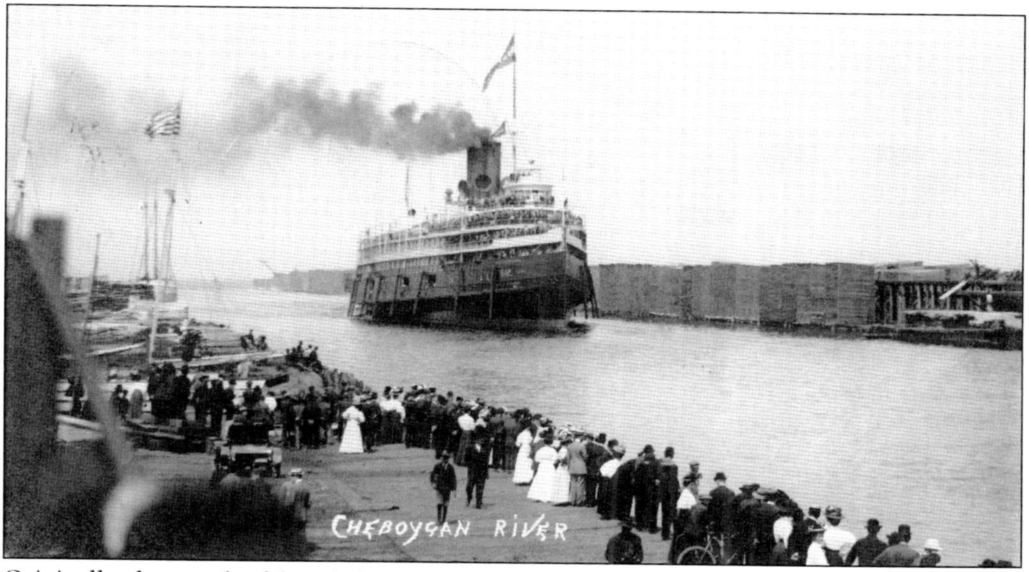

Originally, the mouth of the Cheboygan River, where it emptied into Lake Huron, was clogged by a sandbar. Extensive dredging made it possible for large passenger boats to make a stop in Cheboygan on excursions in Lake Huron to Mackinac Island. This postcard was postmarked 1912 by the Detroit & Mackinaw Railroad. Note the stacks of lumber on the far shore across from the passenger dock.

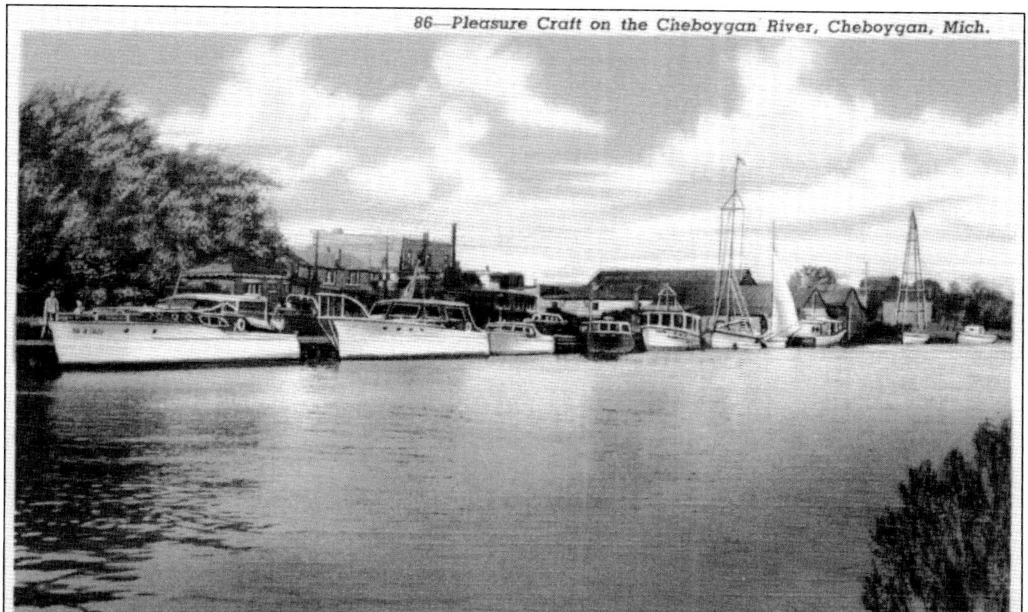

Fancy pleasure craft are moored along the Cheboygan River in a 1948 postcard. This spot marks the end of the Inland Waterway at Lake Huron that originates in Conway, Michigan, almost at the Lake Michigan shore. All kinds of watercraft can be seen navigating their way through the rivers and lakes that connect the waterway. At this eastern end of it, Cheboygan lighthouses are an added attraction.

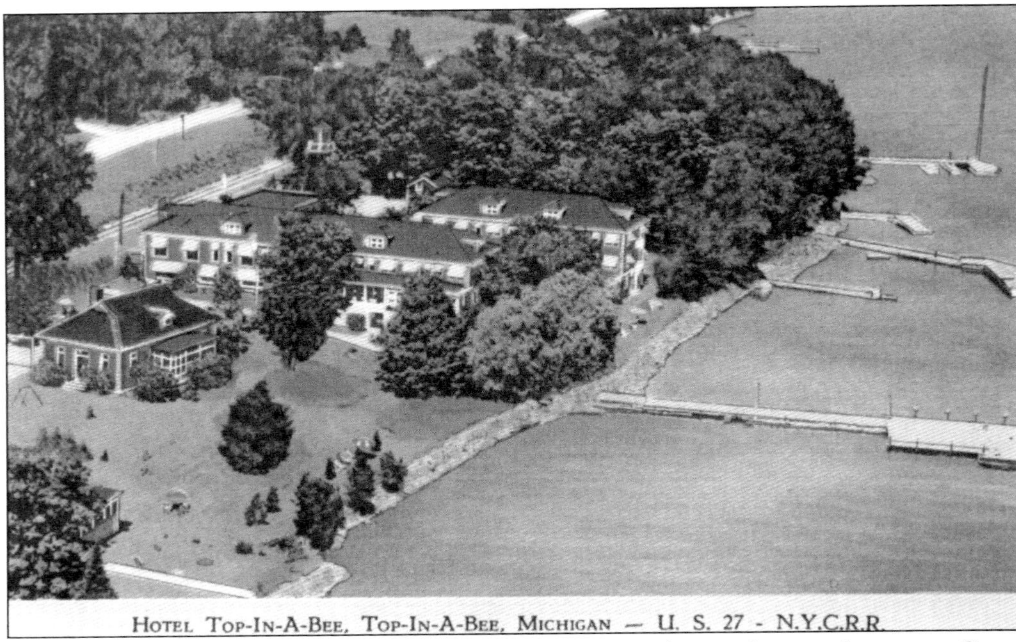

HOTEL TOP-IN-A-BEE, TOP-IN-A-BEE, MICHIGAN — U. S. 27 - N.Y.C.R.R.

Traveling through northern Michigan became an increasingly popular vacation event. Grand resorts were built to accommodate this new tourism industry in the Cheboygan area as well as in Mackinac. Formerly Pikes Hotel in 1881 and later Pikes Summer Tavern, Hotel Top-In-A-Bee (above) was on the shoreline of Mullet Lake. Named after Potawatomi chief Topinabee ("he sits quietly"), who lived near Niles, Michigan, the resort was successful until the 1960s. The Hack-ma-tack Inn (below), on the Cheboygan River near Mullet Lake, was named after the Native American word for Tamarack. Originally a hunting and fishing lodge, it was built with tamarack logs in 1894. Today it is a popular restaurant, still serving residents and tourists with good food and Cheboygan hospitality.

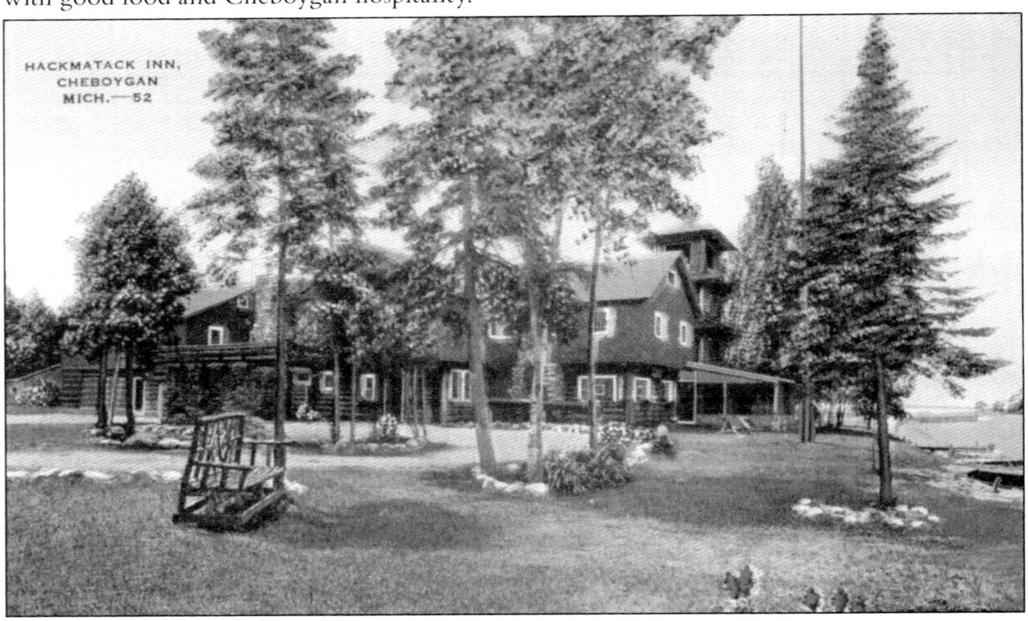

HACKMATACK INN,
CHEBOYGAN
MICH.—52

Six

Let Us Go Boat Riding
Aum-bay Paw-baw-mish-kaw-daw

Water travel on the Straits of Mackinac began with the Native American canoe and most likely originated with the ancient Huron Indian trade route from Montreal and Quebec on the St. Lawrence River through Lakes Ontario, Erie, St. Clair, and Huron to Michilimackinac. Another route brought travelers and explorers across Canada to the Georgian Bay and across the northern end of Lake Huron to Michilimackinac.

A young French man, Étienne Brûlé, was probably the first white man to travel with the Huron and reach the upper Great Lakes. Men who followed Brûlé, like Jean Nicolet, were looking for a trade route to the Orient. Next came more explorers, French missionaries, and couriers de bois, all traveling by canoe. The next vessel to arrive in The Straits was the French sailing ship *Griffon*. Owned by Robert Cavelier, Sieur de La Salle, the *Griffon* set out to explore the great waters. On a return trip to Canada in 1679 loaded with fur pelts, the *Griffon* disappeared, reportedly in a violent storm.

It was not until 1819 that the first steamboat, *Walk-In-The-Water,* came to Mackinac Island. Named after a Wyandot (Huron) chief who lived on the Detroit River, *Walk-In-The-Water* was rigged as a two-masted schooner. In good weather, it moved at six or seven miles per hour. It also met its fate in a Great Lakes storm. Canoes, bateaux, sailing ships, passenger steamers, automobile ferries, coal-fired railroad ferries, pleasure boats, and Great Lakes freighters have all witnessed the scenic splendor of The Straits and have become a part of its history.

Over the years, storms, ice, fire, fog, and explosions have caused many of these magnificent vessels to find their way to the bottom of their nautical highways. The Straits of Mackinac has a good number of shipwrecks, many of which are still undiscovered. The State of Michigan has designated The Straits as part of the Michigan underwater preserve system to protect and preserve historic underwater sites, including shipwrecks.

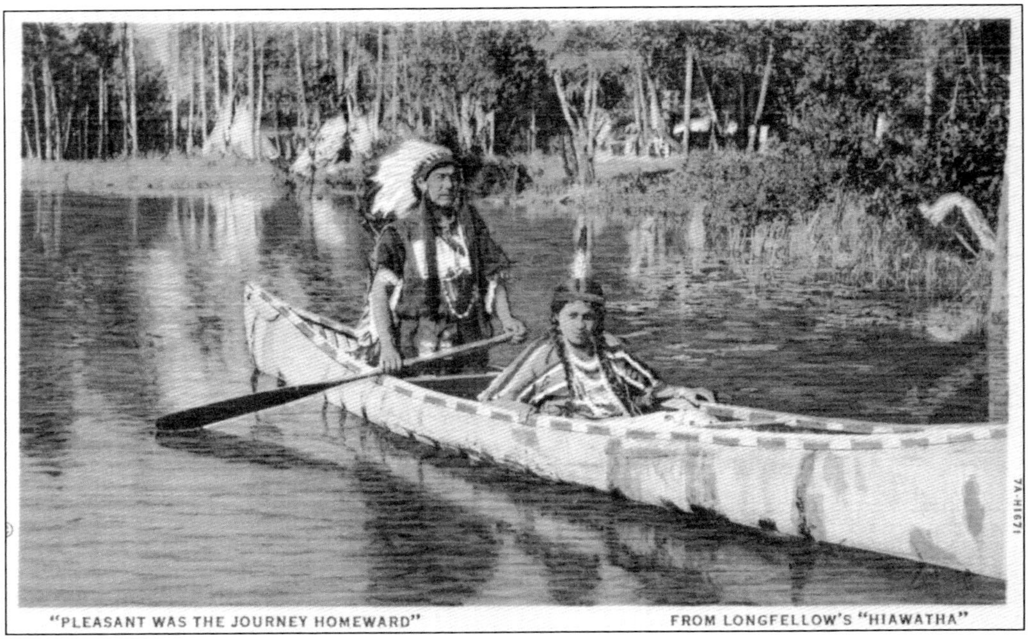

Native canoes traveling in Michilimackinac waters were not like the pleasure canoes of today: some were lighter-weight, for one or two persons to travel swiftly in small streams, and others were much larger, for families and loads of supplies. Jesuit records from 1630 report that "Indian canoes were usually large enough to carry a family of six with all their possessions—blankets, robes, cooking utensils, weapons and food."

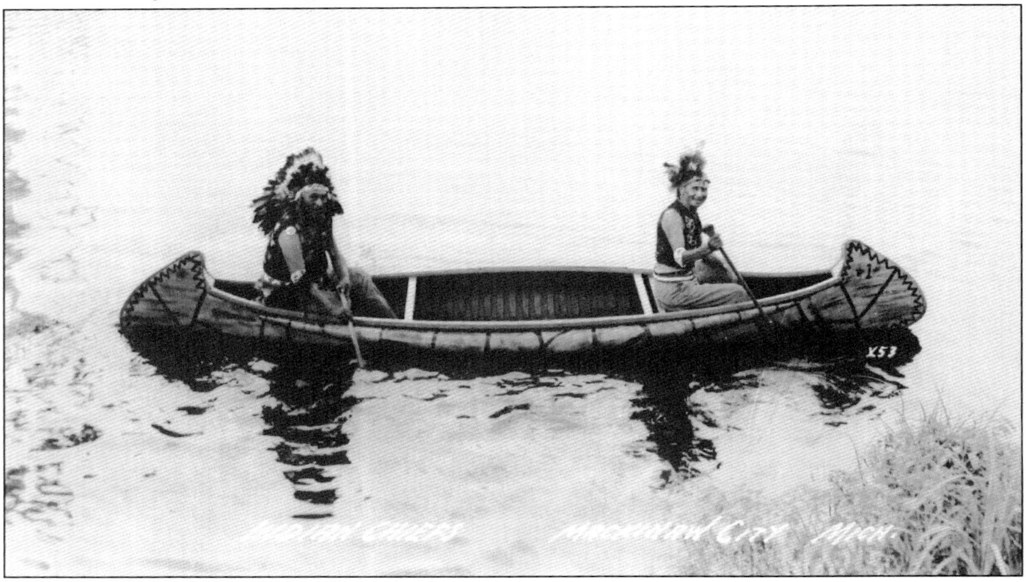

Tribes like the Potawatomi used dugout canoes for traveling on water. Fire was used to char a tree trunk, and then the softened burnt wood was dug out. Years later, canoes were made with wooden frames covered in layers of bark; sap and pitch were used to make them watertight. Huge French canoes (bateaux) conveyed early voyagers though The Straits, carrying thousands of pounds of men and furs.

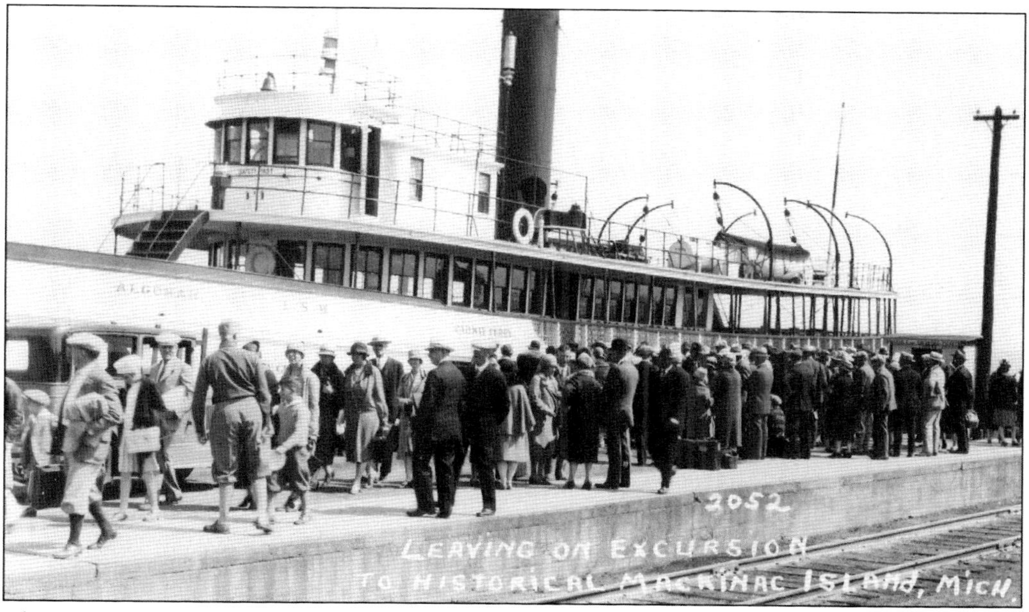

This postcard is titled "Leaving on Excursion to Historical Mackinac Island, Mich." and shows passengers disembarking from the USM Railway Ferry *Algomah* while others wait to board. The wording under the window on the captain's deck reads, "Safety First." Note the rail track in the foreground. Although the image is postmarked "1929 Cheboygan," the dock's actual location is unidentified. (Courtesy of John Marsh.)

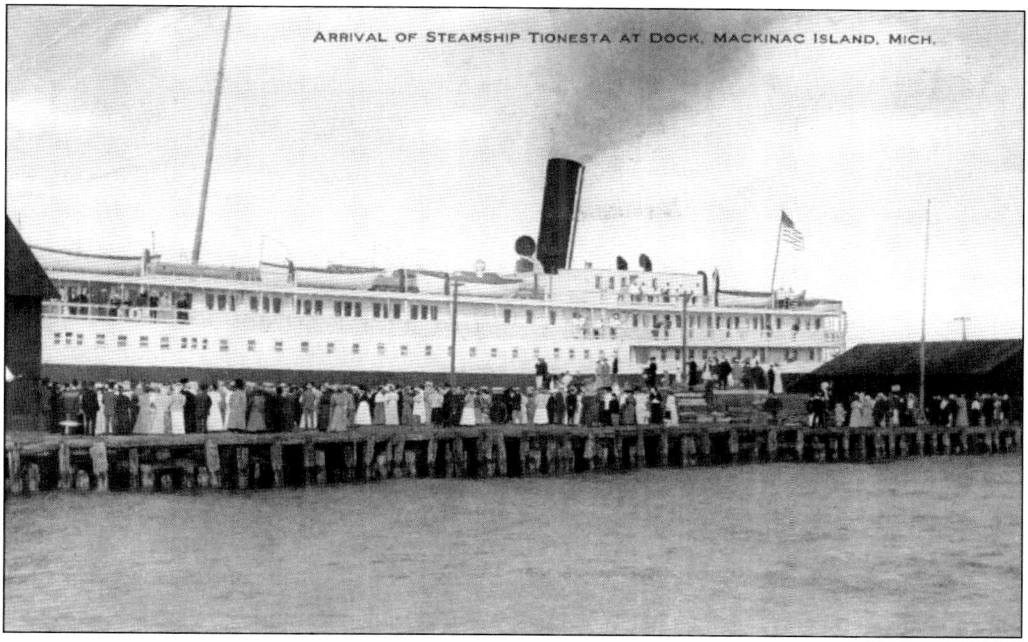

In 1820, there were only four steamers on the Great Lakes, but as demand increased, more were launched. In 1840, the fare from Buffalo to Mackinac was $16 for a cabin and $8 for steerage; horses were shipped at $10 each. Here, postmarked 1914, is the stately steamship *Tionesta* after arrival at a Mackinac Island dock.

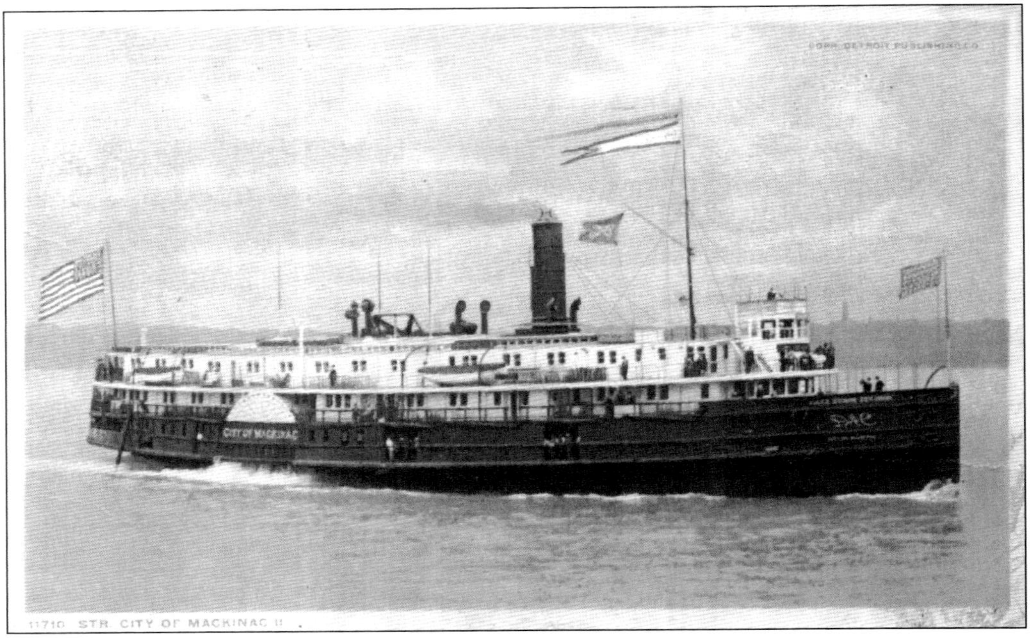

Early steamers belched their smoke and plied their way through calm seas and storms. This 1912 postcard shows the *City of Mackinac* leaving "port" under full steam. This vessel belonged to the Detroit and Cleveland Navigation Company and ran each season from Toledo, Ohio, to Mackinac, with stops at Port Huron, Harbor Beach, Alpena, and Cheboygan. The ship's flags were most probably added by the postcard printer.

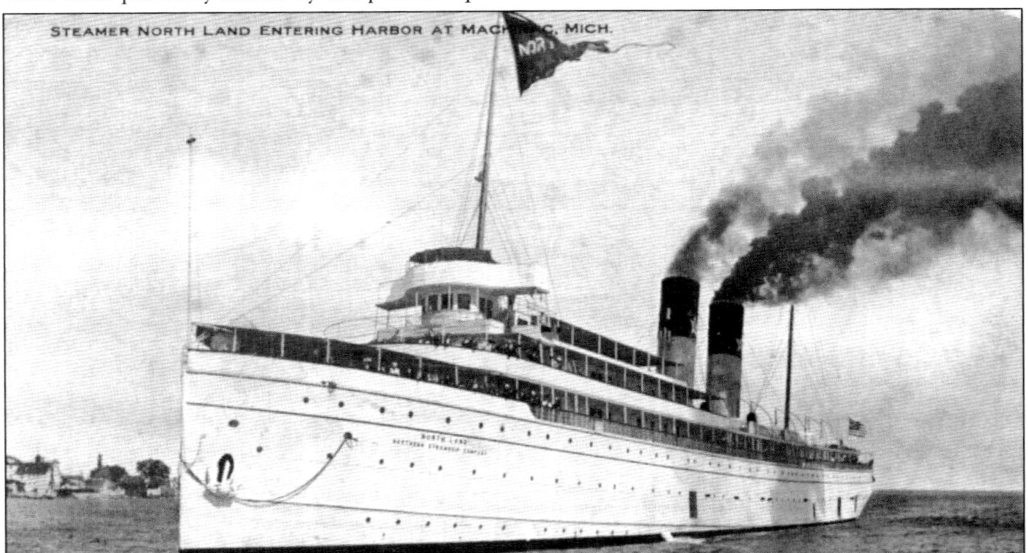

This 1908 postcard shows the *North Land*, part of the Northern Steamship Company's fleet, with smokestacks billowing. The *North Land* was a luxury liner of its time. Unfortunately, the vessels belonging to this steamship company had a reputation for minor explosions in the boiler rooms, which often injured members of the crew. Workers apparently had to be shanghaied from waterfront saloons to hire on.

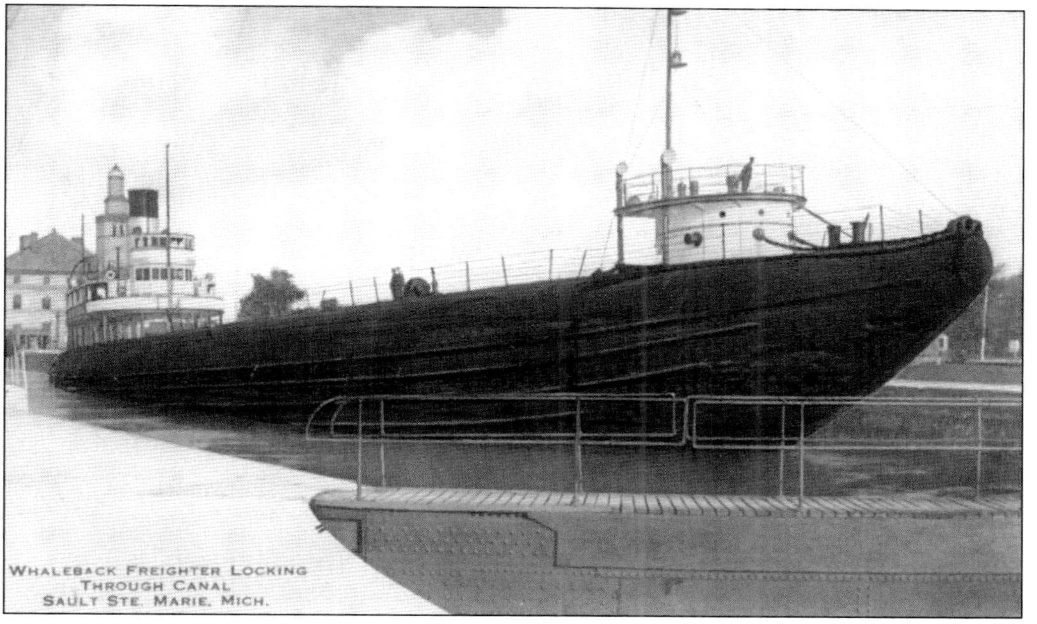

An early forerunner to a Great Lakes freighter was a huge freight steamer called a "whaleback." A cargo ship of unique design, it had a curved hull above the waterline. The sides were rounded, and it had a spoon bow. On the Great Lakes, it usually carried ore or grain. This postcard shows a whaleback locking through at Sault Ste. Marie, Michigan, a northern destination after passing through The Straits.

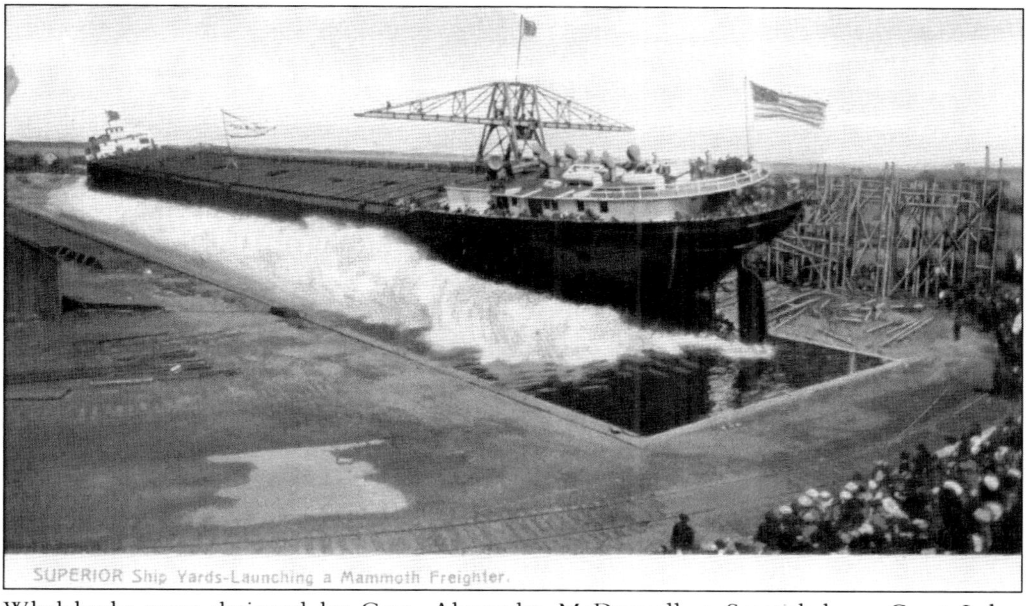

Whalebacks were designed by Capt. Alexander McDougall, a Scottish-born Great Lakes mariner. Between 1887 and 1898, over 40 whaleback vessels were constructed, most of them at West Superior, Wisconsin, which was nicknamed "the home of the whalebacks." Larger freighters superseded whalebacks. Here, this newer freighter is being launched at Superior's shipyard. The American flag was probably added by the postcard printer.

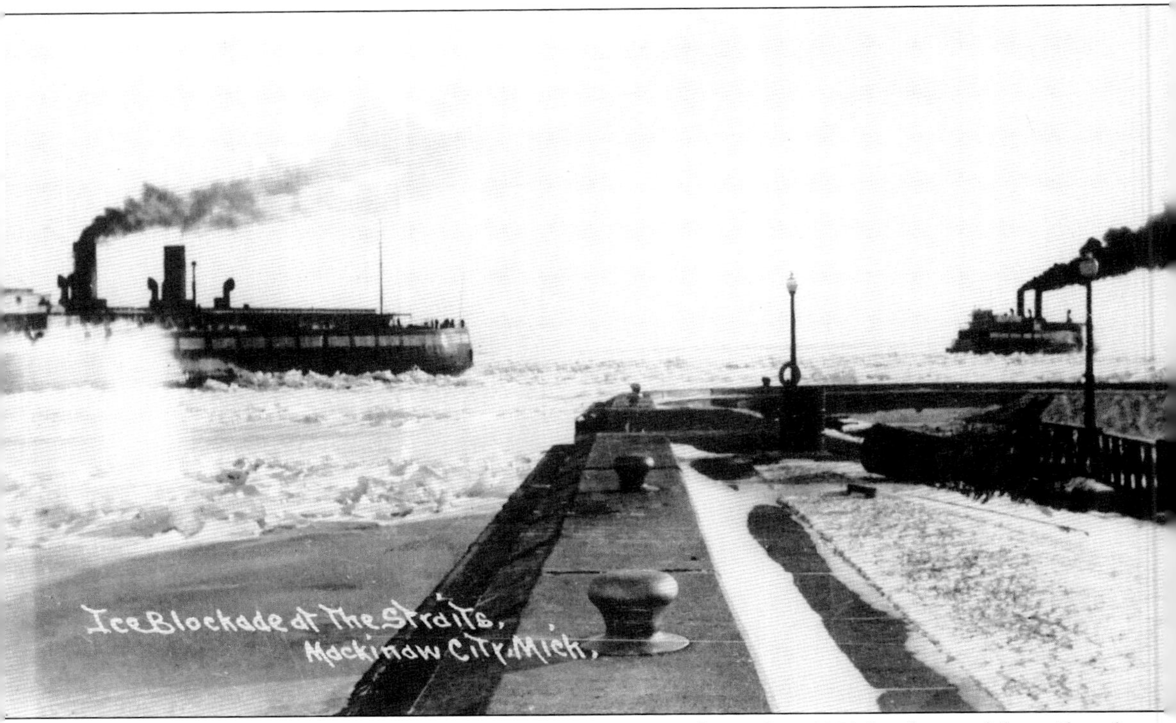

The Mackinac Transportation Company (MTC) was formed in 1881 by three of the railroads that had rail lines to The Straits. In order to make connections and haul freight across the water, MTC built its first large wooden transport ship and icebreaker, *Algomah*. Business was good until winter ice piled up, and when *Algomah* became ice-bound, freight had to be taken off and transported by horse and sleigh. One of the early captains was William Schepler of Mackinaw City, whose family continues to host tourists on passenger ferries to and from Mackinac Island. The first four railroad cars transported across The Straits were on a scow called the *Betsy*, towed by the *Algomah*. Because this only worked in calm waters, the MTC needed a larger, heavier ship and built the *St. Ignace* in 1888—with an engine installed by a young Detroiter named Henry Ford. Later, the MTC added three more icebreakers to its fleet, *Sainte Marie I* and *Sainte Marie II* and *Chief Wawatam*, two of which are pictured here leaving the Mackinaw City Ferry Dock. (Courtesy of John Marsh.)

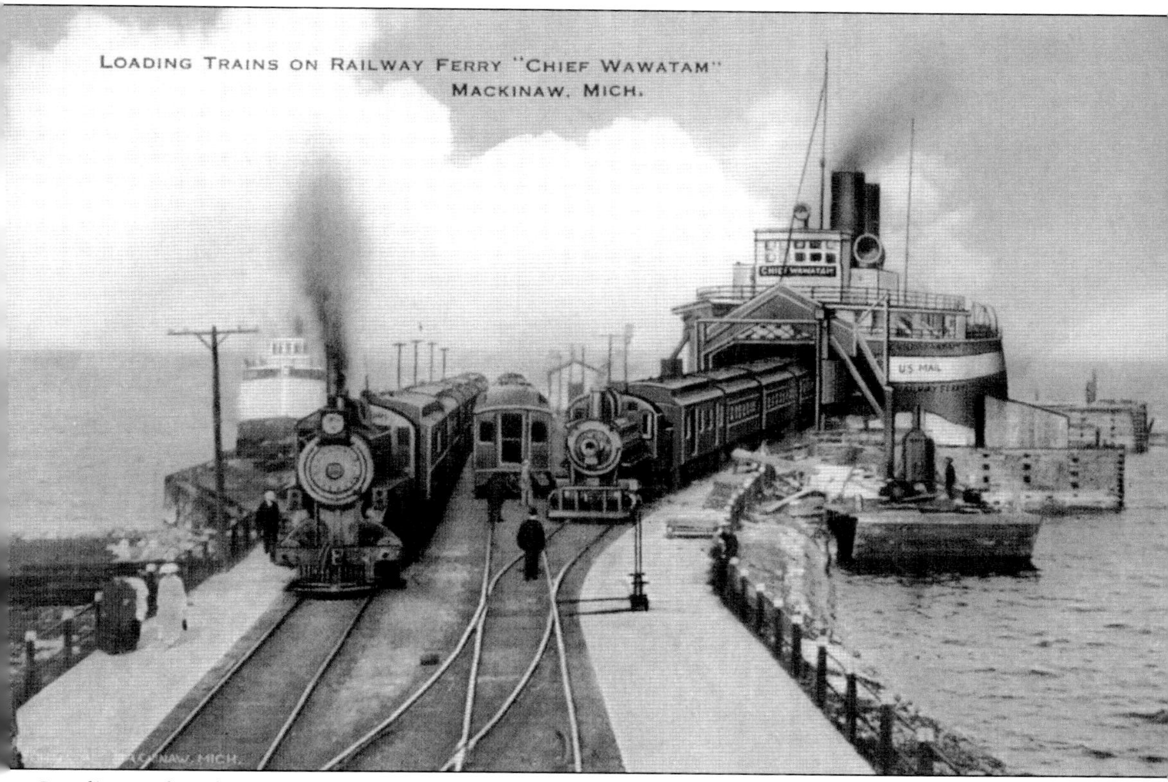

Loading railroad cars on *Chief Wawatam* was a sight to behold. Built in 1911 for the Mackinac Transportation Company for about $375,000, the *Chief* was named after the famed Ojibwa who rescued Alexander Henry, a British trader, in the Native American attack on Fort Michilimackinac in 1763. *Chief Wawatam* (*wa-wa-sum* means "reflections of light") was constructed of steel and was the largest railway ferry plying The Straits. With three engines and a railcar deck with four sets of tracks, it could accommodate more than 20 railcars. The *Chief* usually had a crew of 50 and could carry 350 passengers. Cargo included burlap, food products, mining equipment, iron ore, copper ingots, timber products, fish, flour, and the US mail. *Chief Wawatam* had other duties as well and occasionally teamed with its sister ship, *Sainte Marie*, to help other ships make their way through the ice-choked Straits and the Sault Ste. Marie Locks. As rail freight declined and it became too costly to repair its boilers, the *Chief* ceased operation in the 1960s.

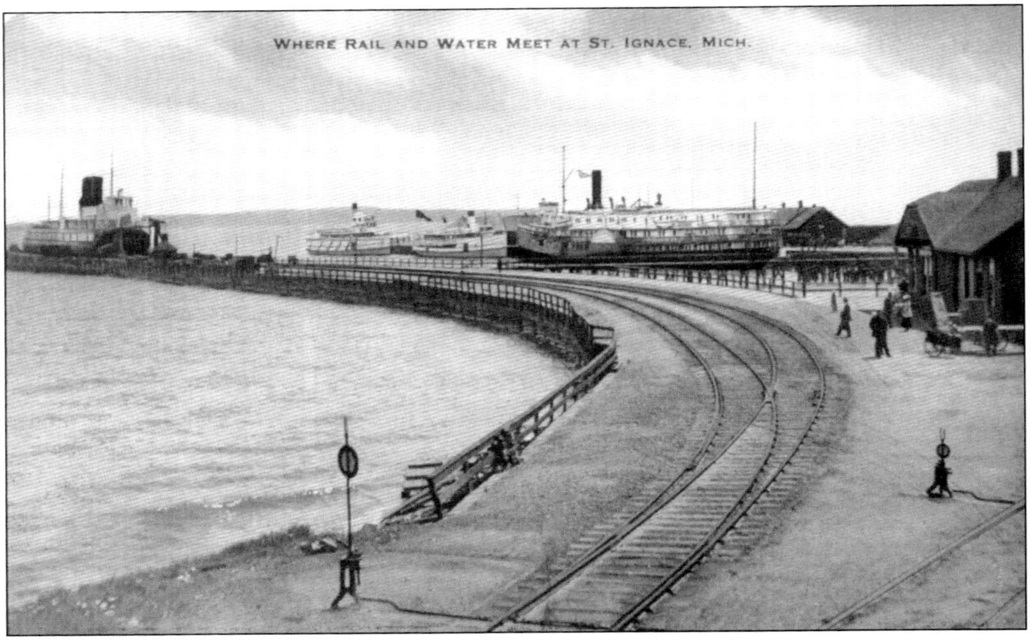

The railroad dock in St. Ignace on the north side of The Straits was just as busy as the one in Mackinaw City. Michigan's Upper Peninsula had rail lines stretching to Sault Ste. Marie, Marquette, and beyond. A railcar ferry sits at the end of the rail spur waiting for its next load. The large passenger ship looks like it could be from the D&C line, and smaller ferryboats are moored nearby.

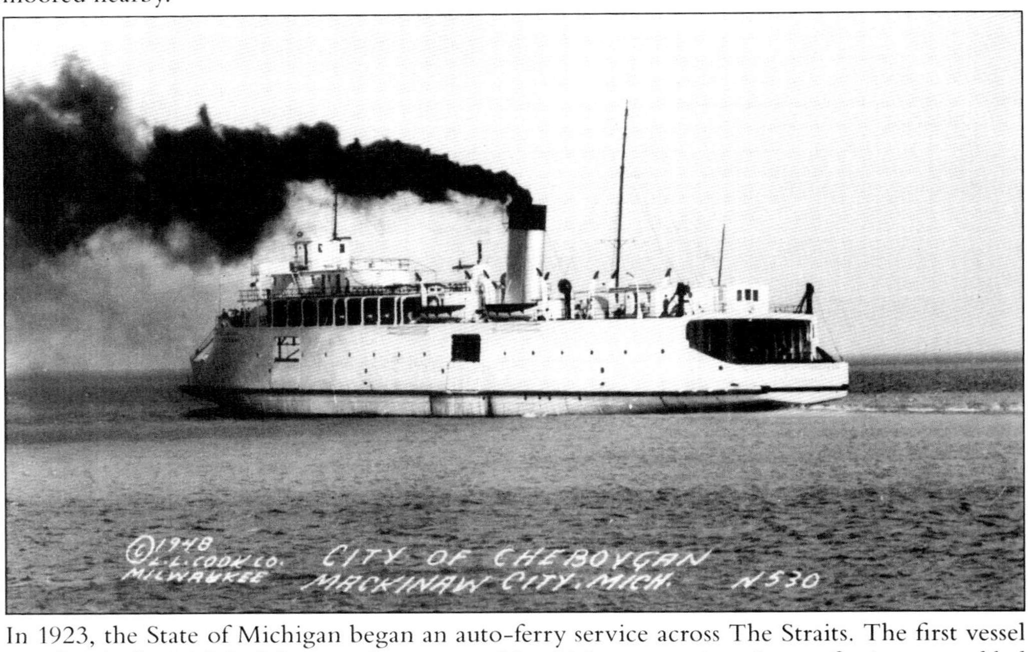

In 1923, the State of Michigan began an auto-ferry service across The Straits. The first vessel was the *Ariel*, which had the capacity to carry 20 vehicles at one time. Larger ferries were added over time, and in 1937, a "remade" Lake Michigan railcar ferry was put into service. It was named *City of Cheboygan* and could carry 85 vehicles.

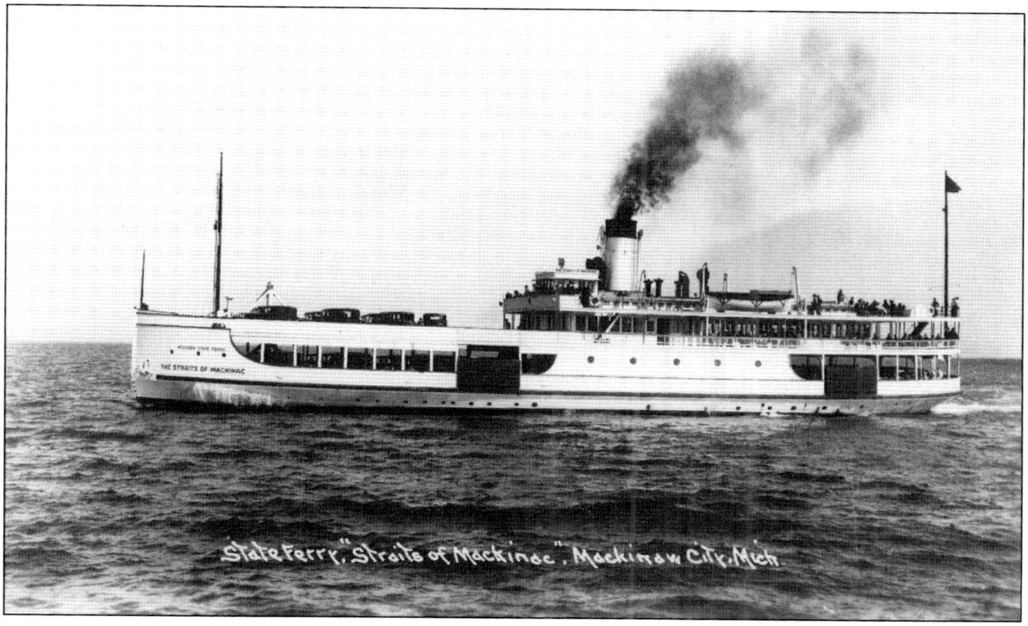

Named after the body of water she plied, the *Straits of Mackinac* appears in these postcards with two deck styles. Initially, the State of Michigan thought it would save money and add capacity to its service by adding an upper deck to its ferries to accommodate more vehicles. And, by enclosing the lower deck, vehicles below were protected from weather elements (above). The *Straits of Mackinac* had her upper deck removed during a World War II scrap-iron drive. As it turned out, it was actually more efficient without the upper deck; waiting time was reduced when the process of the dock elevator hoisting cars to the upper deck one at a time was eliminated. Note the two different spellings of "Mackinaw" in the postcard titles. (Above, courtesy of John Marsh.)

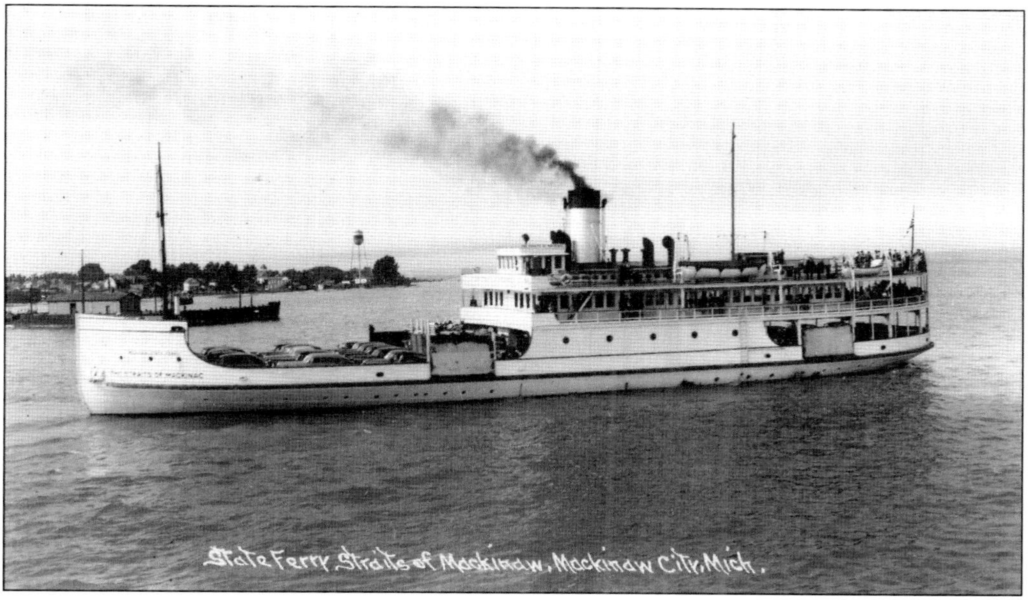

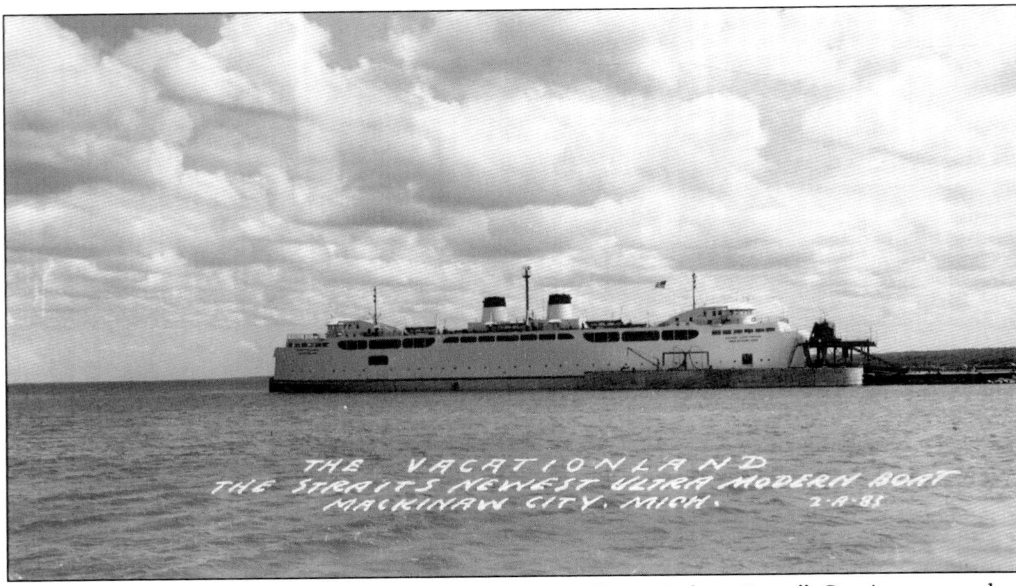

The *Vacationland* was billed as "The Straits Newest Ultra Modern Boat." Costing more than $4 million and christened in December 1951, *Vacationland* made her initial voyage from River Rouge on the Detroit River to St. Ignace. She could carry 650 passengers and 150 vehicles. An amazing site on the water, this powerful ice-breaking automobile ferry served The Straits until the opening of the Mackinac Bridge in 1957.

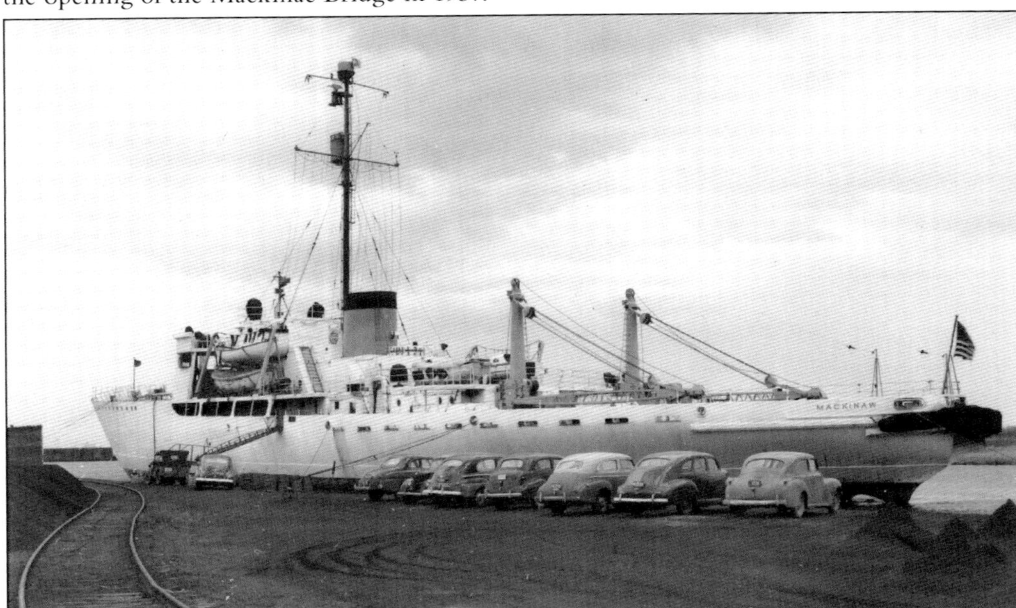

The ultimate boat ride would have been aboard the *Mackinaw* (WAGB83). Called the "Guardian of the Great Lakes," this $10 million cutter and ice crusher was the pride of the US Coast Guard. Built in 1944, *Mackinaw 83* was used to keep shipping lanes open year-round and frequently rescued freighters stranded in the ice. After its decommissioning and replacement by the *Mackinaw 30*, WAGB83 is now a floating museum dockside in Mackinaw City.

Seven

End of Trail
Mee-kuhn-a-boon-tahk

The Native Americans at Michilimackinac, once so numerous, gradually diminished. Many Ottawa moved from the north side of The Straits and settled in Cross Village, Petoskey, and the L'Arbre Croche area, while the Potawatomi moved further south. The Ojibwe remained in Michigan's Upper Peninsula but eventually migrated towards Green Bay. The Huron were either assimilated into other tribes or left with Michilimackinac fort commander Antoine de la Mothe Cadillac to begin a new settlement at Detroit.

Imagine the bewilderment, sadness, and frustration of the native people as they watched their beloved and hallowed Mother Earth invaded, appropriated, deforested, and polluted. Pushed from the homelands that had sustained them, these Anishinabe were devastated by disease, warfare, and a new cultural greed imposed upon them. Those who survived were forced to accept new ways, learn a new white man's language, and attend rigid schools. They were also forced to accept a new religion and were forbidden to practice their traditional sacred rites.

As the white man took over, The Straits became a center of commerce and fortunately remained almost as beautiful as the Native Americans had found it. People are reminded daily of the Anishinabe influence in the heritage of Michigan's place names like Petoskey, Owosso, Otsego, Escanaba, Munising, Ishpeming, Negaunee, Kalamazoo, Tecumseh, and Tekonsha.

There are many more fascinating places in The Straits, particularly the islands: St. Helena, (Mish-aou-o-ning), Round (Nis-sa-win-a-gong), Bois Blanc (Mi-ko-bi-min-iss), and Les Cheneaux (She-baw-o-no-ning), renamed by the French and meaning "the channels." It is said, "Nature was in a lavish mood in the creation of the Straits of Mackinac." There is something mystical and magical about this place that cannot be explained—it has to be experienced.

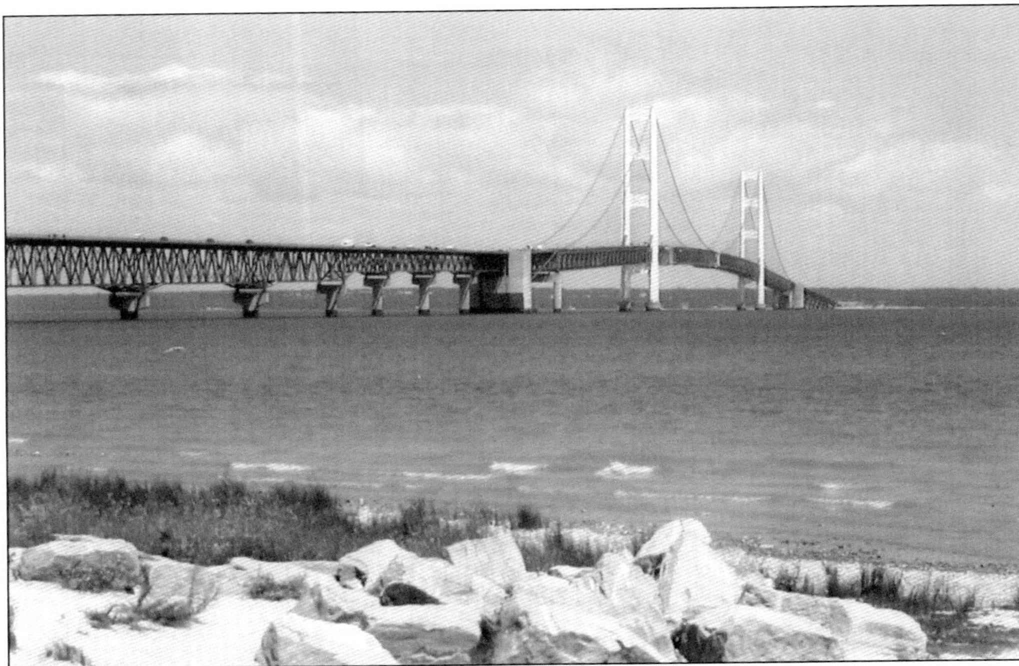

The Straits of Mackinac was a gathering place for early inhabitants of many nations and has been called the "Crossroads of the Great Lakes." It has a unique cultural heritage, having been occupied by the Anishinabe, voyagers, fur traders, missionaries, French, British, and Americans, all who left their mark and contributed to the significant history and magnificent place it has evolved into. It is abundant in hospitality and has been a popular vacation destination for decades, providing busy tourist attractions as well as scenic solitude. The opening of the majestic Mackinac Bridge in 1957 marked the end of one era and the beginning of another. With Michigan's two peninsulas now directly connected, the scenic splendor of the Straits of Mackinac, and its history, continues with an exciting new dimension. (Above, courtesy of Karen Okerman Daddow; below, John R. Okerman.)

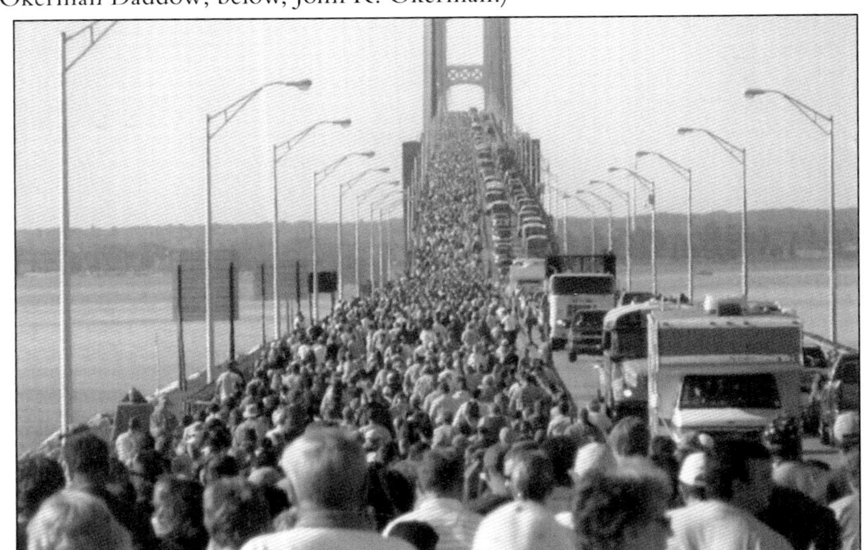

Ojibwa Song

Ma-mo-yu-wum-a-ta, ma-bum

Wan-je-sha-wan-da-goz-e-yung

Wa-os-e-mint, wa-gwis-e-mint,

Gia Pa-niz-it O-je-shag

The following is an Ojibway translation by Rev. Peter Dougherty, Emmet County, Michigan, missionary:

Praise God from whom all blessings flow,

Praise Him, all creatures here below;

Praise Him above, ye heavenly host;

Praise Father, Son, and Holy Ghost.

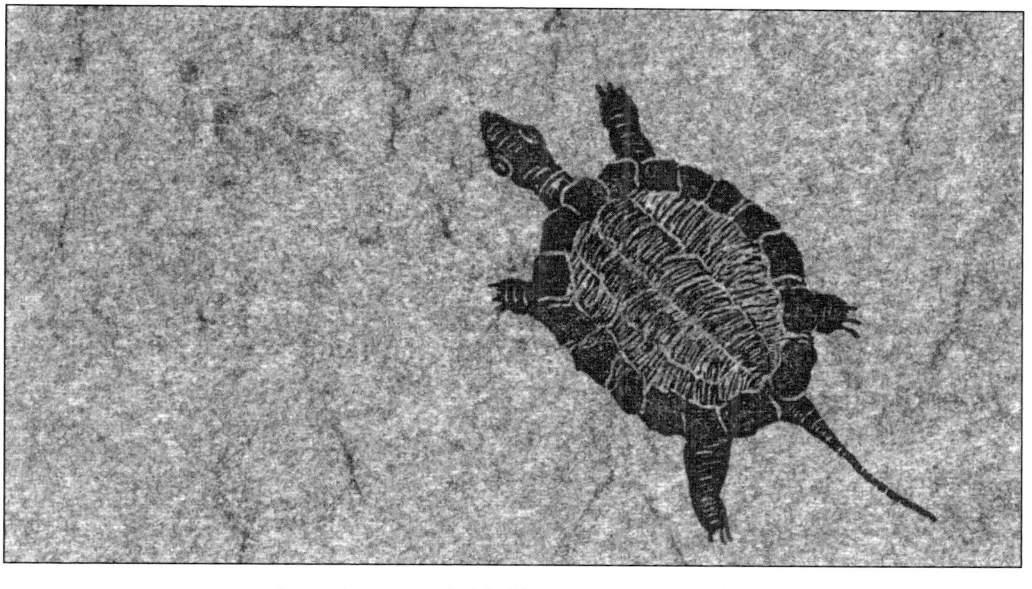

May the Great Spirit bless the Great Turtle,

May the Great Spirit bless Michilimackinac!

SELECTED BIBLIOGRAPHY

Bailey, John R., M.D. *Mackinac Formerly Michilimackinac*. Lansing, MI: Robert Smith Printing Company, 1895.

Barry, James P. *Ships of the Great Lakes*. Holt, MI: Thunder Bay Press, 1973.

Blackbird, Andrew J. *History of the Ottawa and Chippewa Indians of Michigan; A Grammar of Their Language, and Personal and Family History of the Author*. Ypsilanti, MI: The Ypsilantian Job Printing House, 1887.

Boynton, Brother James, S.J. *Fishers of Men: The Jesuit Mission at Mackinac, 1670–1765*. Mackinac Island: Ste. Anne's Church, 1996.

Kane, Grace F. *Myths and Legends of the Mackinacs and the Lake Region*. Cincinnati: Editor Publishing Company, 1897.

Liebner, Mary Davis. *All Aboard the Boat's Leaving*. Cheboygan, MI: self-published, 2008.

Michigan Commission on Indian Affairs. *The Indian in Michigan–Ottawa, Chippewa, Potawatomi*. Lansing, MI: 1970.

Michilimackinac Historical Society. *Michilimackinac*. St. Ignace, MI: Mackinac County Chamber of Commerce, 1958.

Ranville, Judy, and Nancy Campbell. *Memories of Mackinaw*. Petoskey, MI: Little Traverse Printing, 1976.

Sager, Robert C. *The Pageant of Tuscarora*. Burt Lake, MI: Northern Lakes Litho, Inc., 1975.

Schoolcraft, Henry R. *The Hiawatha Legends: North American Indian Lore*. Marquette, MI: Avery Color Studios, 1856.

Van Fleet, J.A. *Summer Resorts of the Mackinaw Region and Adjacent Localities*. Detroit: Lever Print, 1882.

Vogel, Virgil J. *Indian Names in Michigan*. Ann Arbor, MI: The University of Michigan Press, 1986.

Williams, Meade C., *Early Mackinac: An Historical and Descriptive Sketch*. St. Louis: Buschart Bros. Print, 1897.

A Tribute to Mackinac Straits Health System

"A Bridge to the Future"

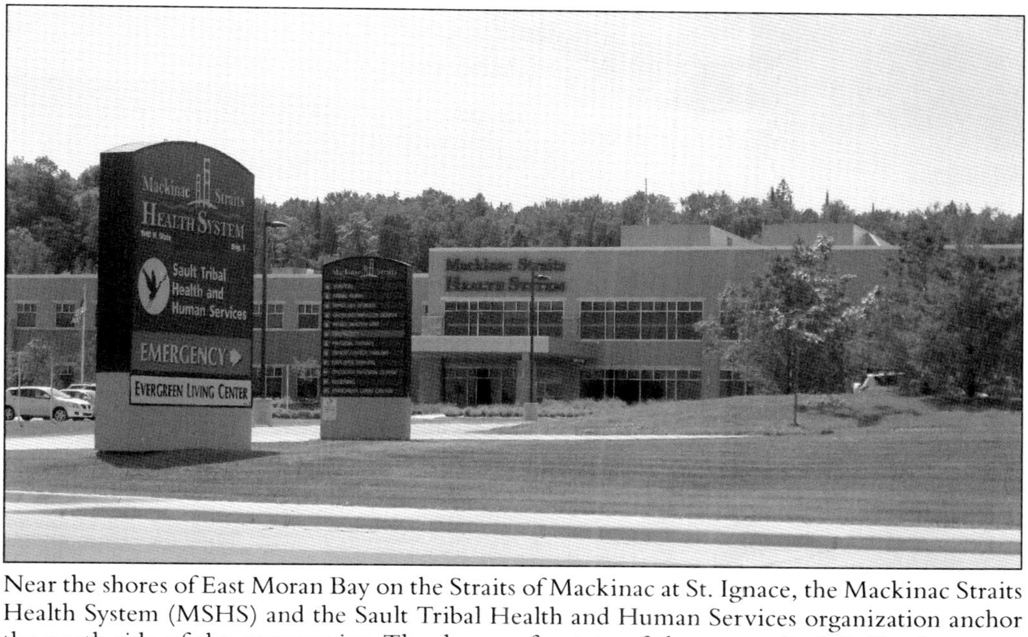

Near the shores of East Moran Bay on the Straits of Mackinac at St. Ignace, the Mackinac Straits Health System (MSHS) and the Sault Tribal Health and Human Services organization anchor the north side of the community. The dream of a state-of-the-art medical facility became a reality in April 2010 with the opening of a new hospital that also offers expanded auxiliary services. In addition, the MSHS operates four satellite clinics: Mackinac Island, Mackinaw City, Naubinway, and Pickford. This commendable community achievement secured expanded health-care benefits for the area for years to come. The land for the project was donated by the Sault Ste. Marie Tribe of Chippewa Indians, who have their own medical clinic on the second floor of the new building. Partial royalties from the sale of this book will continually go directly to the MSHS to help fund small needs within the hospital. Thank you for your support.

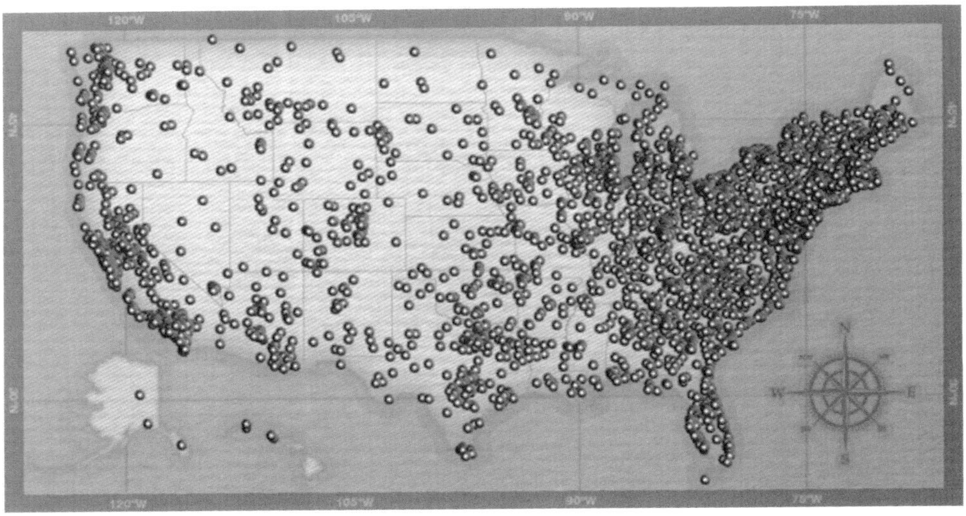

Consistent with our mission to preserve history on a local level, this book was printed in South Carolina on American-made paper and manufactured entirely in the United States. Products carrying the accredited Forest Stewardship Council (FSC) label are printed on 100 percent FSC-certified paper.